Kinship and Diasporas in International Affairs

Kinship & Diasporas
in International Affairs

Yossi Shain

THE UNIVERSITY OF MICHIGAN PRESS   ANN ARBOR

Copyright © by the University of Michigan 2007
All rights reserved
Published in the United States of America by
The University of Michigan Press
Manufactured in the United States of America
⊗ Printed on acid-free paper

2010   2009   2008   2007   4   3   2   1

A CIP catalog record for this book is available from the British Library.

Library of Congress Cataloging-in-Publication Data

Shain, Yossi, 1956–
      Kinship and diasporas in international affairs / Yossi Shain.
         p.   cm.
      Includes bibliographical references and index.
      ISBN-13: 978-0-472-09910-8 (cloth : alk. paper)
      ISBN-10: 0-472-09910-8 (cloth : alk. paper)
         1. Transnationalism.   2. International relations.   3. National
      characteristics.   4. Jewish diaspora.   I. Title.
   JZ1320.S53   2007
   327.101—dc22   2007012896

To my friends Avi & Tali

Contents

Illustrations

Acknowledgments

THIS BOOK IS A culmination of research and writing on kinship and diasporas over the last decade. Most chapters represent an extension and elaboration on previously published materials. Chapters 1 and 2 were written, in the original format, in collaboration with Martin Sherman, whose scholarship and clear thinking enriched me greatly. In chapter 3 I drew, in addition to my own work, on my collaborative works with Barry Bristman. Chapter 4 was originally conceived in a joint project with Tamara Cofman-Wittes, a superb scholar of conflict resolution. It first appeared in Yossi Shain and Tamara Cofman, "Peace as a Three Player Game: The Role of Diasporas in Conflict Resolution," in Thomas Ambrosio, ed., *Ethnic Identity Groups and U.S. Foreign Policy* (Westport: Praeger, 2000). Some ideas in this chapter also appear in Yossi Shain and Ravinatha P. Aryasinha, "Spoilers or catalysts? The Role of Diasporas in Peace Processes," in Edward Newman and Oliver Richmond, eds., *Challenges to Peacebuilding: Managing Spoilers During Conflict Resolution* (New York: United Nations University Press, 2006). Chapter 5 was originally published with Aharon Barth, who taught me so much about international relations theory and its application. I would like to thank the following journals for their permission to reprint material for this book: *International Organization, Political Science Quarterly, Nations and Nationalism, Nationalism and Ethnic Politics*, and *SAIS Review*.

Throughout this work I have benefited greatly from other scholars and students who have worked with me on other projects and writings that are not represented in this volume but influenced my thinking nonetheless. Above all I am grateful to Tanja Flanajan and Ariel Ahram, my superb assistants and cowriters. I am also indebted to my colleagues and friends Robert Lieber, Gil Merom, Josh Mitchell, Aharon Klieman, Avi Ben Zvi, and Azar Gat for their ideas and support.

Fellowships from the Center for International Studies in the Woodrow Wilson School at Princeton University, the Center for Democracy and the Third Sector, and the Posen Foundation have helped me in conceiving and finalizing this project. I am also grateful for all the support I received from Georgetown University's Department of Government and Tel Aviv University's School of Government, my two generous academic homes. Evgeni Kluber and Jessica Gheiler helped in preparing the index.

Finally, I would like to thank Erin Carter and the staff of the University of Michigan Press for their outstanding editing skills; Melissa Spence, my invaluable assistant and deputy director at Georgetown University's Program for Jewish Civilization; and Limor Rachmanov, my devoted assistant at Tel Aviv University.

Abbreviations

ADL-Ramgavars	Armenian Democratic Liberal Party
AIPAC	American-Israel Public Affairs Committee
ANIA	Irish Americans for a New Irish Agenda
ARF	Armenian Revolutionary Federation
ASSR	Armenian Soviet Socialist Republic
BJP	Bharatiya Janata Party
CJF	Council of Jewish Federations
CSCE	Conference on Security and Cooperation in Europe
IDF	Israel Defense Forces
IEIS	Intraethnic Interstate
IR	International Relations
IRA	Irish Republican Army
KLA	Kosovo Liberation Army
NORAID	Irish Northern Aid Committee
SDH	Social Democratic Hunchakian Party
UIA	United Israel Appeal
UJA	United Jewish Appeal
UJC	United Jewish Communities

Introduction

THIS BOOK EXAMINES the role of kinship and diaspo-
ras in the international system. Each chapter delves into different aspects
of "the people," understood as kin members who transcend the boundaries of states and who influence various facets of international and
domestic affairs. The book examines the transmission of religion and culture across frontiers; the dynamics of conflict and its resolution, including the fate of diasporas; the competition among segments of the overall
"people" inside and outside "homelands" for legitimate authority; the
role of transnational financial flows among members of the kin community; and how the concept of collective security stretches beyond the state
system. These overriding issues are examined through the lens of numerous case studies of kin community interactions and diaspora-homeland
relations from a broad variety of theoretical and comparative perspectives. Special attention is paid to contemporary Jewish experiences, in
many ways a paradigmatic case of the role of peoplehood and diaspora-
homeland relations in international affairs.[1]

Undoubtedly, modern nationalism—the idea that people with distinct
characteristics should have the right to govern themselves in a territory
believed to be their homeland—is tied to the Enlightenment and the evolution of the modern state since the eighteenth century. Yet the concepts
of ethnicities, kinship, and the ties between "the land" and "the people"
predate modern nationalism going back much farther. In the Jewish case,
the Israelites under the united Davidic kingdom saw the land—"from
Dan to Beersheba"—as a patrimony of Yahweh to his people. Steven
Grosby writes that "the biblical nation is . . . a form of kinship, signifying
recognition of being territorially related. As such, it posits the criterion of
birth for membership that places the nation within the continuum of

forms of kinship. This recognition of kinship also implies possession and sovereignty over the land."[2] And yet for many generations the idea of returning to the Promised Land was mostly a traditional myth related to the Jewish Covenant with God. In reality, prior to modern Zionism "none dared, and few greatly desired, to subject the matter of the Return to the Promised Land to pragmatic—or even philosophic—examination, it was the case too that for many centuries there was nothing in the actual condition of the Jews that especially impelled or encouraged any of them to do so."[3]

Moreover, the biblical idea that Jews are irrevocably linked (*bnei Israel*) and mutually responsible manifests itself in religious tracts and in communal organization throughout Jewish history. The internal kinship bonds of family ties, common religious observance, language, various cultural practices, and so on were strengthened during much of Jewish history by external pressures that forced Jews to live apart and excluded them from broader society. Kinship ties were always the core of "Jewish politics," but their definition and significance changed dramatically with the creation of the state of Israel. Not only did the state of Israel and its existential challenges become the target of Jewish diasporic mobilization, but the state itself emerged as a major actor on behalf of its kin, albeit not always to their liking. The state created and encouraged diasporic institutions that greatly affect the lives of Jews and their activism in the countries of domicile. This activism is especially intense in times of kinship peril in the homeland and abroad, as exemplified by global Jewish mobilization on behalf of Soviet Jewry during the Cold War.[4]

Robert Gilpin has written that, throughout history, "human beings organize themselves into political groups and are loyal to groups that inevitably conflict with one another. This political process will cease only when individuals fasten their loyalties on mankind as a whole. Except for saints and certain scholars with a more vivid imagination than the rest of us, this transformation in human consciousness has not yet occurred."[5] Indeed, kinship affinities and loyalties remain the hallmark of organized politics and conflict.

In many cases, membership is attributed by birth, rather than earned or chosen. Certainly religion, nationality, and even class are not fully chosen; race is even more primordial. Yet identities and kinship bonds are also liable to shift according to politics and the freedom of choice. Power structures in particular have tremendous impact on the definition of group membership, loyalty, and obligation. Just as inborn identities and kinship ties often defy political boundaries, political structures and in particular sovereign power constantly redefine nascent identities. This process confuses the alleged division of humanity by Providence with the ever-changing designs by humans.

In the era of modern nationalism, when it comes to state-sponsored collective identities, two dynamics come into play. On the one hand, there are notions of shared blood, which traditional ethnofocal visions of kinship stress. On the other hand, there is the notion of blood shed for the state. Often blood spilt in defense of a state reinforces or is made to reinforce the notion of shared blood, as exemplified by the Nazis' *Volksgemeinschaft*. Yet, in other circumstances, spilt blood can come to undermine and trump notions of primordial shared blood, thereby creating new focal points for patriotism and new concepts of membership. This has been especially evident in the evolution of American identity. Despite subscribing to older notions of kinship (such as Providence) and shared blood as forming the basis of the American people, early American leaders like John Jay in the *Federalist Papers* No. 2 already pointed to a much more flexible combination of loyalties. Echoing Shakespeare, Jay said that a sense of common blood could be supplemented by spilling blood, thus making heterogeneous peoples into a band of brothers.

> Providence has been pleased to give this one connected country, to one united people; a people descended from the same ancestors, speaking the same language, professing the same religion, attached to the same principles of government, very similar in their manners and customs, and who, by their joint counsels, arms and efforts, fighting side by side throughout a long and bloody war, have nobly established their general liberty and independence.
>
> This country and its people seem to have been made for each other, and it appears as if it was the design of Providence, that an inheritance so proper and convenient for a band of brethren, united to each other by the strongest ties, should never be split into a number of, unsocial jealous and alien sovereignties.[6]

The fact that shed blood often matters more than the blood of birth was always the hope of modern diasporic Jews who sought to demonstrate their ardent patriotism to their countries of domicile in the face of innate suspicion and anti-Semitism. Thus, shortly after Frederick William III of Prussia finally approved an edict of emancipation that in theory made Jews full citizens, Prussian Jews disproportionately volunteered in the German war of liberation against France. Jewish elders encouraged this outburst of patriotism, "for it was indeed 'a heavenly feeling to possess a fatherland! What rapture to be able to call a spot, a place, a nook one's own upon this lovely earth. . . . Hand in hand with your fellow soldiers you will complete a great task; *they will not deny you the title of brother for you will have earned it.*'"[7]

Scholars have long devoted tremendous attention, both theoretical and empirical, to the "constructedness" and fluidity of such bonds. However, hitherto too little attention has been given to the processes by which these identities are shaped or the raw materials with which such ties are activated. In particular, authors have insufficiently explored the influences of kinship across frontiers and the theoretical implications for international relations theory.

Many questions arise in discussing transnational kinship ties and their political ramifications. For example, where do the bonds of affinity come from? How have they changed over time? How are they transmitted? How do they manifest themselves in political behavior? How does this affinity translate into (political) voices, particularly when in competition with other influences and motivations that shape political allegiance and activity? What are the processes at work? What do kin communities and members owe to one another, and on what basis? What are the long-term trends, and are we witnessing today truly groundbreaking events? When a kin member saves another in a foreign land, what is the significance to each? Are such acts merely part of a grand bargain—for example, every Jew and individual Jewish community looks out for the other's welfare—or is there greater meaning and relevance?

An exploration of these questions enables scholars to better integrate identity concerns as an important element of the study of international relations. This book illuminates the complex interrelationships and ties within ethnonational communities and the far-reaching effects of those relationships on group identity and political outcomes. It highlights the elastic nature of national interest, as defined by constituencies inside and outside the state. It also improves our understanding of how international- and domestic-level forces combine to produce foreign and domestic policy.

Kinship elements have been largely neglected in traditional international relations scholarship, which bases its understanding of state behavior on limited assumptions about a state's identity and interests. *Realist* theorists argue that states are interested primarily in security and therefore search for power, while *liberal* theorists argue that states are concerned also with gains in wealth and other goods. As an increasing proportion of violence within and between states has centered on issues of communal identity rather than power and wealth, international relations scholars have struggled with the nature of national identity and how it shapes states' understanding of their interests. *Constructivist* insights are the most hospitable to this type of analysis, but they are not necessarily the only option for understanding how identity affects interests. This book argues that when it comes to probing the notion of peoplehood, identity may be the primary interest.

By recognizing that "the people" transcends state boundaries and that identity-focused competitions within and between states engage the attention and interests of kin communities that may reside far from the arena of "homelands," this book develops an alternative framework for understanding these dynamics. The importance of "the people" shows that identities are neither fixed and dependent on material factors nor entirely subjective, contingent, and shifting. Many of the ethnonational groups studied here do shift their self-conceptions, and consequently their politics and self-images, in response to geographic separation, life in different types of societies, and other separate experiences. Yet, at the same time, they retain certain objective components of a coherent collective identity: shared history and memory, folkways, and, most important, the objective reality of a territorial homeland. *The homeland* serves as the physical embodiment of the shared national identity, and its political and territorial fate has profound implications for the subjective identity of the diaspora and the transnational community. Thus, both subjective and objective factors combine to shape national identity and transnational communal politics.

Chapter 1 provides an analysis of the logic of the international system based on nation-states. Theoretically, this system should lead to the gradual elimination of transnational loyalties, intranational divisions, and stateless communities. Paradoxically, however, global realities indicate that the reverse is true, with these phenomena becoming more and more prevalent internationally. The discussion offers a comprehensive analytical framework that models the complex relationships among diaspora formation, secessionist and irredentist drives, and the existing nation-state system. A central concern is the formation and disintegration of different nation types (*ethnofocal* or *ideofocal*) and the inner logic of different regime types (democratic or authoritarian).

Chapter 2 explores how financial transfers from diasporic communities to recipients in the homeland are a prime vehicle for fostering changes in collective identities. It provides a conceptual framework for the analysis of these identity-related flows by identifying the various components of national identity, specifying the major channels for the exercise of diasporic influence, and describing the fluctuations of this impact. It shows how, through financial flows, diasporas may be an important stimulus for identity shifts in their homeland and how such flows impact the changing role of the state in the international system.

Chapter 3 deals with the transmission of culture and religion across frontiers through the prism of the Jewish experience and current polarizing Israeli Kulturkampf. From the perspective of conflicting visions of Jewish identity, the interaction between Jewish-Americans and Israel and the evolution of this relationship over time point to how the arena of struggle between secular and religious conceptions is inherently transnational. Reciprocal influences permeate debates among the Jewish people inside and outside "the homeland," Israel, in a process that constitutes the arena in which overall notions of collective identity are formed. This chapter also argues that the growing dependence of diasporic Jewish identity on Israel is fully compatible with attempts to develop a new indigenous Judaism that builds on religious innovations within the American diaspora. Expanding on the theme of evolving Jewish identity, the chapter also assesses the new thinking on Jewish security, both inside and outside the state of Israel, since the collapse of the Oslo Peace Process and in the aftermath of the terrorist attacks of September 11, 2001. The two dominant diaspora-Israeli interactions concern Jewish security and identity, both of which must be analyzed with respect to internal Jewish dynamics (among Jews qua Jews) and external factors affecting Israel and the other countries of domicile. As a result of all of these influences, the content and significance of identity issues are always elastic, contingent, and shifting.

Chapter 4 examines how diasporas function as a distinct third level between interstate and domestic politics in peace negotiations. As the analysis shows, transnational kin communities can have a significant impact on the sovereign decision making by homelands with respect to peace and war. Those in the diaspora are necessarily influenced by the values and experiences of their states of domicile, leading to incongruities of perception between those in the homeland and those abroad. This situation can create complicating cleavages, internationalizing previously domestic political coalitions and agreements.

Chapter 5 concludes by incorporating the study of kinship and diasporas into international relations (IR) theory. It does so by focusing on diasporas as independent actors who actively influence their kin state's foreign policies. Such influences can best be understood by situating them in the theoretical space shared by constructivism and liberalism, two approaches that acknowledge the impact of both identity and domestic politics on international behavior. It also maintains that the exploration of diasporic activities can enrich both constructivism and liberalism. First, diasporas' identity-based motivations should be an integral part of the constructivist effort to explain the formation of national identities. Second, diasporic activities and influences in their homelands expand the meaning of the term *domestic politics* to include not only politics *inside the state* but also politics *inside the people*. For the liberal approach, this is a "new fact." Finally, it contends that the extent of diasporic influence on homeland foreign policy is determined by three components that make up the balance of power between homelands and diasporas, buttressed with examples taken from the relations between the newly established Armenian state and the strong Armenian diaspora as well as between Israel and diaspora Jews.

Although the chapters uphold the centrality of the nation-state and the power of sovereign governance, they also show how issues pertaining to the kin community as a whole inside and outside national borders may be as critical for the formation of modern collective identities and international relations. This analysis also produces a much more precise understanding of collective identities, a concept that has long suffered from imprecise and intuitive definitions.

ONE

Dynamics of Disintegration: Diaspora, Secession, and the Paradox of Nation-States

Diasporas and Secession: An Anomaly in the World of Nation-States?

At the center of the national ideal is the belief that people with a distinct character should possess their own territory. Thus, over time, a world consisting of independent nation-states should, by definition, obviate such phenomena as separatist movements and diasporas. In this sense both diasporic existence and secessionist claims are what might be termed *countertheoretical* concepts, inconsistent with the structural rationale of the global system.

The ensuing chapter proposes a broad analytical framework for the study of the complex relationships between diaspora formation, secessionist (and irredentist) drives, and the existing nation-state system, tracing the genesis and subsequent effects of these processes to the interplay between two distinct independent variables: nation type and regime type. Nation type deals with the nature of the intranational bonds that forge the unifying sentiment of national identity, defining its limits and the span of the heterogeneity of its membership. Regime type deals with the manner in which the nation is governed, particularly in terms of the pluralism and accountability that prevail in its polity.

The mutual interaction between respective nation types and regime types not only determines which variant of secession motivation and diaspora formation will be dominant, but it also generates a perennial source for the rejuvenation of old identities and the awakening of new ones. This process of identity creation and re-creation is a persistent challenge to the prevailing state system.

The ethnopolitical dynamic described here seems to lead to a paradox whereby the ceaseless quest for self-determination begins to threaten the feasibility of the very idea of self-determination. The accelerated proliferation of new nation-states will almost certainly promote continual disintegration, or at least erosion, of existing states. Clearly, if unarrested, this process may imperil no less than the very concept of the nation-state as a viable political entity. Rather than fading away as anomalies, anachronisms of the past, diasporas and separatist sentiments appear to be not only an endemic feature of the international system but a pivotal element in comprehending the direction of present and future trends in it.[1]

The ensuing attempt to impose theoretical order on the elaborate interplay between the dispersion, fragmentation, and amalgamation of political communities may ultimately help in illuminating broader issues of identities and membership in our time.

A Genealogy of Nationalism, Diaspora Formation, and Secession Incentives

In general, one may identify a twin mechanism in the formation of diasporas and secessionist movements. On the one hand, incomplete implementation of the principle of self-determination—in which "the political borders of states have been superimposed upon the ethnic map with cavalier disregard for ethnic homelands"—may leave ethnocultural groups with unfulfilled aspirations for political independence.[2] These groups may remain either stateless diasporas, and/or secessionist claimants, sometimes with ties of allegiance to an already independent political unit.[3] An example of the former is the Kurds, of the latter, the relations between Nagorno-Karabakh and independent Armenia. On the other hand, the successful implementation of the national idea may not preclude, and may even foster, the resurgence or reawakening of national aspirations within ethnic groups, thereby engendering secessionist or irredentist drives. Thus, neither the *birth* nor the *maturation* of the nation-state seems able to stem the apparent self-generating potential of secession sentiments and diaspora formation.

In the ensuing genealogy, I adopt a distinction between two different forms of nationalism: the ethnofocal and the ideofocal. The *ethnofocal* variant sees the nation as an organic division of humanity, decreed by some divine or natural edict; in contrast, the *ideofocal* variant perceives the nation as "a community formed by the [exercise of subjective] will [of its individual members] to be a nation" not dependent upon "race or descent, but upon a common thought and a common goal."[4] This distinction parallels in many respects the familiar concepts of ethnic versus civic nations, but it deviates in two substantive ways: First, while this ethnic/civic paradigm focuses more on the *end results* of political process (the kind of states and/or nations that reflect the *culmination* of a process of nation building), our terminology places greater emphasis on the *causal origins* of political process (the nature of the nuclei around which national collectivities coalesce and that seed the nation-building process). Moreover, *ideofocal* is more inclusive than *civic*. While the latter is almost universally associated with multiethnic-libertarian connotations, the former is intended to incorporate multiethnic-authoritarian contexts as well, in which the use of the term *civic* would be at best misleading if not entirely misplaced.[5] The ideofocal notion of nationalism includes both libertarian multiethnic societies as well as those that focus on the allegedly unifying ideal, rather than the rights exercised by those alleged to be unified by it (such as Soviet communism).

Our analysis of diasporas and their formation is intimately linked to these alternative concepts of the nation. I define *diaspora* as a people with a common origin who reside outside their perceived homeland, whether independent or not. They regard themselves, or are regarded by others, as members or potential members of the national community of their homeland, a standing retained regardless of the actual status of their citizenship inside or outside their homeland.[6]

The dichotomous distinction between the two archetypal paradigms of "nation"—ethnofocal and ideofocal—constitutes the conceptual foundation for the ensuing analytical framework. This framework illustrates how different processes of diaspora formation and secessionist desires are linked to various paths of nation building and maintenance. As noted before, there is a duality in the processes of diaspora formation and secession motivation that corresponds to differing flaws in either the generation of a new principle of nation identity or the maintenance of an existing one. These deficiencies (or "aberrations" from theoretical ideals) may be rooted in sociocultural divisions, ideopolitical rifts, and/or geoeconomic inequities.[7]

Table 1 traces the major failures that produce processes of diaspora formation and secession motivation. It shows how in an ethnofocal setting, diaspora formation and/or secessionist drives may be the result either of the failure to create (or impose) a monoethnic national identity (Class A) or the failure to maintain one (Class B). By contrast, in an ideo-

TABLE 1. The Influence of Nation Type on Diaspora and Secession Processes

Generic Principle of National Building	Failure to Create/Maintain Generic National Principle	Resultant Diaspora and Secessionist Processes	Empirical Examples
Ethnofocal Class A	Failure to create a monoethnic national identity; significant disparity between geopolitical borders and ethnopolitical allegiances	(a) Migration—voluntary or forced. Formation of "stateless" ethnic diasporas (b) Rebellion and secessionist efforts by indigenous minorities (c) Irredentist minorities	(a) Tibetan refugees in India (b) Kurdish rebellion in Iraq, Turkey, and Iran (c) Sudeten Germans
Class B	Failure to maintain a monoethnic national identity after largely monoethnic state established without separatist pressure along ethnic lines	1. Disputes over ideological issues regarding the manner in which monoethnic state should be governed (a) Diasporic communities result of political not ethnic persecution. Political refugees not stateless people (b) Separatist pressures for division of state result in two states for one monoethnic group (c) Strong propensity to reunification after resolution of ideological rifts 2. Large-scale inflows of alien populations	1. (a) Iranian exiles, Vietnamese refugees (b) China/Taiwan (endogenous ideological generated rift); East/West Germany (exogenously imposed ideological rift) (c) German and Vietnamese reunification 2. North Africans in France; population dumping (Filipinos in Indonesia)
Ideofocal Class C	Failure to create a supraethnic national identity; rejection of attempts to impose a supraethnic national identity on multiethnic community resident with geopolitical frontiers of a political unit	(a) Secessionist pressure almost inevitable, especially if accompanied by weakening of the central regime that initiated imposition of supraethnic doctrine (b) Postsecession diaspora result due to internal migration (forced or voluntary) during period of attempted imposition of supraethnic doctrine	(a) Baltic States, Sikhs in India (b) Russian communities in post-Soviet Baltic states
Class D	Failure to maintain a supraethnic national identity—disintegration of a previously unifying panethnic ideofocal principle that may be democratically generated or authoritarian imposed	(a) Secession pressure only if disparate ethnic groups territorially concentrated (b) (i) Postsecession diaspora result only if internal migration occurred during period of validity of supraethnic doctrine; (ii) Otherwise multiethnic society uniformly diffuse and only ideological separatism likely (c) Diaspora in ideofocal host state may foment secession in distant homeland	(a) Quebec, former Yugoslavia (Milošević) (b) (i) Balkans; (ii) Multiculturalism (c) Slovak diaspora

focal setting, diaspora formation and/or secessionist drives may be the result of either the failure to impose a supraethnic national identity (Class C) or the failure to maintain one (Class D).

In light of the definition of *nation*, the failure to create or to maintain a national identity will occur whenever there arises an effective challenge that disputes the legitimacy of the prevailing source of sovereign authority. If this challenge arises with the inception of a sovereign political unit, the failure will be one of creation (or imposition). If it arises after such a unit has effectively stabilized, the failure will be one of maintenance. Challenges that dispute the unitary nature of a single source of sovereignty and call for its division into two or more sources will express themselves as secessionist claims. Challenges that call for the adoption of an alternative *existing* source will express themselves as irredentist claims. Coercive rejections of such challenges are liable to generate migratory flows and exilic and/or diasporic communities.

The development of a theoretical model to account for the occurrence of such failures, with sufficient generality, elegance, and parsimony to elevate it above a mere description of the actual historical events that brought them about, is an ambitious task beyond this study's more modest scope. Rather, I confine myself to laying the foundations for a conceptual frame of reference for the causal analysis of the formation of secessionist claims and diasporic communities. From the underlying rationale of such a framework, I then propose a functional typology for a classification of these phenomena and processes—which is a fundamental prerequisite for almost any scientific endeavor. A taxonomical endeavor is a less glamorous but indispensable preliminary for a more sophisticated venture in model building.[8]

Class A: Failure to Impose a Monoethnic National Identity

The major causal stimulus in this category is the attempt by certain nation-states to implement an ethnofocal principle by imposing the identity of a dominant ethnic group as the national identity of the state, even though the boundaries of geopolitical sovereignty do not coincide with boundaries of ethnopolitical allegiance. Resistance to this imposition and subjugation may in principle result in one of two diametrically opposed processes, or a combination of both.

1. Migration (forced or voluntary) of the ethnic minority, and the creation of diasporas outside its indigenous homeland. Some of

these diasporas may be granted citizenship in host states, potentially facilitating their assimilation to a new national identity,
while others may remain stateless refugees, deprived of such
opportunity.

2. Rebellion and endeavors by an ethnic minority to extricate itself
   from foreign domination by secession or irredentism—that is,
   either to establish a separate ethnofocal sovereignty or to unite
   with a contiguous neighboring state of compatible ethnic
   makeup. Here again, these secessionist and irredentist tendencies need not necessarily be mutually exclusive, and both may
   occur simultaneously, as the Moldovan case exhibits.⁹

Claims for self-determination of indigenous populations may involve
diasporas abroad or kindred states with strong ethnonational ties to the
minority claimants. For example, the support of Armenia and diasporic
Armenians around the globe in the secessionist struggle of Armenians in
Nagorno-Karabakh has been critical in the efforts of the latter to resist
Azerbaijani hegemony.¹⁰

Extreme attempts to impose ethnofocal identity have taken the
extreme forms of genocide and population transfer. The struggle
between Turks and Armenians over the possession of a single homeland
led to the Armenian holocaust of 1915, when a million and a half Armenians perished. Population transfer—which was once considered an
acceptable norm in the creation of new nation-states—was another
method in the implementation of the monoethnic Turkish ideal. The
Greco-Turkish exchange of populations after the Treaty of Lausanne set
a precedent for compulsory transfer of populations in our time.¹¹ More
than a million Greeks were sent from Turkey to Greece, and a smaller
number of Turks from Greece to Turkey, thereby drastically reducing
diasporic presence on both sides of the border.

In addition, the failure to impose a monoethnic Turkish nationality
and erase the quest for a separate Kurdish entity has generated a for-
midable stateless community, thereby setting the stage for chronic
secession drives. Kurdish pursuit of self-determination came close to
realization after World War I, when the principle of self-determination was sanctioned at the Versailles Peace Conference. Thereafter, in
the Treaty of Sèvres in 1920, the Kurds were promised an independent
state to be carved out in "areas lying east of the Euphrates."¹² Yet Kurdish hopes were quickly shattered when Mustafa Kemal Atatürk

founded the modern Turkish state, which flaunted the international convention by refusing to recognize ethnically based minorities. Since then Kurds remain scattered in many states, suffering from their host governments' efforts to deny and crush their identity. Undoubtedly, "if there is one thing that united all [Kurdish contiguous host] countries— Iraq, Iran, Turkey, and Syria—it is their hostility to the Kurds and their unwillingness to see the emergence of a Kurdish state in their midst."[13]

Class B: Failure to Maintain an Ethnofocal Identity

Even states in which the implementation of the ethnofocal principle has largely been successful (with or without the use of force) are not immune to divisions that may lead to exiled diaspora and political separatism. Unlike cases of impaired implementation of the ethnofocal idea, in this case the division and dispersion are the result of ideological, not ethnological, rifts that override the sense of unity engendered by common ethnic affiliation. Several such disputes, particularly in the latter part of the twentieth century, have resulted in the splitting of nation-states into two or more sovereign entities. The divisions of East and West Germany, North and South Vietnam, and North and South Korea are all instances of largely uniform ethnic states breaking up into independent political units, not because of the rivalry over ethnocultural dominance, but over paradigms of politico-socio-economic organization. Whether endogenously generated or exogenously imposed, such rifts have also produced large flows of exiles and refugees turned diasporas.

Political exiles who contested the government in their monoethnic home nation without challenging the boundaries of the state or its ethnobased identity are a common feature of modern world politics. Such exilic groups, however, should be distinguished from stateless diasporic communities that aspire to create a new (additional) state, rather than displace an incumbent regime in an existing state.[14] While in the former case, centrifugal stimuli for secessionists' division and dispersion are rooted in ethnic disparities, in the latter instance they are rooted in polemics of political predilections. Empirical evidence in recent years suggests that once these ideological disputes are settled and one socioeconomic doctrine triumphs over another, the centripetal stimuli rooted in ethnic uniformity and the widely accepted concept that one nation should have no more than one nation-state will militate toward eventual reunification.

Reunification, in turn, may also promote the repatriation of diasporas and exiles from other countries.[15]

Another variant of failure to maintain ethnofocal national unity may arise from incoming migratory pressures, resulting in expatriate ethnic communities that may develop into incipient diasporas. Such phenomena are often the consequence of economic exigencies that compel ethnofocal states to open their gates to foreign workers whose remittances may frequently be crucial to the well-being of their compatriots in their country of origin, as in the case of the Turks in Germany, or the large influx of Asians, Africans, and Eastern Europeans into Israel.[16] This variant of identity-maintenance failure is differentiated from that previously discussed because it rarely gives rise to secessionist pressures and because the diaspora is usually (although not exclusively) the result of voluntary inflows into an ethnofocal state, rather than coercively induced outflows from it, as in the previous ideological induced variant.[17]

Perhaps one of the most distinct instances of such a process of immigrant-generated erosion of an ethnofocal identity is the case of the American nation. This is described most succinctly by Lind in the following excerpt.

> The First American Republic, then, was a nation-state, based upon an Anglo-American Protestant nationalism that was as much racial and religious as it was political. Most Americans before the Civil War did not think of theirs as a melting pot nation. The plot of the national story was the expansion across North America of a nation of virtuous, republican, Protestant Anglo-Saxons, a master race possessed of the true principles of government and religion. The Anglo-American nation had a great future ahead of it; but that future did not include cultural hybridization or genetic transformation through amalgamation with other, lesser stocks. This conception of the American identity and destiny would be changed, by massive European immigration.[18]

In this regard, Myron Weiner has pointed out that "countries in which societal membership is based on notions of 'indigenousness' or consanguinity are likely to have a greater sense of threat from migration than societies that have a political definition of membership."[19] Although secessionist claims are rarely associated with this process, the deliberate dumping of diasporas in a neighboring country may be used as a pretext for ensuing irredentist claims by the dispatching state. For example, the influx of Filipinos into the Sabah state of Malaysia encourages the Philippines' claim to the region.

*Class C: Failure to Create (Impose) a Supraethnic
National Identity*

When historic events such as the breakdown of empires, termination of colonial rule, or war produce states whose boundaries include diverse indigenous ethnic groups, efforts may be made by ruling elites to override these disparities by attempting to impose a supraethnic state identity.[20] Such identity may be based on some universal ideal that transcends ethnonational solidarity altogether (e.g., USSR),[21] or on the insistence that loyalty to an imagined nationality should override all ethnocultural or religious affiliation (e.g., India's "secular nationalism" or Syrian and Iraqi Ba'athism).

Note that Class C must be differentiated from Class A where a dominant *existing monoethnic* identity (as opposed to a *new supraethnic* one) is imposed as the national identity on other ethnic communities, such as the one Ethiopia imposed on Eritrea during the dictatorship of Mengistu Haile Mariam. The failure to force a hybrid multiethnic national identity onto an ethnically diverse distinct society, either by administrative/legalistic means in libertarian regimes (i.e., civic nationalism) or by authoritarian coercion, is liable to incite secessionist demands and produce a refugee-based diaspora.[22] An exception to this dynamic may be when ethnic groups are well dispersed throughout the confines of the state without significant geographic concentration in defined regions.[23] Not surprisingly, one of the tactics of ideofocal imposition has been to encourage or to coerce population blending via resettlement in order to achieve ethnonational heterogeneity (as opposed to Class A where population transfer is intended to achieve ethnonational homogeneity).

Class D: Failure to Maintain a Supraethnic Identity

In this category the principal causal impetus is likely to be the obsolescence or loss of relevance of a former unifying ideal. A supraethnic ideal may be accepted and even internalized in authoritarian settings as well as libertarian ones. Thus, for analytical purposes, one must distinguish between the *failure to achieve* a widespread internalized acceptance of the supraethnic national identity and the *failure to maintain* such internalization (after it has been achieved). Susanne Hoeber Rudolph and Lloyd Rudolph have made a similar distinction in their analysis of conflicts in the former Yugoslavia and in India, where Hindu nationalism has been on the rise.[24] Rather than focus on the question of why old conflicts are flaring up anew (Class C), they asked why traditionally harmonious mosaics have been shattered (Class D).[25]

In Class D processes, the disintegration of a unifying ideofocal principle may be closely linked to a process of regime transformation and state dissolution. Declining authoritarian regimes that initiated and sustained an ideofocal imposition over ethnically distinct minorities (residing in defined areas) are particularly susceptible to secessionist drives.

The Influence of Regime Types

In the following section I elaborate on the basic nation type (ethnofocal/ideofocal) categorization by demonstrating how the influence of differing regime types (libertarian/authoritarian) affects the various classes of diaspora- and secession-related processes, generating several subvariants of these classes.

Autocratic regimes' limited plurality and accountability affords them greater freedom of action in dealing coercively with challenges to their sovereign authority relative to libertarian regimes.[26] Clearly this difference in "coercive latitude" in the different regimes is likely to express itself in the treatment meted out to ethnic dissidents or separatist claimants, tending to make certain diaspora-formation- and secession-related processes more prevalent in one type of regime rather than in another. I thus expect that the interaction between the various categories in the foregoing nation-type-based genealogy, on the one hand, and differing regime types, on the other, will produce additional sources of variation in the basic categories developed here. (It should of course be emphasized that these postulated regime-induced variations should be interpreted in terms of differences in *probable propensities* rather than *deterministic dichotomies.*)

In addition to the influences of nation type and regime type, those influences that are rooted in the composition of the population (i.e., immigrant communities versus indigenous peoples) have important effects on the diasporas and secession-related processes, which cut across, and are superimposed on, the divisions discussed hitherto.[27] Consequently, it is a factor that impinges significantly upon the nature of the nation-state and the concept of national allegiance. As such it is incorporated in the ensuing analysis, receiving extensive attention in the discussion of the various categories in the elaborated genealogy.

Libertarian and Authoritarian Influences on
Ethnofocal Processes

Very few libertarian states with ethnofocal aspirations have been able to maintain a monoethnically homogeneous community. More frequently, ethnofocal libertarian states were established by a dominant group that incorporated indigenous minorities who were reluctant to forgo the perception of congruence between their ethnic affiliation and their own national identity. Some of these indigenous groups may have been previously self-governing societies, while others were diasporas of existing nation-states. The birth of Israel as a Jewish state is to a large degree an exceptional case, in which the genesis of a ethnofocal libertarian state involved the simultaneous repatriation of a stateless diaspora (Jews) and the partially coercive dispersion of a partially indigenous ethnic minority (Palestinians). Palestinians have consequently perceived themselves as a stateless diaspora with ethnonational aspirations, similar to those previously harbored by the Jews.[28]

In ethnofocal libertarian states, especially those uncomplicated by ethnically disparate minorities, a high value is placed on preserving the uniformity of the community. State authorities strive to avoid "tainting" the ethnic composition of the population by restricting immigration of nonnationals and/or preventing ethnically "incompatible" residents from acquiring citizenship rights. Some ethnofocal countries, like Germany and Israel, may also encourage the repatriation of their kindred diasporic communities.

Broadly speaking, therefore, libertarian states without disparate indigenous ethnic populations are less susceptible to diasporic or exile politics, let alone to secessionist challenges by disgruntled ethnic minorities. They may, however, face secessionist threats on ideopolitical grounds. During the American Civil War, for instance, the Southern Confederacy made no claim to a separate ethnicity but rather to a separate ideology that supported slavery, thus casting doubt on some of its "libertarian" propensities.[29] The move toward political secession—as opposed to ethnonational secession—may take place under different types of political regimes. However, it is more likely to occur during civil strife or regime transition when forces in the periphery are in a position to defy the center.

Despite their basic reluctance to admit nonnational immigrants and refugees, many homogenous libertarian states have opened their gates to aliens for economic or humane reasons—as they are liberal democracies after all. Though such immigrant communities are not likely to become secessionists (as they have no generic ties to a defined region in their new country), they tend to cultivate minority consciousness in their host societies and often develop diasporic identities.[30] In reality, many immigrant groups have asserted their identification with their native lands in large measure, as a result of their communal experience abroad. Even in relatively free settings, immigrants face exclusion and hardships in their new countries of domicile, and they may feel alienated because of religious differences with their host community.

In the United States, especially at the turn of the twentieth century, many diasporas whose group identity had been dormant became ardent nationalists, much more than they ever had been in their native lands. With the outbreak of World War I, ethnic Americans became increasingly preoccupied with the independence of their countries of origin. Inspired by Woodrow Wilson's proclamation of the principle of self-determination, Poles, Ukrainians, Lithuanians, Armenians, Albanians, and Croats mobilized their diasporic energies into a powerful force in promoting the cause of national independence of their homelands, carefully blending Wilson's postwar vision into their home country's agenda. To a large extent, the Eastern European immigrants were permitted (and even encouraged) to display their attachment to their homelands because they were ruled by German-speaking nations. President Wilson's sympathy for the independence of Eastern Europeans was however also linked to his personal political ambition to build supportive constituencies among ethnic Americans for electoral purposes.[31]

By juxtaposing the liberal ethos of their host state against the ethnofocal definition of the community, immigrant groups may pose a challenge to the ethnofocal identity of their host countries. Recent examples of this phenomenon are the identity and citizenship debates in Germany and France. Both countries were founded on the equivalence of nationality and citizenship, and have refused, in principle, to think of themselves as countries of immigrants. These countries have markedly dissimilar approaches to national identity and citizenship. France has adopted the principle of *jus soli* (place of birth constituting the determining factor) and has naturalized nonnational newcomers with a universalist and assimilationist vision of turning foreigners into Frenchmen. In Germany, by contrast, citizenship is ethnically based and blood-transmitted (*jus sanguinis*). However, both countries have witnessed an anti-immigrant xenophobic backlash and a growing resentment at the prospect of a pluralistic society.[32] Indeed, libertarian ethnofocal countries that open their gates to nonnationals—even without granting them citizenship—may in time evolve into "poly-ethnic democracies," to use Will Kymlicka's term, or even reconsider their own ethnofocal distinctiveness.[33] Indeed, Germany is the classic example of a country that has moved away from the status of a "reluctant land of immigration" to a more multiethnic state. Due to its openness to guest workers and its liberal asylum policies, Germany is now one of Europe's leading recipients of foreign nationals (about 9 percent of its total population). Despite the Kohl government's efforts to reduce the numbers of foreign residents in Germany and to curtail the access of asylum seekers, Germany could not stem the tide, especially given declining demographic trends in the German indigenous population. The growing reality of a multiethnic society has pushed Germany to adjust its national identity by adopting a more legal-liberal approach to citizenship that undermines the ethnicity principle as the sole criterion for access.[34]

Though many ethnofocal Western democracies have moved to halt migration, they are still loath to deport "rejected asylum seekers or individuals given temporary asylum." Western democracies have also granted foreign workers many social rights and benefits usually provided to citizens. Nonlibertarian ethnofocal states, by contrast, have imposed many civil restrictions on migrant workers. Since migrant workers "are unencumbered by protests from human rights organizations in their own country and unrestrained by liberal ideology," the nations may quickly deport their foreign populations once they consider the populations politically dangerous or economically ineffective.[35] The massive expulsions of foreign laborers by Saudi Arabia and Arab principalities during the Persian Gulf crisis are examples of this phenomenon.

Moreover, when ethnofocal libertarian states are founded or coalesce in the process of incorporating indigenous populations (as opposed to ethnofocal states that opened their doors to ethnically disparate immigrants), the potential for cleavages and political tensions between the dominant group and the incorporated minorities is immanent. Even if "common citizenship" is offered to the minorities, the claim that "there is more than one people, each with the right to rule themselves" is likely to endure.[36] Indeed, the increasing autonomy and struggles for self-determination of aboriginal nations in Western countries in recent decades have challenged "the way political rights are to be understood within liberal democracies."[37]

Controversy over kindred populations may arise when neighboring states take a strong interest in the fate of their respective diasporas across the border. The Hungarian minority in postindependent Slovakia (Hungarians make up 11 percent of Slovakia's population) has been targeted by Slovak nationalists, which has raised tensions between the two countries.[38] When democracies confront each other on this score they are more likely to collaborate to defuse tensions; they may mutually agree to grant cultural autonomy to their respective diasporas or may even promote peaceful population exchanges. Yet when such confrontation develops between more autocratic countries, a conflagration of violence and even ethnic cleansing is more likely to ensue.[39]

Concern, real or otherwise, for indigenous minorities in neighboring states (perceived to be kindred diasporas) may be exploited by extremists to foment nationalist fervor and/or to fuel irredentism. The Nazis' support of the Sudeten German demand for self-determination from Czechoslovakia was a pretext to undermine the existence of the Czechoslovak state itself. More recently, the fate of Russian minorities in post-Soviet states has been exploited by Russian nationalists, in an attempt to challenge Russia's fragile polyarchy.[40]

Coercive attempts to assimilate indigenous populations into the majority have taken place under all types of regimes, although authoritarian governments are far less scrupulous than democracies in imposing cultural hegemony or in ignoring minority cultural demands. The example of the Kurds in Turkey illustrates clearly the impact of regime type on the fate of diasporas and the accompanying complex of political processes such as separatism, perceptions of national identity, territorial boundaries, and definitions of homeland. Turkey's harsh treatment of its large Kurdish minority has repeatedly undermined its attempts to present itself as a Western-style libertarian state. Its refusal to recognize a separate Kurdish identity and its uncompromising efforts to impose a monoethnic Turkish nationality are widely perceived to be inconsistent with the norms of modern liberal regimes and have often strained Turkey's relations with the United States and its European partners in NATO.[41]

As Arend Lijphart points out, the imposition of a dominant national identity tends to spur claims for autonomy or self-government and to breed tensions of dual loyalties. Ethnofocal liberal states may choose to abandon the option of assimilation in favor of "consociational solutions which accept the plural divisions as the basic building blocks for a stable democratic regime." If such arrangements are implausible or were tried and failed, "the remaining logical alternative is to reduce pluralism by dividing the state into two or more separate and more homogeneous states . . . [Indeed] secession into sovereign statehood goes a significant step beyond the segmental autonomy, of course, but it is not incompatible with the basic assumption underlying the consociational model."[42] While libertarian regimes have been generally amenable to peaceful consociational arrangements, the nature of authoritarian regimes militates against their implementing similar measures. Such nonlibertarian regimes in ethnofocal states will have a higher propensity to resort to extreme coercive measures to eradicate the ethnic identity of dissenting minorities and suppress any expression of aspirations for self-determination. These may include forcible expulsion of ethnic elites, mass transfer of indigenous minorities, and even genocide.

Libertarian and Authoritarian Influences on the Ideofocal Process

Unlike the ethnofocal libertarian states where in principle the indigenous population rejects ethnically discriminatory domination, in ideofocal libertarian states the rejection focuses on inclusion into a larger ethnically heterogeneous entity under the banner of alleged civil "homogenization."[43] In other words, while in an ethnofocal setting the rejection is of perceived ethnic subjugation, in an ideofocal setting the rejection is of perceived ethnic egalitarianism, according to which sociocultural diversity must be subordinated to civic-legal equality in the dispensation of governmental authority. In this regard, it is perhaps appropriate to recall Lord Acton's distinction between the demands of allegiance that ethnofocal and ideofocal nationalism can legitimately place on the individual. In the former case, these demands are unlimited, embracing all walks of life, but in the latter case they are limited only to the political sphere, with a "firm barrier" emplaced against the "intrusion . . . into the social department."[44]

In principle, two major variants of this latter class, which I have designated as a "harmony of diversity," may be identified—either a harmony of *discrete* ethnicities or one of *diffuse* ethnicities (see fig. 1). In practice, it is likely that the former variant will pertain to a population composed of geographically distinct indigenous ethnicities (as in India), while the latter is more likely to pertain to a largely immigrant society comprising a diffuse cosmopolitan mélange (as in the United States). The Canadian example reflects a combination of both.

The nature of a harmoniously diffuse ideofocal variant has been well articulated by Michael Walzer. He wrote that in the U.S. model,

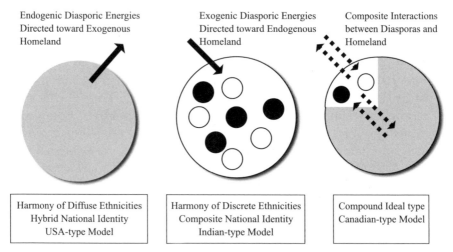

Endogenic Diasporic Energies Directed toward Exogenous Homeland

Exogenic Diasporic Energies Directed toward Endogenous Homeland

Composite Interactions between Diasporas and Homeland

Harmony of Diffuse Ethnicities
Hybrid National Identity
USA-type Model

Harmony of Discrete Ethnicities
Composite National Identity
Indian-type Model

Compound Ideal type
Canadian-type Model

Fig. 1. Diasporic conditions in ideofocal libertarian states—ideal-type variants

> the singular [political] union claims to distinguish itself from all the [ethnic] plural unions, refusing to endorse or support their ways of life or to take an active interest in their social reproduction or to allow any one of them to seize state power, even locally . . . there is no privileged majority and there are no exceptional minorities.[45]

By contrast, Nehru characterized the harmonious discrete variant in his description of India's secular nationalism as follows.

> Unity was not conceived as something imposed from outside, a standardization of beliefs. It was something deeper, and within its fold, the widest tolerance of belief and custom was practiced and every variety acknowledged and even encouraged.[46]

These structural differences tend to generate divergent influences on the nature of diasporas, their political objectives, and their modes of operation (see fig. 1). With respect to the ethnically discrete model, the diasporic condition involves *indigenous* ethnicities residing *outside* the borders of the ideofocal nation-state (such as Punjabi Sikhs and Kashmiris outside India). In the ethnically diffuse variant, the diasporic condition involves *foreign* ethnicities residing *inside* the borders of the ideofocal nation state (like many hyphenated Americans). In the former case, diasporic energies are directed *inward* from outside the ideofocal state in which the homeland lies. In the latter case energies are directed *outward* from within the ideofocal state toward the homeland abroad.

Thus in the latter case secession claims of ethnicities are highly unlikely prospects. Concerns over diasporic identities and actions are mostly associated with the "threat" of multiculturalism and/or dual loyalty. In the United States, for example, critics of the growing "cult of ethnicity" in American civic culture articulate an old American anxiety that the devotion to ancestral homelands undermines national cohesiveness by encouraging subnational loyalties.[47] My own analysis, however, has shown that diasporic involvement of ethnic Americans in homeland issues generally tends to enhance the integration of immigrants, reinforce the value of democracy and pluralism abroad, and temper rather than exacerbate domestic ethnic conflicts.[48]

By contrast, territorially based minorities like the Sikhs and Kashmiris in India or the Quebecois in Canada will be a fertile breeding ground for secessionist ambitions frequently encouraged by outside diasporas. In this respect, kindred ethnic groups (sovereign states or diasporas) may play multiple roles. On the one hand, they may be actively sought after as potential sources of support for secessionist claims. On the other hand, they may themselves be a powerful stimulus in encouraging separatism. Sikhs in North America have played this role for Punjabi aspiration inside India, while France has fulfilled both these functions for Quebec separatists.

In his controversial visit to the province, President de Gaulle energized the nascent secessionist movement in Quebec when he publicly pronounced the call *"Vive le Quebec libre!"* Since then, leaders of the Quebec separatist movement have traveled repeatedly to Paris seeking (and often receiving) the endorsement and encouragement of their French cousins. Indeed, in spite of France's official policy of noninterference, such leaders have been granted treatment and ceremony usually reserved for heads of sovereign states.

In ideofocal authoritarian states, a pan-ethnic vision is invoked to erase previous ethnonational/tribal loyalties of indigenous peoples included in the geopolitical boundaries of the state. Soviet socialism, Titoism, and to some extent Arab Ba'athism fit this model. Attempts to blur the ethnodistinctiveness of regions may lead to a large-scale relocation of population. As regions secede, often because of radical ethnonationalists gaining the upper hand against the sentiment of the general public, attempts to rebuild lost national identities may result in transformation of settler communities into ethnic diasporas. This has been the case in Transdniestria, where ethnic Russians united with Russian-speaking Ukrainians against Moldovian radical ethnonationalists.[49]

The forcible annexation of sovereign nation-states and attempts to impose new identity naturally generate resistance and/or mass departure of indigenous populations that create organized diasporas abroad. Such diasporas are motivated to preserve the original national identity, while their leaders often play a major role in keeping the flame of nationhood alive for their kinfolk in the annexed homeland. Led by the Dalai Lama, the Tibetan diaspora has nurtured an alternative democratic polity in India and, in the words of Franz Michael, has "provided a beam of light and hope . . . for the six million Tibetans remaining in the Chinese-dominated Tibet."[50] Indeed, diasporic leadership may remain, even after generations of displacement, the driving force in the international struggle for reinstating independence and may ultimately assume a central role once sovereignty is regained. The crucial role played by the diasporic Dashnak Party in Armenian modern history is a case in point.[51]

Diasporas as Cause and Effect in Ideofocal Disintegration

The overriding goal of ideofocal imposition is to erase and deny the existence of indigenous group identities, as noted earlier. History has shown this to be an immensely difficult task. In the former Soviet Union, while some observers consider the policy of pluralist integration to have been quite successful before being frustrated by the collapse of the state, others have argued that the inadequacy of Soviet nationalism was immanent in its very nature, "made manifest by the collapse [of the old state] but not caused by it."[52]

However, at times, the ideofocal goal of fusing diverse identities into genuinely internalized supraethnic national sentiment seems attainable in both in a libertarian and an authoritarian context.

Thus as a libertarian example, the American people, according to some observers who have rejected the multicultural vision, "constitute a genuine nation, with its own nation-state, the USA, with its own genuine, if largely inarticulate, nationalism." According to this view, "most Americans of all races are born and acculturated into the American nation; most immigrants and their descendants will be assimilated into it. The American nation is different in detail from [other] . . . nations. It is not, however, different in kind."[53] Among authoritarian states, Yugoslavia under Tito was perceived by some as a country that successfully attained a supranational goal of constructing a multinational state in the Balkans.

Clearly, there may be justified debates over the empirical accuracy of these assessments.[54] However, for analytical purposes one should distinguish between the rejection of the imposition of a supraethnic identity prior to its genuine internalization and the disintegration of a genuinely internalized supraethnic identity that allows the resurgence of previously "suspended" ethnonational sentiments. The fact that the unequivocal classification of any particular empirical case into one or another of these categories may be open to controversy should not diminish the fundamental conceptual validity (or utility) of this analytical distinction. Nor should it obscure the fact that they point to two substantially different political conditions under which diasporas may form and secession sentiments arise. If the identity is rejected, the failure to attain the goal of a stable nation may be cited as the cause for diaspora formations and secessionist claims. If the identity disintegrates, this indicates that the successful achievement of this goal guarantees no termination of these processes.

The Balkan reality is illustrative of this point. Tito's relatively successful imposition of the supraethnic Yugoslav identity diminished the political profile and intensity of diasporic aspirants for ethnic-based self-determination. However, Slobodan Milošević's subsequent seizure of power in 1987, wherein he played the Serbian nationalist card, turned out to be a watershed in the course of Balkan nationalism. It ignited interethnic conflict by thrusting the issue of diaspora and secession to the forefront of the national agenda. Likewise, his suppression of ethnic Albanians in Kosovo mobilized Albanians around the world to a common cause.

For diasporic Croats in particular, it was difficult to espouse the cause of independence during Tito's period because of Croatia's fascist legacy and collaboration with the Nazis during World War II. Moreover, Croat diasporic proponents of self-determination were widely regarded in Europe and North America as extremists advocating terrorism to obtain their goal. These exiles did not enjoy wide support among overseas Croats and were hunted by Tito's secret police. The disintegration of Yugoslavia's nationalism and the pursuant intercommunal war galvanized the diaspora at large into action in the service of the seceding state. The emergence of Croatian independence in 1990 was a turning point in the awakening of the Croatian diaspora. The lobbying of Croat nationalists in Germany was instrumental in Germany's early recognition of the new state. Diasporic Croats were also critical in raising money for the 1990 election campaign of Franjo Tudjman.[55] Croats in North America began

to assert their ethnic pride primarily by identifying with the political cause of their kin in the former Yugoslavia. Regardless of their
specific relationship to the mother country, they now speak of
their transformation as a people from . . . a historically repressed
minority group in former Yugoslavia to a proud, new nation that
has successfully shrugged off the yoke of communist rule and
asserted a new sense of purpose and pride.[56]

Tentative Conclusions

Our analysis shows that the idea of the nation-state, even when successfully realized, is patently unable to generate durable stability either internationally or intranationally. A world order of nation-states is seemingly
incapable of preventing either the dispersion of stateless minorities or the
continuing rebellion of ever-emerging ethnicities. These ethnicities per-
petually demand new vehicles to express their own distinct national aspiration as independent political entities, separate from the existing array of
nation-states.

According to the nationalist ideal, an international system of nation-
states should, by the very definition of *state* and *nation*, eliminate ethnically motivated transnational loyalties and do away with intranational
strife. In theory, any disgruntled diasporic ethnic group, whether resident
in an alien monoethnic state or an unsatisfying ideofocal one, could then
immigrate to its own nation-state, while contented diasporas that have
forsaken aspirations of self-determination could be absorbed into the
sociopolitical fabric of host nations either on an ideofocal basis or as willingly incorporated minorities in an ethnofocal one. This view, however,
is based on an underlying assumption of a static equilibrium of political
loyalties. If this were indeed true, then one could well expect that an
appropriate division of humanity into nation-states would generate a tendency by which transnational bonds and intranational insurrection would
eventually die out.

Yet this static perspective fails to capture the dynamics of a reality in
which political loyalties and national identities are constantly changing,
even after stable nation-states have coalesced. These dynamics, which
may include processes such as ideofocal disintegration and ethnofocal
rupture (to name but a few of the possibilities), suggest that diaspora formations and secession claims are in fact endemic to a world order of
nation-states, rather than anomalous anachronisms doomed to extinction.
Indeed, the scope for the revival and reconstruction of political alle-

giances and ethnonational identities can be gauged from the fact that the number of homelands and potential nations "is many times larger than the present number of nations with or without a state and infinitely larger than the number of states."[57] This perpetual challenge to the validity of existing political entities may eventually undermine the very conceptual well from which states draw their own legitimacy. The unrestrained invocation of the principle of self-determination challenges the feasibility of its continued implementation in practice. It creates a constant menace of instability and fragmentation of already established states, thus imperiling the viability of a global system based on the dominance of nation-states as the overriding principle of world order. Rather than becoming an anomalous anachronism, diasporas and separatist sentiments appear to be not only an endemic feature of the international system, but a pivotal element in comprehending the direction of present and future trends in it.

TWO

Diasporic Financial Flows and Their Impact on National Identity

Financial transfers from diasporic communities to recipients in the homeland have long been a vehicle for preserving or inducing changes in identities of indigenous kin communities. As early as Hellenic and Roman times, diasporic life was a normal feature of many communities in the Mediterranean region. Members of all sorts of ethnic and religious communities, including Jews, had settled elsewhere in the open and pluralistic Hellenistic world, adopting the local identities (Athenian, Macedonian, Phoenician) of their new homes. In addition to the absence of regret, embarrassment, or low self-esteem, Mediterranean Jews of the time developed no theory, identity, or consciousness of diaspora. Moreover, like many Jewish-Americans today, Jews living outside of Palestine during the Hellenic and Roman period felt no tension between a duty to Jerusalem, the symbolic and real embodiment of their faith, and a loyalty to their place of residence.

This symbolic attachment to Jerusalem manifested itself in a yearly tithe for the maintenance of the Temple, paid by Mediterranean Jews after the Selucid and Ptolemic overlords ceased subsidies. This tithe quickly became a symbolic obligation and a major means through which diaspora Jews affirmed their identity and faith. The importance of this tithe to Jews living across Europe and Asia cannot be overemphasized—a fact not lost on contemporary observers like Philo, Cicero, Josephus, and local Roman authorities, who faced substantial criticism when they tried to curtail the substantial sums being sent to Jerusalem.

In his account of the ancient Jewish diaspora, Erich Gruen writes:

> The size of [diasporic] contributions over the years had brought substantial wealth to the Temple. Josephus proudly observes that

the donations had come from Jews all over Asia and Europe, indeed from everywhere in the world, for a huge number of years. When that activity was interfered with by local authorities, Jews would send up a howl to Rome.[1]

In contrast to interpretations of the tithe that see it as evidence of the abnormal, temporary status of life in the diaspora, these contributions signified a normalization of diasporic life. Such payments simultaneously revealed the diasporic community's confident integration into their new homelands and their commitment to their faith. According to Gruen, "The gesture did not signify a desire for the Return. On the contrary: it signaled that the Return was unnecessary."[2]

Today, even in the era of globalization and the widespread homogenization of culture, people remain dedicated emotionally and politically to the life and well-being of their kin communities in other parts of the world; diasporic attachment to ancestral homelands remains a vital force in international affairs. This attachment is usually expressed openly and unapologetically, mainly by those residing in modern liberal states where allegiance to both the country of origin and the country of domicile exist without conflict. In the United States, for example, the meaning of ethnic identity has been transformed. Old nativist fears—that Americans with emotional ties to their ancestral homelands cannot be fully loyal to the United States—are rapidly disappearing. Those once disparagingly called "hyphenated Americans" feel increasingly free to organize and lobby on behalf of the "old country" as long as they are marketing the American creed abroad.

Signs of a world more hospitable to multiple loyalties are easy to find. Homeland countries that previously restricted their kin abroad to single citizenship now permit dual citizenship. These countries have also enabled their kin diasporas to retain broad economic and political rights in their kin states, even though the individuals clearly have established themselves as loyal citizens in other states. Moreover, with "the deregulation of international financial markets coupled with new technologies [that] has made sending money back home easier and cheaper than ever," the money flowing back from diaspora members has become an important economic force for the homeland.[3]

This chapter focuses on the *identity-related* impact of these flows, particularly with regard to their effects on sentiments of national affiliation and the manner in which they may be molded by those providing the funds. While the impact of identity-related issues is a topic that is gaining increasing importance in international relations theory, particularly within the constructivist school of thought, the full significance of identity in world affairs has yet to be adequately developed by scholars in this field.

I elaborate on the general observation that identities are a potent force in international politics by (1) formalizing the concept of national identity and specifying its distinct components; (2) broadening the focus of identity beyond the traditional demarcation of states to include diasporic kin residing in far-removed lands who participate in the process of homeland identity formation; (3) establishing that diasporic financial flows are an important vehicle through which diasporic influence impinges upon the various components of identity; and (4) identifying structural channels through which diasporic financial influences are transmitted to affect the various components of identity, and how the importance of these channels changes over time in accordance with the evolutionary stage of homeland identity and agenda, and diasporic perceptions thereof. A systematic elaboration of these issues enables a structured articulation of the manner in which issues of identity affect the stability of the nation-state system and hence the very foundations of international relations.

It is precisely these diaspora-related influences in general, and financially related ones in particular, together with their ramifications for national identities, that place the subject matter of this chapter firmly at the center of relevance for debate on international relations today. In the final analysis, the sense of identity, affiliation, and loyalty constitutes the glue of nations and thus the underlying foundation upon which the nation-state system rests. In this regard Holsti observes that "reasons of affinity and sentiment rather than . . . [realist considerations of] power or more hard-headed cost-benefit analyses" are liable to determine state conduct in the international system.[4] Realists would not necessarily disagree with this observation. They recognize the "reciprocal relationship between identities and conflict, arguing that conflict both grows out of and stimulates the perception of differences among groups."[5] Thus, the mechanisms that either engender change or preserve stability in national affinities and sentiments necessarily comprise a major element for comprehending some of the most significant contemporary developments in global politics today.

For this reason, in the subsequent survey of diasporic monetary transfers to homeland recipients, I draw a clear distinction between those that are motivated mainly by economic considerations (such as remittances and profit-driven investments) and those that are purposefully intended to influence perceptions of identity. I commence the analysis with a brief survey of the broader dynamics of diaspora-homeland interaction, under-scoring how this impinges on issues of national identity and hence on the cohesiveness and stability of existing nation-states, as well as the relations between them. In subsequent sections, I propose a conceptual framework to impose some analytical order on the wide-ranging empirical diversity of diaspora-homeland financial transfers and their impact on issues of identity—and on the state system.

The model proposes a specification of (1) the components of national identity, (2) the channels through which financial influences may be exerted on these identity components, and (3) how the relative importance of the various transmission channels may vary over time. I employ numer-ous empirical examples drawn from a wide range of contexts for purposes of comparison in order to elucidate various aspects of the theoretical framework. I also find it instructive to delve in greater detail into the case of the Jewish diaspora–Israel interaction. This particular case study may be seen as a *fully developed paradigm* of relations between expatriate com-munities and the country of origin (from pre-independence via attainment of statehood to the period of state consolidation), portions of which often reflect other diaspora-homeland experiences, that do not (or do not yet) exhibit the same range of evolution. This, of course, does not indicate that they are qualitatively different but rather that they manifest only part of the full range of the paradigmatic diaspora-homeland nexus. Moreover, the case of Jewish diaspora–Israel interaction is often looked upon and sin-gled out by other diasporas and their kin states as a model to be emulated.

The chapter concludes with a brief synopsis of the possible method-ological merits of the model and offers some tentative conclusions that arise from it, particularly with regard to the effect of diaspora-homeland financial flows in international politics today. The final section also sug-gests ways in which the model and the conclusions that flow from it con-tribute to the ongoing debates on identity within international relations today.

The Dynamics of the Interaction between the Diaspora and the Nation-State

A world order of nation-states is incapable of eliminating either the dis-persion of stateless minorities or the recurring rebellion of ever-emerg-ing ethnicities demanding vehicles to express their own distinct national aspirations as independent political entities separate from the existing array of nation-states (as outlined in chap. 1). At the base of this seemingly perennial political instability, there appears to lurk an inherent volatility in the way national identities are defined and perceived. Diasporas and the influences they exert have a central role in this dynamic of disintegration and regeneration of sentiments of national cohesiveness, suggesting that diasporas are endemic to a world order of nation-states, rather than anomalous anachronisms doomed to extinction. Certainly, far from being fading echoes of unfulfilled political aspirations of stateless communities, diasporas often are the driving force behind the reawakening of such aspirations.

Diasporic efforts to affect issues of national identity in their country of origin, kin state, or symbolic homeland stem from a variety of motives. Such motives may derive from the desire to change the character of the prevailing regime and/or of national institutions that determine identity-related realities in a manner that will enable return of expatriates to the homeland. Other motives include the fact that the perceived image of the kin state impinges on diaspora status in host societies, both in terms of the cohesiveness of the diasporic community itself and in terms of perceived image in the eyes of others.

Diasporic financial support of causes in the kin state may also stem from a desire to feel part of the homeland experience, to assuage guilt, or to provide a focus for activity on the part of diasporic organizations. For example, the manner in which Israel defines its national identity and conducts its domestic and foreign policies has immediate ramifications on the lives of many Jews abroad. For years, Israel has relied on American Jews for financial and political support, while Jews in America have received psychological comfort from Israel's continued existence and successes. Money raised to influence homeland causes is also an integral part of the process of institution building and identity formation (preservation) in the diasporic communities. Accordingly, during the early years of the Oslo Peace Accords, some American Jews expressed concern that without the danger of war in the Middle East, American Jewry would no longer feel the urge to donate to kin causes *inside* the United States.[6] It is thus only natural that American Jews continue to be keenly interested in influencing the politics of identity in their historic homeland in a manner concordant with their preferences. However, the very attempt to exert influence on national identity inside the homeland via fund transfers may in itself affect diasporic status.

Transnational Flows, Diasporic Effects, and National Identity

Three major categories of diasporic transnational flows may be discerned: flows directed from kin communities abroad toward the homeland; flows from the homeland to the kin communities in hostlands (broadly defined as countries of domicile); and finally, flows within transfrontier diasporic networks. In this chapter, I focus principally on the first of these categories—financial flows from diasporic communities into the homeland, which I term *intraethnic interstate* (IEIS) flows.[7] The subsequent discussion is thus a preliminary endeavor to conceptualize the effects that such IEIS monetary movements may have in accentuating, attenuating, and otherwise reconfiguring perceptions of national identity, including the style and substance of national sentiments in the homeland—thus influencing the behavior of nation-states in the international system.

It should be noted that although the propagating forces, both technological and psychological, of globalization tend to facilitate easier and more rapid transfer of diasporic funds, such monetary movements and their concomitant effects have been prevalent for decades, even centuries. Diaspora financing has constituted a critical resource base for the conduct of the struggle for national sovereignty since the nineteenth century. Early Fenianism in Northern Ireland, for instance, "was to a great extent the creation of the Irish diaspora in the United States. . . . in its first generation [Fenianism] depended on . . . [diasporic] American money."[8] Diasporic funds were also responsible for domestic consolidation and economic well-being in Greece and Italy. One scholar has commented that in the establishment of modern Greece, the "diaspora functioned more or less as an 'absentee bourgeoisie.'" Another has noted that at the turn of the twentieth century, Little Italy in New York City contributed "more to the tax roll of Italy than some of the poorer provinces in Sicily or Calabria."[9] A particularly dramatic illustration of how diasporic funds are intertwined with the formation of national identity is the interaction between the leaders of the Polish independence movement and the Polish-American community known as Polonia on the eve of World War I. The prewar links between Polish-American "peasant" immigrants and Poland were primarily familial or based on regional ties. National consciousness had not developed, and class differentiation undermined the sentiment of Polish unity. The leaders of the Polish independence movement strove to overcome this lack of national cohesion by granting the

Fig. 2.   The link between diasporic financial flows and International Relations

less affluent Polish-Americans inclusion and upgraded status in the national endeavor in return for their financial contributions. By 1918, Polish-American contributions to the independence movement totaled the huge sum of over $87 million and earned the diaspora the title of the "fourth province of Poland."[10]

More than ever before, today the "democratization" of technology, finance, and information amplify the density, range, and impact of transnational links. The influence of these effects is transmitted into the prevailing state system and impinges upon the functioning of the international system. This causal chain linking diasporic financial flows to issues of international relations is schematically depicted in figure 2. It is my contention that while high-speed, widespread transfrontier communal contact and international money flows between diasporas and their kin states are frequently associated with globalization and the blurring of indigenous identities, they can also generate the antithetical phenomenon of localization and the sharpening of ethnonational sentiments.

Even the most superficial examination of diasporic-related monetary flows in today's world reveals the immense significance that they have for economic, political, and sociocultural developments in both home and host countries—as well as for international relations in general. These effects may range from state- and nation-building processes in the homeland to discriminatory alienation of diasporas in host societies. Diasporic-related funds have been used to promote struggles for self-determination and for state and/or nation building in Eastern Europe, the former Soviet Union, Africa, and the Indian subcontinent. They have been crucial to the consolidation of newly independent Armenia and have played an important role in the struggle for a Palestinian state.

In some Latin American countries, such as Colombia, the Dominican Republic, Nicaragua, and El Salvador, remittances and other financial investments by kin communities located in the United States have been among the most important factors in shaping the character of political organizations and state institutions, as well as deeply influencing daily life and culture.[11] Some have even compared the impact of diaspora financial influences on Latin American reality to that of the Spanish Conquest. In the case of the Dominican Republic, Levitt noted that the reliance on diaspora money has prompted Dominican legislators to approve dual citizenship and expatriate voting rights. She predicts that diaspora "influence over national politics is likely to increase with their economic contribution. The more the Dominican Republic needs the economic injections they provide, the more the Dominican government will take steps to ensure their continued involvement."[12]

In China, the financial flows from expatriates have generated much of the volume of foreign investment in recent years. These flows brought about significant changes in the perception of the national status of Chinese diasporic communities, both inside China and in their countries of domicile—especially in Southeast Asian countries such as Indonesia, Malaysia, and the Philippines. Indeed, Asian diasporic entrepreneurs in the high-tech sectors "bring back [to their homeland] not just money but an infusion of entrepreneurial spirit and skills that their home countries often sorely lack."[13]

Political economist Devesh Kapur shows how, in the last two decades, diasporic financial flows, investments, and business links with homelands have challenged (if not reversed) the migratory vision known as "brain drain" with the notion of a "brain gain." According to Kapur, the diaspora links with the homeland defy the Western idea of capitalism's universal impartiality, since diasporic capitalism builds in large part on family control and on long-term trust-based relationships. Such network-based capitalism has increased the impact of diasporic nationalist identity on the production of cultural politics inside the homeland. The growing impact of diasporic South Asians and Indians in particular on the reshaping of the nationalist creed of their homeland highlights these phenomena.

In January 2003 India's government, in an effort to draw upon diasporic money and political power, held the Global Indian Family conference in New Delhi. In a three-day display of kinship celebration the government marked the achievements of over two thousand "prominent" diaspora members. Addressing the conference, Prime Minister Atal Bihar Vajpayee called on the diaspora to strengthen their ties with India, preserve their Indian identity abroad, and use their resources to uplift their ancestral homeland. He offered people with Indian origin dual citizenship and urged the diaspora to continue to invest their money in their homeland.[14]

The money of Indian diaspora does more than advance India's economy. In recent years many accounts describe how the Indian-Hindu communities in the United States are raising substantial funds for Hindu nationalist agendas of the Bharatiya Janata Party (BJP), promoting a movement of Hindu religious nationalism that has increased the level of sectarian tension in the homeland.[15] In 1998, in an excellent example of this kind of nationalist "social investment," the Indian government tested five nuclear devices, an act that was followed by various economic sanctions being placed on the country by the United States and other powers. The immediate result was a deteriorating financial situation that the Indian government fought through the issuance of Diaspora Bonds (specifically called Resurgent India Bonds). These bonds, marketed exclusively to diasporic communities in Europe and the United States, raised over US$4 billion and greatly alleviated the crisis in the homeland. However, complicated issues of dual loyalty surfaced: "In purchasing the bonds, Indian Americans deliberately flouted the stated policy of the United States—to sanction India for its nuclear testing—and joined India in celebrating its newfound military prowess."[16]

It is interesting to note that this financial instrument differed from many of the State of Israel bond issues, which were SEC compliant and, although bought primarily by American Jews, were open to all buyers. Diasporic money has long been a major influence on the Israeli economy in general. In recent years, however, diaspora groups have begun to funnel their resources to specific political and sociocultural factions, rather than donate to the general federations and appeals whose distributions of funds is determined mainly by the Israeli government. This shift has had a substantial impact on the conduct of the public debate and has affected perceptions of national identity.

Conversely, some home countries are investing directly in kin communities abroad to enhance sentiments of national affinity, with the purpose of creating a "bridgehead" for the promotion of commercial and political activities in their host countries. One study of the relations between diasporic Eritreans in Europe and the new Eritrean state shows how the homeland invested greatly in institutionalizing and guiding diasporic contributions and political involvement abroad, including a regular payment of 2 percent of diasporas' annual incomes. This created a culture of contributing to the state that was critical during the war with Ethiopia (1998–2000) when diaspora contributions reached their climax.[17]

These examples constitute only a sample of a far more pervasive and complex phenomenon. It is against the backdrop of this highly varied empirical profusion that I approach the principal objective of this chapter: to devise an analytical structure that imposes a measure of intellectual order on the wide range of diasporic-related monetary transfers and the attendant ramifications on the nation-state and its current status in the international system.

Profit-Oriented versus Identity-Oriented Flows

The first step in this endeavor is to limit our attention to flows that are purposefully intended to influence the formative processes of national identities inside and outside the homeland. This aspect of diaspora-related financial flows has received little attention relative to the extensively researched areas of emigrant remittances and other capital flows such as expatriate investment in the homeland.

What distinguishes IEIS funds that are purposefully intended to affect the "politics of identity" from commercially motivated flows is the fact that IEIS funds are not intended to produce direct economic profits for the source, but rather to promote specific sociopolitical causes that relate directly to issues of national identity. Economically motivated funds may influence identity, but this is an externality or by-product, not its primary purpose. Thus, while on the empirical level, both identity-related and commercially motivated features may be manifest (making unequivocal characterization in any given instance problematic), on the analytical level, this is a conceptual distinction that is both theoretically pertinent and potentially useful.

Some examples elucidate the point. Overseas Chinese are the dominant source (up to 80 percent) of foreign investment in mainland China and to some extent are responsible for the growing spread of China's burgeoning capitalism. The fact that overseas Chinese commercial networks are overwhelmingly based on ties of kinship and/or subethnic regional relations reflects the significance of identity in the conduct of Chinese business affairs.[18] Although this feature may have far-reaching sociopolitical repercussions within China, "overseas Chinese capitalism" is motivated more by considerations of profit rather than by an explicit desire to mold aspects of political or national identity.

The case of the Polish diaspora is another instance in which profit-oriented investments from kin communities abroad served as a vehicle for political change. Private entrepreneurs of Polish origin abroad funneled considerable investments into the homeland economy with the purpose of moving the regime away from a centralized socialist structure to a more open liberal one.[19] A similar phenomenon may be identified in Israel's early years, when Jewish businessmen abroad channeled money into the

Israeli economy, thereby propagating a more liberal, free-enterprise set of values relative to those prevailing in a country that at the time reflected a predilection for pervasive state control of much of the economic activity. Although these financial flows were in part a reflection of a desire to induce changes beyond the purely economic sphere, they also had a profit motive.

Likewise, while remittances from migrant communities to kinfolk in the homeland are motivated oftentimes by considerations of economic livelihood, rather than a conscious intent to shape indigenous national identity, they have tremendous impact on all walks of life in the homeland. In some Central American states, where remittances have at times actually exceeded revenue from exports, they also appear to have had a stabilizing effect after years of civil war. Like economic transfers, remittances can have secondary effects on identity.[20] Actors within the homeland that benefit economically from diasporic remittances may act to change the perceptions of such communities from alienated outsiders to accepted insiders. However, the overall impact of remittances should be perceived as falling within the economic sphere, being directed specifically to the family or clan, rather than to the nation or state.[21] While I am mindful of such secondary, identity-related effects of economically motivated money transfers, I exclude them from the ensuing analysis and confine our attention to those IEIS flows specifically intended to impact issues of politics and identity.

The Conceptual Framework: Specifying the Components of National Identity

I begin by attempting to remove the term *national identity* from the sphere of plausible intuition and imprecise colloquialism in order to establish a clearly defined substantive content for the term. In this regard, it is natural that our specification of *national identity* be tied to our specification of the concept of nation. If the term *national identity* is virtually synonymous with the term *national character*, then changes induced (by, say, IEIS funds) in the defining characteristics of the nation would imply a corresponding change in *national identity*.[22]

In this context, I adopt John Stuart Mill's seminal characterization of a nation as "a portion of mankind . . . united among themselves by common sympathies which do not exist between them and others and which make them co-operate with each other more willingly than with other people, desire to be under the same government and desire that it should be government by themselves, or a portion of themselves, exclusively."[23]

Accordingly I assign the term *nation* to any segment of humanity if it possesses *both* of the following two characteristics.

(1) There exists a bond of community between its members that does not exist between them and those outside the group.

(2) The group members are prepared to accept as legitimate a source of sovereign authority if and only if it emanates from within the group itself (i.e., any source of authority external to the group will be rejected as not legitimate).

In what basic ways can these characteristics vary without a "segment of humanity" losing its status of nation? This is a question of consequence for the purposes of this chapter because the answer also defines the ways in which the parameters of national character or national identity can change.

Given that the first trait is one manifested in several human collectivities, such as social clubs, sports teams, and trade unions, it must be the second trait, namely, the rejection of alien sources of sovereign authority of origin external to the group, that is the quintessential litmus test of "nationness." Accordingly, changes that do not undermine the nation status of a collectivity must relate to either variations in (1) the nature of the bonding by which the collectivity coalesces and/or (2) the modes of dispensing its sovereignty. This latter element relates to two separate aspects: the internal dispensation of sovereignty—that is, the internal (hierarchical) configuration of the polity or regime type; or the external dispensation of sovereignty—that is, the conduct of the collectivity vis-à-vis other sovereign collectivities in its external (anarchical) environment.

The delineation of these realms of variation (composition of the national entity, its external conduct and internal configuration) generates the conceptual space within which differing variants of national characteristics, and changes that may be induced therein by agents such as financial transfers, can be mapped as depicted in figure 3. Let us now take a closer look at these various components of national characteristics and their range of variation.

Variations in Composition of the Nation: The Nature of the National Bond

This component of identity relates to the definition of the self-other distinction, that is, who is embraced within the community bond and who is not. The crucial issue is how IEIS funds contribute to the (re)creation, alteration, and/or consolidation of this bonding. I conceptualize the

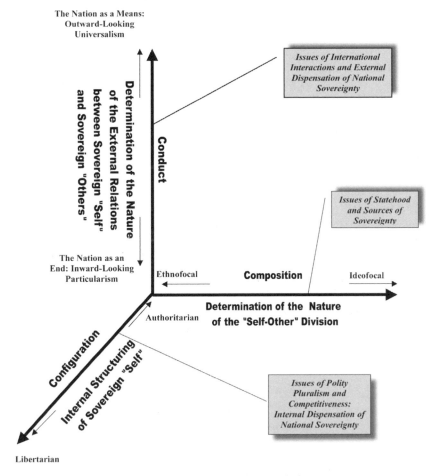

The Nation as a Means:
Outward-Looking
Universalism

Determination of the Nature
of the External Relations
between Sovereign "Self"
and Sovereign "Others"

Determination of the Nature

Conduct

*Issues of International
Interactions and External
Dispensation of National
Sovereignty*

*Issues of Statehood
and Sources of
Sovereignty*

The Nation as an
End: Inward-Looking
Particularism

Ethnofocal   **Composition**   Ideofocal

Determination of the Nature
Authoritarian   **of the "Self-Other" Division**

Configuration

Internal Structuring
of Sovereign "Self"

*Issues of Polity
Pluralism and
Competitiveness:
Internal Dispensation of
National Sovereignty*

Libertarian

Fig. 3.   The components of national identity

range of variation of community bond as being bounded by two antithetical polar archetypes, one homogeneous, the other ethnically heterogeneous. This notion of antipodal paradigms of the national bond has been developed in various versions by several scholars over the years. Lord Acton, for example, drew a distinction between the two opposing concepts of nations and nationalism, the one founded on the principles of *national unity*, the other on the principle of *national liberty*.[24] Kedourie presents a distinction between "objectivist" and "subjectivist" perceptions of nation.[25] A similar differentiation is implicit in Juan Linz's distinction between a monoethnic "nation state" and a multiethnic "state nation."

Others have distinguished between categories such as "civic" and "primordial," "national civic" and "organic," state-centered versus ethnocultural, and "liberal" versus "communitarian."[26]

However, as argued in chapter 1, in specifying the legitimate range of variation of *nation* I opt to use the terms *ethnofocal* and *ideofocal* to denote the antipodal endpoints of this spectrum. The term *ethnofocal* serves to denote a genus of nationalism in which the principal component in national bond is based on ethnic homogeneity; *ideofocal* denotes a genus of nationalism in which the national bond exists in spite of ethnic heterogeneity and is based principally on the identification with a common ideal.[27] Diasporic money often is mobilized in attempts to influence the positioning of national identity along this continuum. In this regard it should be noted that within a given diaspora, especially if the homeland is multiethnic, there may be differing perceptions and preferences pertaining to the desired composition of the national identity. For example, while some Sikh expatriates may prefer to dissociate themselves from a pan-Indian identity and cultivate their own specific ethnoreligious identity, giving both political and financial backing to the cause of secession, other Sikhs abroad are supportive of a united India. Similar opposing preferences are mirrored in the wider Indian diaspora, some backing the more ethnofocal emphasis of the Hindu nationalists, while others support a more multiethnic vision of the Indian nation and state.[28]

Variations in the Configuration of the National Polity: The Nature of the Internal Dispensation of National Sovereignty (Regime Type)

This component of national identity relates to characteristics of the internal structuring of the sovereign self (which could be thought of as the internal political anatomy of the sovereign self). Here, the important issue is how IEIS funds influence the way the internal dispensation of national sovereignty is structured—that is, how they affect the internal configuration of the polity or regime type of the homeland state. I conceptualize this component in terms of varying degrees of centralization or decentralization of the homeland polity. This may range from an ideal-typical hegemonic authoritarian regime, in which power in a noncompetitive, nonpluralistic polity is concentrated in the hands of a few, to an ideal-typical polyarchic libertarian regime, in which power in a competitive pluralistic polity is widely distributed among various independent political actors, over and beyond the executive authority. In order to avoid ambiguity, I shall consider the degree of authoritarianism or libertarianism of any given regime on the basis of the seven defining polity parameters as specified by Dahl.[29]

Thus, any IEIS monetary influence that increases the intensity of one of these parameters will have the effect of moving the regime type closer to the libertarian pole of the range, and conversely any reduction in them will move the regime type toward the authoritarian pole. In this context, the ability of a diaspora to achieve such effects may be linked to the motivations of other elements of the international system, including the host country, to promote regime changes in the homeland. For example, the Cuban diaspora in the United States, which for the most part has undergone a transition "from exiles to immigrants," is now perceived as a major source of financial impetus toward regime reform in the homeland.[30]

Variations in the Conduct of the Nation: The Nature of the External Dispensation of National Sovereignty

This component of identity refers to the characteristics of the interaction between the collective homeland self and external collective others in the outside environment. This is a characteristic more fundamental than the nuts and bolts of the everyday conduct of foreign policy and relates to a perception of the "proper" role of the nation in terms of historic destiny. As such, it reflects a collective sense not of what is worthwhile (in terms of political pragmatism) but rather worthy (in terms of moral merit). Notable examples of such conceptions include the American "manifest destiny," Britain's "white man's burden," the French "*mission civilisatrice,*" and above all, the imperial German slogan used to justify the dissemination of German influence, "*am deutschen Wesen soll die Welt genesen.*" On a theoretical level, Steven Krasner articulates the essence of this distinction.

> All political and social environments are characterized by two logics of actions, what James March and Johan Olsen have called logics of expected consequences and logics of appropriateness. Logics of consequences see political action and outcomes, including institutions, as the product of rational calculating behavior designed to maximize a given set of unexplained preferences. . . . Logics of appropriateness understand political action as a product of rules, roles, and identities that stipulate appropriate behavior in given

situations. The question is not how I can maximize my self-interest but rather, given who I am, how should I act in this particular circumstance.[31]

In this context the external relations of a nation would be seen as more than a means to further political interest and would be considered a vehicle for transmitting spiritual values and ideals. This perception of the "role of the nation among nations" is not an immutable feature and may change over time as a function of historical experience and events such as military victory or defeat (as in cases of Japan and Germany).

In defining the range of variation of this component, I draw on Hans Kohn's distinction between the perception of the nation as an *end* in itself and that of a nation as a *means* to accomplish a more lofty function, beyond promotion of its own egoistic interests. The implication is that the perception of the "proper" role of a nation ranges between two antithetical poles. On the one hand the nation can be conceived of as having no other historic role or duty other than of "looking after one's own collective self." This constitutes an inward-looking particularistic view of the nation's role. At the other end of the spectrum, the nation is conceived of as a means by which to serve mankind as a whole, with a mission beyond the pursuit of its own (collective) interest. This view is reflected in the writings of Giuseppe Mazzini: "Every people has its special mission, which will co-operate toward the fulfillment of the general mission of humanity. That mission constitutes its nationality." I therefore conceptualize the third component of national identity as one ranging between two opposing perceptions of the proper conduct of the collective self toward collective others, one characterized by inward-looking particularism, the other by outward-looking universalism.

In this regard it is interesting to note that Jews' perceptions of their "proper" national role vary between these two antithetical notions. Gil Merom has observed that on the one hand, Israel's "sense of inherent exceptionalism, which emanates from concepts such as the chosen people, also include the belief that the Jews would become a 'light unto the nations' (or *la'goyim*) or a beacon to the world." On the other hand, Israel's "experience of isolation is bolstered by the belief that the Jewish people was preordained to 'dwell in loneliness' [*sic*] (*am levadad yishkon*)."[32] When Jewish philosopher Martin Buber challenged the early Zionist vision of creating Israel as a "nation like other nations" he argued that the realization of such an idea would render the new state empty and meaningless. Instead, Buber promoted the notion of "Hebrew Humanism" as the core idea of the Zionist renaissance. He envisioned Israel as a state that serves a unique role in world politics stemming from God's demand that the Jews champion truth and righteousness "for the whole life of man, for the whole life of the people."[33]

The Relationship between the Different Components of Identity

For the purpose of this chapter, the important issue is how IEIS funds are intended to influence perception of this role and how diasporic money is mobilized in attempts to influence the "positioning" of national identity along this continuum. As pointed out earlier, the representation of the three elements of national identity (composition, configuration, and conduct of the sovereign self) as a triaxial system generates a three-dimensional cubelike space in which the political effects of IEIS flows can be depicted (see fig. 3).

These elements are analytically distinct variables and, although intuitively it may appear likely that increasing the intensity of one component (e.g., inducing a more ethnically heterogeneous ideofocal type of national bond) will also affect the intensity of other components (e.g., induce a more polyarchic libertarian regime and a less inward-looking particularistic perception of the national role), this is not necessarily the case. The ethnic heterogeneity of the Soviet nation did not induce elements of libertarianism into the nature of the regime. Rather, the collapse of totalitarianism spurred a plethora of more ethnically uniform identities (re)asserting themselves in regimes generally more open than the Soviet predecessor. Likewise, ethnically heterogeneous nations in South America have few pretensions of fulfilling a wider global role beyond dealing with the affairs of the nation per se. In light of these examples, it would be more accurate to talk of the connection between the various components as being one of *plausible correlation* rather than of *necessary causality*.

The Channels through which IEIS Funds Impinge on Identity

Identity-motivated diasporic financial flows may be directed into the homeland via organizational vehicles in the three major institutional categories of society: state (including pre-state precursor organizations), political society, and civil society. This process and the resulting impact on the components of identity—together with the possible subsequent

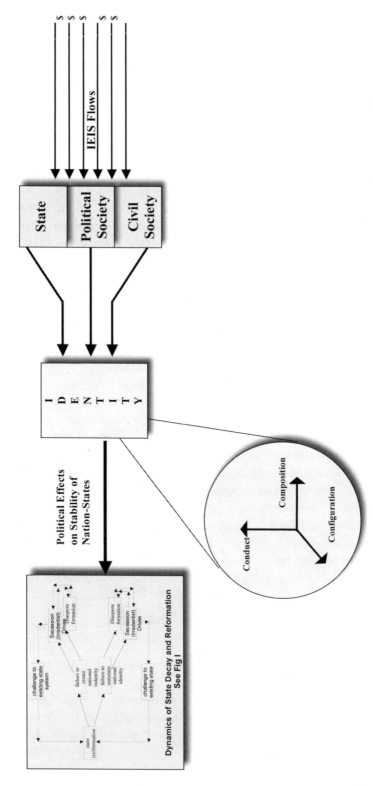

Fig. 4   The vehicles for transmission of the effects of IEIS flows on national identity

ramifications for political stability—are schematically depicted in figure 4. In this regard, I adopt three broad distinctions.

State. The organizational and institutional apparatus for the external exercise of (national/collective) sovereignty beyond defined territorial limits, and the internal administration of such sovereignty within them. In this category I include the principal pre-state bodies engaged in the propagation of demands for self-determination and in the embryonic infrastructure of the nascent state.

Political Society. Those bodies competing for power over the organs of government that control the state apparatus.

Civil Society. The organizational and institutional apparatuses of society not included in the state and political society.

The relative importance of these societal sectors as channels for IEIS funds and the mechanics of their transfer are affected by several factors, such as the stage of state building in the homeland, the nature of the political regime there, and the circumstances of the diasporic communities in their lands of domicile. Diasporas that enjoy the relative freedom accorded by liberal democratic states are more likely to utilize the forces of globalization to channel funds to homeland causes.

Certainly the policies of the host country regarding the transfer of funds to recipients in the homeland are of cardinal importance. The transfer of diaspora-related funds may cause international tensions when they are perceived by either the home or host governments as promoting causes inimical to their interests. Indeed, these funds' importance has been reflected in the vigorous response of the U.S. administration in several cases. For example, complaints from Yasir Arafat regarding large-scale transfer of funds from Arab diasporic sources in the United States to radical Islamic groups were among the factors that prompted the Clinton administration to issue an executive order on January 24, 1995, entitled "Prohibiting Transactions with Terrorists Who Threaten to Disrupt the Middle East Peace Process." The prohibition included the transfer of funds to Jewish extremist groups as well.[34] After September 11, Western states paid even more attention to transfers of funds from the Muslim diaspora to Islamist networks in the homeland.

In the period prior to and immediate following the establishment of statehood, the dominant emphasis is usually on funds channeled to state (or pre-state) organs, driven by motives associated with (re)generating, consolidating, or maintaining sovereignty for the nation, that is, creating or underpinning the viability of the self-other distinction. The national leadership—in the homeland or in exile—will appeal for diasporic funds by accentuating the self-other divide to include diaspora members as part of the national collective. Susan Woodward has observed that it would be difficult to imagine Croatian independence and Franjo Tudjman's nationalist program without the financial role of the Croatian diaspora. "Without the $8 million sent to Tudjman and his party, the Croatian Democratic Union (HDC or 'party of all Croats in the world'), by Croatian émigrés when no other party in Croatia had any funds," Tudjman's 1990 hard-pressed electoral success would have been unlikely.[35]

Indeed, in the pre-state and early state-building periods, diasporic funds are designated principally for purposes that contribute to the overriding goal of establishing a sovereign state. This involves efforts to decouple homeland society from dependence on "alien" rule. Typically such activities include armament procurement, land redemption, settlement construction, education and invigoration of language, and the immigration (repatriation) of kinfolk abroad. This has been the case with the Armenians, the Palestinians, the Croatians, and Albanian Kosovars.[36] When rival aspirants for power in the homeland attempt to promote different paradigms of statehood, nationhood, and political vision, the channeling of diasporic funds is likely to diverge and be distributed among the various contesting bodies, both in the pre-state and early postindependence stages. In the years prior to Israel's independence, such a split in American Jewish diasporic support occurred, with funding for military procurement being channeled to both the Haganah (affiliated with the mainstream Zionist establishment) and the Etzel (Irgun Zva'i Leumi— linked with the opposition Revisionist movement).[37] As mentioned previously, in the case of the Palestinians, diasporic financial support is similarly divided among the different organizations including the mainstream nationalists, the Left, and the Islamic factions.[38]

In the struggle for independence, an aspirant leadership tends to stress kinship across frontiers, equating diasporic funding of the efforts in the homeland with "national loyalty." Funds are often solicited for procurement of military material or support for political organs, as the intended precursors of official state bodies after the attainment of independence. In her memoirs, Golda Meir recounted her appearance before American Jewry in early 1948, where she described the imminent threat to the Jewish community in Palestine on the eve of the declaration of Israel's independence and recalled her emotive rallying of financial support from her audience: "You cannot decide whether we should fight or not. We will. . . . That decision has been taken. Nobody can change it. You can only decide one thing: whether [we] shall be victorious . . . or whether the mufti will be victorious." She described the outpouring of support in vivid terms: "They listened, and they wept, and they pledged money in amounts no community had ever given before. By the time I came back to Palestine . . . I had raised $50,000,000, which was turned over at once for the Haganah's [the major Jewish underground] secret purchase of arms in Europe."[39]

In the early postindependence stage it is likely that the bulk of IEIS funds will be directed toward official state organizations aimed at the consolidation of national independence—that is, to enhance and secure the status of the sovereign self versus external others. State-related organs try to establish a monopoly and usually remain the major recipients of diasporic funds whenever an imminent threat is perceived to menace the security of the national collective. Nevertheless, there may be circumstances that foster exceptions to this general tendency. In these cases, expatriate money is likely to be channeled to other aspects of state consolidation in the realm of civil and political society, with or without the home regime's direction. However, such independent initiatives are more likely when diaspora sources wish to mold kin-state identity in ways that run counter to the vision of the home regime.

The case of Armenia is a good example of such potential conflict. The Armenian diaspora, especially its highly mobilized U.S.-based community, has always been dedicated to homeland affairs, often serving as a critical lifeline for Armenian security and welfare needs—as was particularly well illustrated after the 1988 earthquake and throughout the years of conflict in Nagorno-Karabakh. By the mid-1990s, contributions to Armenian relief from the diaspora community amounted to $50 million to $75 million a year. Razmik Panossian has written that since the time of Armenia's independence from Soviet rule in 1991 *"sending financial and material aid to Armenia has become [the] operative paradigm of homeland-diaspora relations."*[40] The Armenian president Ter-Petrossian sought to channel the diaspora fund-raising efforts into the government-controlled Armenia Fund—allegedly to "keep politics out" of the process of the building of the country, but actually to neutralize the influence of traditional diaspora parties on it. While the moderate Armenian Democratic Liberal Party (ADL-Ramgavars) and the Social Democratic Hunchakian Party (SDH) generally lent unqualified support to the government, the Dashnak bloc, the Armenian Revolutionary Federation (ARF), assumed an opposition role. The Dashnak, with its pan-Armenian orientation and a long-established prominence in carrying the torch of Armenian nationalism in exile, challenged the home regime's monopoly in defining Armenia's foreign interests (especially vis-à-vis Nagorno-Karabakh and relations with Turkey), its religious and cultural practices, its national mythology (particularly with regard to the Armenian genocide), and even the very notion of "Armenianness." These disputes led to the withdrawal of the century-old Dashnak organization from the Armenia Fund and intensified the dissension in homeland-diaspora relations.[41]

As state existence becomes increasingly secure, diaspora financial allocations begin to be directed increasingly toward nonstate segments of the homeland institutional framework in the realm of civil and political society. Again, Armenia provides an excellent illustration of this phenomenon. The diaspora-based Dashnak Party poured several million dollars (a significant sum in post-Soviet Armenia) into newspapers and other civil society organs, to help sustain the ideological position supporting the notion of Greater Armenia, which held that any concessions over the Karabagh issue, as intended by President Ter-Petrossian, were close to treason. The *Financial Times* reported that in February 1994, the Dashnaks raised $1.5 million for the struggle in Karabagh in a single California telethon. This vigorous diaspora-led campaign heightened nationalist fervor inside Armenia and eventually brought about Ter-Petrossian's resignation.[42]

Financial support may be provided directly to political organizations engaged in overt competition (in polyarchic libertarian regimes) or covert struggle (in hegemonic authoritarian ones) in order to try to effect a change in the mode of government at home. This intended change may involve a qualitative change of regime or a change in the dominant values by which the homeland is governed within a prevailing regime type—either in terms of the degree of internal inclusion by which the composition of the national unit is defined, or in terms of the basic behavioral parameters that characterize the conduct of the nation's external posture. Each of these cases can be conceptualized as moving the configuration of the homeland polity further from, or closer to, one of the ideal poles specified in the previous section (i.e., along the axes of composition, configuration, and conduct).

Diasporic elements often try to influence identity components via civil society agencies by supporting causes concordant with their own worldview or emotional proclivity. Civil society embraces "the arena of the polity where self-organizing groups, movements and individuals, [largely] autonomous from the state, attempt to articulate values, create associations, and solidarity and advance their interests."[43] Indeed, a higher degree of civil society autonomy has been the aspiration of many groups that have challenged centralized regimes. Accordingly, diasporic flows to civil society agents may seek the promotion of specific sociocultural and/or economic organs that reflect desired traits of identity. Even in cases where countries of origin are governed by nondemocratic rule, diasporas often channel funds to civil society agencies in order to circumvent prohibitions imposed by the regime and to create a parallel society dominated by values other than those propagated by the incumbent government.[44] In open polyarchic homelands, diasporic funding of civil society institutions is part and parcel of the routine societal pluralism, in which there is overt and ongoing interaction between such civil agencies and the organs of political society and those of the state. While polyarchies usually tolerate diasporic funds to civil agencies, even when they conflict with the core values of open society, such freedoms are not always unmitigated. Even polyarchies have blocked diasporic money transfers by taxation or outright prohibition on the grounds that such transfers are inimical to state security, the basic fundamentals of the society, and the democratic political system. Indeed, in this regard, governments in home countries may collaborate with authorities in the hostland to impede the flow of diasporic funds to undesirable recipients.

The organizational infrastructure through which IEIS funds are provided serves as a channel or conduit by which influences are exerted on the previously specified components of national identity: (1) the configuration of the homeland polity, (2) the external conduct of the homeland nation, and (3) the inclusiveness of the national collective. It should be noted that financial support to a given recipient may influence more than one of these components. Thus, backing a liberal-oriented civil society institution may affect issues that relate to regime structure (configuration), attitudes toward ethnic minorities (composition), and the tenor of interactions with the outside world (conduct). This correlation, however, is not a causal necessity. In terms of our conceptual framework these influences are expressed by a displacement of any given status quo identity along one (or more) of the three axial dimensions of identity.

An Illustrative Case Study: The Case of Israel and the Jewish Diaspora

I now move on to examine the application of the scheme in the case study of Israel and the Jewish diaspora. This case (presented as illustration rather than conclusive corroboration of the model) is chosen not only because it demonstrates an integration of all the aforementioned components, but also because it exhibits the evolutionary role and mechanisms of diasporic transnational funds and their impact on national identity. In this sense the Jewish diaspora–Israel link constitutes an archetypical example and is often referred to as such by scholars and activists alike.

Funds related to the Jewish diaspora have been crucial in all three of the previously mentioned categories of kin-community interactions— those directed from kin communities abroad toward the homeland, those directed from the homeland to the diaspora community in hostlands, and those which take place within transfrontier diasporic networks. Interdiasporic flows were responsible for the preservation and redemption of Jewish identity among "lost tribes" in the former Soviet Union, Ethiopia, and other parts of the globe. The state of Israel (as the homeland entity), by means of its various agencies, has funneled funds to many diasporic centers to foster Jewish identity, encourage immigration to the homeland, establish pro-Israel lobbies, or in extreme cases even "buy" kindred diaspora from oppressive regimes using Jews as bargaining chips (e.g., Romania during the Ceauşescu era or Ethiopia under Mengistu).[45]

Jewish communities worldwide contributed financially to virtually every aspect of life within Israel. As early as 1830, American Jews established organizations to assist Jews in Palestine. In 1854 Judah Touro left $60,000 of his estate "to ameliorate the condition of our Jewish bretherin in the Holy Land, and to secure to them the inestimable privilege of worshiping the Almighty according to our religion without molestation."[46] Since the 1940s, the manner in which Judeo-diasporic flows were channeled into the homeland largely reflect the patterns set out in our proposed scheme, both in terms of the institutions through which they were routed, and in terms of the objectives to which they were directed (see table 1).

As long as a severe threat to the physical survival of Jews in the homeland was believed to exist, Zionism was perceived and pursued as an overarching ideology, encompassing all variants of Jewishness. Since in many respects the question of security and state building was predicated on the idea of a strong military and "the ingathering of exiles" (*kibutz galuyot*), the major thrust of diasporic contributions (and state efforts to mobilize them) centered on these primary issues of survival. Other issues of identity were downplayed under the ideopolitical hegemony of the mainstream Zionist leadership of the time. Civil society, political society, and organs of state were to a large measure intertwined and enlisted in the state-building effort.[47]

Diasporic financial contributions to the newly established state were of two major types: philanthropic gifts and repayable loans raised via state bonds. Initially, diasporic aid came in the form of donations, which were channeled via the subsidiary organization of the United Jewish Appeal (or UJA, an umbrella Jewish fund-raising organization in North America) to the Jewish Agency for Israel. In order to receive tax deduction benefits in America, money transfers were made to U.S.-based charitable bodies, which operated via affiliated organs in Israel. For all practical purposes the Israeli government determined the use of these funds. They were directed toward resettlement and rehabilitation of Jewish refugees, the building of housing, educational facilities, as well as agricultural and scientific institutions. Ben-Gurion wanted "to demonstrate Israel's sovereignty with respect to foreign Zionist funding, and to insulate its political system from targeted cascades of foreign Zionist votes."[48] He moved swiftly to reduce the political role of American Zionists and to ensure that the distribution of American Jewish funds was conducted in ways determined by his government. The division of labor between the homeland and the diaspora was designed to emphasize the Zionist view that Jewish existence in Israel was superior to Jewish life outside the homeland and that Israel now dominated the terms of Jewish identity. Arthur Hertzberg pointed out that the Zionist narrative ignored diasporic contributions to Israel's War of Independence and relegated diaspora Zionist efforts, "no matter how . . . helpful they might be to the Jewish State, . . . [to] lower status in the hierarchy of Jewish values."[49]

The migration of Israel toward the center of Jewish-American consciousness and identity did not occur overnight. Earlier divisions within the diaspora over the legitimacy and necessity of the Zionist experiment in Palestine largely ended with the establishment of the state of Israel. Yet for most Jewish-Americans it was clear from the outset that their Jewish experience as Americans was not going to recede into insignificance but would continue to develop alongside the Jewish revival in the newly established state. The definitions of this duality vary according to ideological camps in the homeland and the diaspora.[50] Many American Jews, notwithstanding the very real emotional attachment they felt to Israel and their view of Israel as a center of Jewish spiritual identity and authority, feared that political expressions of support for Zionism would bring charges of dual loyalty that could not be allowed.[51] However, while local community needs became a larger focus for American Jewish fund-raising in the 1950s, contributions to Israel remained at impressive levels. Though direct pledges to Israel through the UJA declined steadily from a high of $150 million in 1948 to a low of $60 million in 1955, this was in

part due to a diasporic perception that the critical danger to Israel's existence had passed for the time being and to the channeling of diasporic
funds into alternative forms of contribution and investment.[52]

One new channel for diasporic funds was the issue of government
bonds (Israel Bonds), introduced by Prime Minister Ben-Gurion
together with several U.S. Jewish and Israeli leaders on September 3,
1950, in order to bolster Israeli independence and sovereignty. The
Knesset (the Israeli parliament) accepted the proposal and passed legislation authorizing the flotation of Israel's first bond issue—the Israel Independence Issue. The significance of this move was to introduce the device
of public loans as a vehicle for raising development capital, rather than
philanthropic gifts, which hitherto had been the sole means for tapping
diasporic money. The first issue was launched in May 1951 and received
an overwhelming response with $52 million worth of bonds sold. Israeli
leaders went to great lengths to underscore the close linkage between
Jewish identity and Jewish contributions to the development of the
homeland. Golda Meir, in a tribute to the Israel Bond program,
described this linkage of kinship in glowing terms: "You have a stake in
every drop of water we pour into our land, in every mile of road built, in
every kilowatt of power, in every field, in every factory."[53] By 1967,
America had purchased $850 million worth of Israeli bonds, and Ameri-
can Jews had donated around $1 billion more through the UJA.[54]

The notion of a symbiotic existence between diaspora Jews and Israel
continued to grow, reaching its zenith with Israel's victory in the Six-Day
War, which "produced the greatest flood of financial contributions in
American Jewish history," amounting to sums unprecedented at that
time.[55] Since that time, many Jewish-Americans have lived vicariously
through the state of Israel. Lord Beloff observed that after 1967, "Israel
had become the new religion of American Jews. . . . Jews were to be found
less often praying to God than raising funds . . . on behalf of Israel."[56]
Indeed, the period between the late 1960s and the late 1980s can generally be seen as the Israelization phase of the Jewish-American diaspora,
characterized by uncritical support of the state and the embrace of secular Zionism as a major feature of Jewish-American identity and culture.
The structure of the organized Jewish community in the United States
was built around philanthropy and political activism on behalf of the
homeland, and Israel became the most attractive selling point of Jewish
fund-raisers. During these years the UJA evolved into "America's Jewish
religion." The peak of the UJA-Federation fund-raising drive was in the

early 1990s with around $1 billion raised in an "emergency campaign" to help Israel resettle the massive post-Soviet immigration.[57]

However, as Israel's existence as a state appeared more secure, controversial topics, previously suppressed by the exigencies of survival, began to force themselves onto the national agenda. Open dissension regarding the boundaries of the state, Israel's policy toward the Arab world in general and the Palestinians in particular, and questions of sociocultural and political pluralism became increasingly dominant in the public debate, both within Israel and among the diasporic kin. The growing diversity of perspectives at home and abroad created a new reality in which Israel was no longer idealized by the diaspora, and by the 1980s public dissent by American Jews against Israeli policies was already visible. Many Jewish-Americans were critical of Israel's behavior during the 1982 war in Lebanon, were anxious in the wake of the Pollard Affair, and were strongly opposed to Israel's handling of the Palestinian uprising (*intifada*). The idea of helping Israel help itself, as opposed to the notion of unconditional support while staying away from Israeli domestic and foreign affairs, took root in the 1980s, with American Jews overcoming their reluctance to speak out critically against Israeli official policies.[58] This new posture expressed itself in public disapproval of Israel's conduct by both left- and right-wing diasporic circles, especially after the signing of the 1993 Oslo Accords. Earlier American Jewish reluctance to criticize Israeli policies was based on the notion that those who do not move to Israel forfeit the right to pass judgment on matters that for Israelis are matters of life and death. Yet in the last two decades the diaspora is claiming the status of full partners in the national project whose views must be weighed by those seeking their money. Diasporic claims to a voice vary according to conceptions of diasporic and Israeli Jewish identity and Israeli behavior. Overall, the new divergence of public postures found expression in shifting patterns of diasporic monetary support of homeland causes, and hence in changing and less monolithic influences on components of homeland identity.

While in the early days of state building, different variants and interpretations of Jewishness were no more than a marginal factor in determining how diasporic funds were distributed, in the last two decades there has been a perceptible shift in the nature of the recipients of diasporic money within Israel, with civil and political society becoming increasingly significant in determining issues pertaining to homeland identity, relative to the previous dominance of the state. Questions of internal composition (e.g., citizenship and religious identity), external conduct (relations with outside entities in the international system, including the debate on the universalistic versus particularistic paradigms of international affairs), and regime characteristics (particularly the debate over religious orthodoxy versus secular liberalism in domestic political affairs) are major foci of diasporic interest and money. This new pattern was reflected in the call of Conservative and Reform rabbis and leaders of Jewish organizations to stop contributions to Israeli bodies not recognizing non-Orthodox movements. When the "Who is a Jew" crisis first erupted in 1988, the Boston and Atlanta Jewish Federations voted to withhold $16 million in Israel-bound UJA contributions. A decade later, U.S. Reform rabbis called on their congregations at Yom Kippur services to give to pluralist causes in Israel instead of donating to the UJA. By the late 1990s a number of Jewish federations drastically reduced financial support to the UJA and increased backing to bodies in both the political and civil realms that promote values concordant with those of the fund providers. In this case, such constituted an effort by the diasporic community to fundamentally alter the concept of Israeli citizenship.

As early as 1979, liberal Jewish groups in the diaspora created the New Israel Fund to promote issues of religious pluralism, Jewish-Arab equality and coexistence, civil and human rights, and advancement of the status of women.[59] In the early 1980s, the organization raised about a quarter of a million dollars each year; by 1999, it reported annual collections of $19 million. More significantly, in the past decade, the portion of funds raised by the Council of Jewish Federations and allocated to Israel via the UJA dropped from 60 to 40 percent. The San Francisco Jewish Federation slashed its support to the UJA. Instead, it initiated a new fund-raising campaign to finance programs aimed at promoting tolerance, pluralism, and democracy. The Boston and Cleveland Jewish Federations adopted similar positions, with some members advocating severance of all financial ties with Knesset members who supported or acquiesced to the conversion law. In this regard it is interesting to note that in response to its fund-raising crisis, the UJA itself has begun emphasizing its commitment to religious diversity and pledged itself for the first time to ensure the Conservative and Reform movements' financial support from the Jewish Agency.[60]

In light of all this, it is understandable that Thomas Friedman urged U.S. Jews to help build an Israel in which they would want their children to live.[61] There is, however, no consensus among the diaspora as to just what that Israel should be. For example, as Reform and Conservative

Jews expand their financial and political efforts to introduce pluralism into Israel's religious practices, they challenge the previous politics and distributive criteria of Jewish-American giving, which conformed largely to the prevailing status quo in Israel. In so doing they have begun to undermine Israel's Orthodox sector and its endeavor to monopolize the concept of Jewish identity.[62]

In the late 1990s, demands to overhaul diaspora charity to Israel became the most important point of contention between Jewish-American local federations and the Jewish Agency—traditionally the main Israeli recipient of diasporic funds. As the latter became suspected of being a politicized organ for channeling money to Orthodox institutions that deny the legitimacy of Reform and Conservative denominations, federation leaders demanded greater autonomy in determining allocation policies inside Israel. Significantly, in November 1999, activists of the General Assembly of America's Jewry, held in Atlanta, moved to establish a single umbrella organization, the United Jewish Communities (UJC). The new body not only unified all Jewish communities across America—through a merger of the UJA, the United Israel Appeal (UIA), and the Council of Jewish Federations (CJF)—but also aimed at redirecting funds intended to bolster Jewish identity, so as to empower U.S.-based local federations and give them greater say over spending inside Israel. To a large extent the assembly was the culmination of a decade-long debate on Jewish pluralism.[63] The Israeli daily *Ha'aretz* reported that Reform and Conservative representatives were "trying to take advantage of the assembly to define the aspiration toward religious pluralism in Israel as one of the major goals of American Jewry, with all the implications this would have for the allocation of funds."[64]

Thus diasporic sponsors have exercised considerable leverage in promoting the implementation of their own values in Israeli society and in shaping aspects of national identity in a manner consistent with their worldview. Business magnates such as the Australian Habad leader Yosef Gutnik and Miami-based Irving Moskowitz have not only financed cultural and economic activities that promote their ideological predilections—including building settlements in territories claimed by Palestinians and sponsoring traditional religious rites for new immigrants—they have also directly backed right-wing political parties in the Israeli polity and former prime minister Benjamin Netanyahu.[65]

Indeed, the economic power of the diaspora is also an important element in the political arena with diasporic funds often being the principal source of finance for several rival candidates in national elections. Typically, this is done by channeling money via so-called voluntary associations that endorse their own political platforms (and visions of Judeo-Israeli identity) or oppose those of their adversaries. Some observers even estimate that the reliance of right-wing parties and former prime minister Benjamin Netanyahu on financial support from like-minded religious Jews abroad has made the diasporic donors more significant than domestic constituencies in terms of ideological posture and accountability.[66] Likewise, former prime minister Ehud Barak was reported to have raised much of the financing for his successful bid for the premiership from diasporic sources, including expatriate Israelis. As early as 1997, candidate Barak began courting Jewish-American donors who sought to oppose trends toward Orthodox sectarianism in Israel and to foster greater religious pluralism and a more compromising peace agenda. In January 2000, Israel's attorney general ordered a police investigation of Prime Minister Barak's fund-raising election drive after Israel's state comptroller implicated Barak and his One Israel/Labor Party in a massive—and possibly illegal—fund-raising scheme that funneled millions of dollars from diaspora donors into his electoral campaign.[67]

Altogether, by 2000 the process of decentralization in American Jewish philanthropic contributions to Israel showed some fascinating developments regarding the impact of the shift to identity-oriented funds. First, there was an increase in targeted diasporic philanthropic flows through proliferating Jewish-American foundations and independent donor-advised funds. Large sums of this money are intended to promote religious, social, and political causes, "amplifying the influence of American-based agendas in Israel in the form of strengthening the various agencies and programs that are being supported with the help of Jewish-American philanthropic funds."[68]

A survey carried out on behalf of the Jewish agency identified a diaspora-led "grassroots cultural-social movement" in the proliferation of organizations intended to impact Jewish identity in Israel's "secular arenas" as their key mission. These organizations are linked to the Movement of Progressive Judaism, the Conservative (Masorti) Movement, and some Orthodox bodies. They promote the increasing role of civil society in Israel's secular arena where the crisis of Jewish identity and Judaism as culture was at its height.[69] Nir Boms's study of diaspora giving and the redefinition of Israeli Jewish identity estimates that, in 2000, diasporic funds amounted to a record $2.6 billion. The increase in targeted diasporic financial involvement also led to the creation of numerous newly established diaspora-Israeli interactions, with representatives of American Jewish federations opening dozens of offices in Israel under a new framework called Partnership 2000 that granted diaspora representatives the ability to set priorities and supervised the allocations of their donations.

Finally, the outbreak of the second intifada in September 2000 and events of the last few years and their consequences deeply affected the thinking and organizational efforts of the Jewish diaspora and its relations with Israel. The new posture in which Israel and the Jews found themselves was broadened beyond the seemingly manageable proportions of a national dispute largely about borders to one encompassing religion and fundamentals of Jewish national identity. The growing tendency of Arabs and Muslims to broaden their political language to express hostility to Jews (not just to Israel) that was intensified after September 11 produced greater Jewish unity and the revival of a new Zionist vision. This unity manifested itself in political mobilization by diaspora groups, and the Israeli government focused on the core issue of anti-Semitism. Indeed, mobilization on this scale, involving national and international informational, lobbying, and solidarity campaigns had not been seen in many years. The newfound unity around the issue of "Jewish security" and the rise of anti-Semitism was used by Israel and diaspora organizations as a unique opportunity to heal (at least temporarily) the breach between Jewish communities on such issues as who is a Jew and to undo Israel's apparent retreat from Zionism and Jewish identity into "post-Zionism." The widespread feelings of vulnerability recorded among American Jews compounded by the reality of an external threat to Israel's existence as a Jewish state once again strengthened the ties to the homeland as a "whole."[70] An influx of emergency donations came to support victims of suicide bombing and to improve security measures in Israeli schools. The emergency funds raised by the UJC—which totaled around $300 million by the summer of 2002—ended, temporarily, the UJC's "long-standing policy of refusing to spend money over the Green Line" (i.e., West Bank and Gaza).[71]

These examples illustrate the mechanisms by which funds are funneled via institutions of the state, political society, and civil society, by diverse diasporic groups that strive to influence the various components of national identity (composition, configuration, and conduct). The common aim of all these diaspora efforts was to change Israel in accordance with the diaspora's worldview. These diaspora-sourced effects may have far more consequential ramifications than the identity changes themselves. While Jewish groups calling for secession from Israel are presently marginal, there is no guarantee that they will remain so. Given sufficient monetary backing from like-minded diasporic sponsors, it might be possible for ultranationalist proponents of a separate, strongly ethnofocal secessionist state of "Judea" in the West Bank, or the increasingly heard advocates (whether ultrareligious or ultrasecular) for the establishment of a separate entity for the ultra-Orthodox population of Israel, or the members of the radical left-wing supporters for the redefinition of Israel as a "state of all its citizens" rather than a "Jewish State," to acquire enough power to become more than insignificant murmurs of political eccentricity. This would constitute a serious challenge not only to the stability of the state of Israel in its present form, but to its raison d'être in any form.

Tentative Conclusions

In this chapter I have proposed a conceptual framework for the analysis of how diaspora-sourced financial funds affect national identity in the homeland and thereby the international system. The point of departure of this effort was a schematic delineation of the components of *national identity*, derived from a widely acknowledged mainstream definition of *nation*, and a general specification of the vehicles through which diasporic financial influences may be transmitted. This scheme serves as a useful instrument for comparative analysis of diverse empirical cases involving diasporic financial influences on homeland identity.

However, beyond the methodological merit of the scheme, more substantive inferences appear to emerge from our analysis of the effects of diaspora-related financial flows, which address some criticized aspects of the identity debate in international relations. For example, although the constructivist approach to international affairs emphasizes how "variation in state identity, or changes in state identity, affect the national security interests or policies of states," some scholars claim that this approach has yet to fully address the issue of how identities are shaped and how interests become defined as they do.[72] Checkel asserts that constructivism is more a "method" or "style" than a structured theory and as such is plagued by "empirical ad hocism."[73] Furthermore, when IR theory incorporates issues of identity, it tends to concentrate primarily on the role of domestic formative processes, giving only limited emphasis to the transnational impact of diaspora communities that have normalized and embraced life outside their countries of origin or symbolic homelands, but play a crucial role in the politics of identity of their kin states.

It is on several of these issues that our model suggests some avenues of advancement.

1. It removes "national identity" from the realm of imprecise and intuitive characterization by specifically defining what is in the concept and its component elements. By so doing it provides a means for a more systematic investigation of the issue of identity, its effects, and agencies of change.

2. It offers the constructivist school a general and formally structured framework for the analysis of identity, the domestic institutions that mold it, and its impact on IR parameters. Precisely this structured generality provides constructivism some aid in contending with charges of "empirical ad hocism."

3. It outlines a specific mechanism that articulates the causal nexus between transnational influences on identity and IR by showing how such influences (particularly financial ones) may impact on the (re)definition of the most basic foundations of the nation-state system—that is, on the sentiments of affiliation and loyalty that ultimately determine the cohesiveness of nations.

Overall, the model demonstrates that transnational communities and transnational financial flows, typically associated with the phenomenon of globalization and the blurring of national identities, often produce diametrically opposite effects, involving the awakening, invigoration, and reinforcement of a discrete national identity and separateness. This phenomenon underscores the ubiquitous and enduring role diasporas have in the ongoing process of disintegration and reformation of the global state system. If diasporic money is indeed a major source of influence on national identity, it would almost by definition also be a major force in the (re)determination of the political allegiances at the very foundations of nationhood and statehood. Thus, the variability of such identity-defined allegiances suggests that any configuration of nation-states in the international system at a given period in time is one whose foundations are built on shifting sands. As a discernible agent of influence on these allegiances, diasporic-related financial flows may serve as metaphorical winds of change that drive these shifting sands.

THREE

Transnational Religion and the Struggle for Jewish Pluralism

On MARCH 31, 2005, after six years of debates, Israel's supreme court—sitting as the High Court of Justice—ruled that non-Orthodox conversions in which the study process was conducted in Israel but was finalized in the United States by Reform or Conservative Rabbis will be recognized. This ruling broke the monopoly of the Orthodoxy over recognized conversions inside Israel. The court accepted the petition filed by the Religious Action Center, the extension arm of the U.S.-based Reform movement, and allowed for the first time in the state's history non-Orthodox converts to be fully recognized by Israel as Jews deserving Israeli citizenship based on Israel's law of return. The ruling, which drew harsh criticism from Orthodox leaders, was the latest manifestation of a culture war over Jewish identity inside and outside Israel. Part of the debate is over the dilemma of who is a Jew, and the question of who has the ultimate religious authority among Jews to determine membership.

The clash at the heart of the debate over Jewish identity inside Israel within the diaspora and between Israel and diaspora Jewry also involves dilemmas of Jewish politics and geography—including who speaks on behalf of the Jews and where the boundaries of the state of Israel or the Jewish homeland end. These dilemmas have far-reaching implications for the dissemination of religious values across frontiers and the role of kinship in international affairs. For example, just a few days before the Supreme Court's decision on conversion, a group of forty people, mostly Orthodox Jews from New York and New Jersey, arrived in Tel Aviv to demonstrate solidarity with settlers in Gush Katif, the main Israeli settlement bloc in the Gaza Strip. The group included bankers, two state supreme court judges, and doctors, and was comprised of both Democrats and Republicans. Their leader, Dov Hikind, a member of the New York State Assembly, promised to bring thousands of American Jews to Gaza in the summer of 2005 to obstruct the Israeli government's plan to evacuate Gaza. Helen Friedman, head of Americans for a Safe Israel, vowed to return in the summer with her family to organize resistance, which she described as civil disobedience. "Our slogan is 'let our people stay,'" said the primary school teacher, invoking the famous biblical call of "Let my people go," which Moses addressed to Pharaoh. "The land belongs to all the Jewish people and not only to Israelis," said Friedman.[1] At the other end of the religio-ideological spectrum, the Association of Reform Rabbis in the United States declared their support for Sharon's government, emphasizing that the sanctity of life precedes the sanctity of the land. The president of the Hebrew Union College, David Ellenson, welcomed Sharon in New York, saying that the courage shown by the prime minister in evacuating settlers from Gaza improves diaspora-Israeli relations.[2]

The identity of U.S.-based diaspora groups is made up of elements that are shared with the homeland, elements that are unique to the American experience, and elements shared with kin in other countries. Diasporic interests in homeland affairs are the product of a multiplicity of motivations, among them the desire that there be harmony and a confluence of interests between them and their kin in their respective homelands. Debates between diasporic and homeland elements may arise over the interests of "the people" and the interests of the homeland, including the extent to which the diaspora should have a voice in defining the terms of the homeland's existence, well-being, and international behavior. These issues are constantly contested, subject as they are to developments on the American domestic scene, the realm of international politics, and homeland affairs. For diasporas that are part of the rich and accommodating tapestry of American society, the difficulty of maintaining the content of their respective ethnocultural and religious identities in America has led to an increasing dependence on ties to the homeland for identity sustenance. Homeland societies, for their part, which have been struggling against economic and military challenges, as well as with core questions concerning ideational foundations, have turned to diaspora communities for material, psychological, and spiritual assistance to ensure their viability and inform national identities and goals. The fact that many U.S.-based diasporas and their respective homelands often see their character and interests intertwined in some fashion underscores the elastic and flexible nature of identity and interest across frontiers.

This interaction is particularly powerful and durable when diasporic and homeland (ethnonational) identities are strongly linked with religious affiliation, as in the case of the Hindus, Punjabi Sikhs, Catholic Poles, Irish, Armenians, and Jews vis-à-vis Israel. The saliency of the religious component in the identity of these groups is strengthened by its ties to their ethnonational origin and the strong resonance of a homeland, which is deeply intertwined in the religion. In the American context, the religious component of these diasporic identities is also embellished because other ideational components and forces of communal cohesion—ethnicity, language, geography, and nationalism, which form the core of identity inside the homeland—are constantly eroded in the face of a strong assimilationist culture. In addition, in the current U.S. context, religion is appreciated and culturally valued much more than ethnicity. In fact, "religious organizations become the means of maintaining and expressing ethnic identity [in the United States] not just for non-Christian groups such as Hindus, but also for groups such as the Chinese Christians, Korean Christians, and Maya Catholics."[3] In some respects religious affiliation provides a lower cost for the creation and assertion of homeland-related identities as part of the American way of life that greatly respects religiosity. If we add religion to occasional concerns of kinship security (e.g., Armenians and Nagorno-Karabakh, Hindus versus Pakistanis in Kashmir, or the struggle of Irish-Americans over Northern Ireland), these are the twin concerns that mobilize diasporas today.

Indeed, the interaction between Jewish-Americans and Israel is a model for both decision makers and scholars of interactions between diasporas and their kin states on political, economic, and religious affairs. The growing fluidity and diversity of Jewishness in the United States and in Israel, the two largest centers of world Jewry, compounded by a renewed sense of threat to Jewish security worldwide (emanating from the violence in the Middle East and the concomitant anti-Semitic campaign of the early twenty-first century), make the study of the mutual influences between American and Israeli Jews a valuable study in the overall analysis of diasporas in world affairs.

This chapter examines the Israeli-diaspora relationship from the perspective of an evolving Jewish identity. The question of Jewish identity in Israel and in the United States, the continuing insistence of many Jewish-Americans on perceiving Israel as a critical source of their own identity—and therefore as a crucial target of their influence—and Israel's direct or indirect involvement in the lives of all Jewish communities create a dynamic in which reciprocal influences mutually constitute Jewish identity. The chapter underscores the reasons for Jewish-Americans' increasing involvement in and impact on the Israeli identity battle. It also analyzes the growing openness of Israeli society to both Orthodox and non-Orthodox diasporic influences. The new modes of Jewish-American participation in Israeli affairs—domestic and international, on the one hand, and Israeli rethinking of its own position vis-à-vis the diaspora in terms of legitimacy, status, power, and identity, on the other—has opened the way for greater negotiation over, and coordination of, the meaning and purpose of Judaism in our time.

While many speak of the widening "gulf between the two centers of world Jewry" due to divergence of identities, or of "the waning of the American Jewish love affair with Israel," I argue the opposite.[4] Today, Jewish-Americans influence the nature of Jewish identity in Israel more than ever before, and Israel is reaching out to diasporic voices in an unprecedented manner. This mutual reinforcement draws the two communities closer together, reinvigorating Jewish identity in both countries. Indeed, American Jews, from those most deeply and directly involved with Jewish communal life and with Israel to those who habitually shunned synagogues and other Jewish institutions and eschewed involvement with anything Israeli, found themselves by the beginning of the twenty-first century confronted by myriad issues ranging from identity to physical security that were catalyzed or radically intensified by the Middle East's newest war of attrition, and further exacerbated by the terror attacks of September 11 and their aftermath. The new conflict raised uncomfortable questions for American Jews, not least for the unaffiliated. These questions included, among others, the direct and personal meaning to themselves of an existential crisis in Israel and among threatened Jewish communities elsewhere; the moral component of Israel's war and the United States' war and their responsibility for it, if any; and, based on these two dilemmas, what they owed their country—or countries—and how it would be possible to navigate their several obligations.

A deeper understanding of these questions sheds light on the broader phenomena of ethnoreligious American impact on the identity and politics of other countries via their diasporas. As will become evident, the two issues that dominate diaspora-Israeli relations are security and identity, both in the United States and in Israel. The perceived significance of identity issues on both sides is elastic and always determined by concerns with security. When security is threatened, debates over identity recede.

Equally, when security threats recede, debates over identity resurface. Indeed, perceptions regarding the acuteness of the security issues are not always shared between and within the two countries, and the debates will directly correspond to the differing emphases on Jewish identity. Yet when perceptions of acute insecurity are evident, they rapidly create a sense of kinship solidarity that overwhelms other dimensions of identity. Thus, an examination of the interplay of these two issues with the Israeli–Jewish-American case also generates important theoretical lessons.

Judaism and the Homeland Dimension

Throughout the 1990s the Israeli-diaspora relationship had been evolving in different directions. For almost a decade, many Israelis and diaspora Jews believed that a comprehensive Middle East peace would alter fundamentally both Israel's Jewish character and relations between the sovereign Jewish state and Jewish existence in the West. Peace would have enabled Israel to achieve a level of normalization that would have loosened the bonds of involvement with and responsibility for the diaspora, while releasing the diaspora from burdensome entanglements with Israeli security issues that had overshadowed their lives in their countries of domicile for over a generation. As late as the summer of 2000 the prevailing sense among observers of Jewish-American affairs was that "the Israel agenda" of American Jews and Jewish advocacy groups "has changed radically. Whatever the serious problems and deep pitfalls in the peace process, the issues that have come to the fore are related more to the relationship between Israel and America's Jews than with the physical security of Israel."[5]

Indeed, far from representing a process of detachment, the 1990s were marked by a growing involvement of Jewish-American liberal movements in the backlash against and coercion by Israel's religious establishment, which led many Israelis to shed their religious identities even beyond their secular Zionist socialization. In 1999, U.S.-based Reform and Conservative movements funded a public campaign on Israeli billboards and in the media, calling on secular Israelis to embrace religious pluralism under the slogan "There is more than one way to be a Jew." The campaign, financed by a grant from a Jewish family foundation in San Francisco, met with a harsh response from the Israeli ultra-Orthodox sector. This campaign was part of a growing Jewish-American involvement in the battle over Israel's Jewish identity. This battle, often described in general terms as the struggle between secular and religious

Jews,[6] or between "Israeliness" and "Jewishness," was the most controversial domestic theme in Israeli politics and civic culture in the 1990s,
with far-reaching political, economic, and legal ramifications. Only the
al-Aqsa intifada, which erupted in late September 2000, and the ensuing
wave of Palestinian terrorism that brought security back to the center of
the Jewish agenda were able to heal this rupture that threatened Israeli
society from within.[7] Ari Shavit, one of Israel's famous writers, said,

> today the Jewish people is waging two existential wars simultane-
> ously. One for the body, against the Arabs, and a second war for
> the soul, against itself. The identification of Judaism with a reli-
> gion from which people are trying to dissociate themselves is cre-
> ating a very serious vacuum [in Israel]. That is why there is a deep
> recoil from everything Jewish. But without Jewish identity, we will
> not be able to exist.[8]

As Asher Arian has noted, since the 1980s "there has been a parallel
growth of both secularism and religion in the country, decreasing the
spirit of coexistence and pluralism, and increasing the anxieties and fears
of a 'war of cultures'—or worse—among the Jews of Israel."[9] Certainly
by the mid-1990s violence has become a common feature of the Israeli
Kulturkampf, most dramatically expressed in the assassination of Prime
Minister Yitzhak Rabin. Religious ultranationalists saw Rabin's willingness to trade Jewish land for peace with the Palestinians as a sin against
divine law.[10] Indeed, the religious aspects of the Israeli Kulturkampf link
dilemmas of Jewish identity boundaries with attachments and commit-
ments to the physical ancient and modern boundaries of the Jewish state.
On June 24, 2000, with secular-religious tensions rising, religious
extremists set a Conservative synagogue in the heart of Jerusalem on fire.
Former prime minister Ehud Barak declared the attack "shocking . . . a
horrible act that chills the souls of all Jews."[11] Yet, just months later, after
the apparent collapse of the Oslo Peace Process, and as the identity issues
among Jews were pushed to the side in the face of a renewed Arab-Jewish
conflict, Israeli president Moshe Katsav said that the violent clashes
between Jews and Arabs helped reduce the divisions that exist in Israeli
society.[12]

Before the eruption of violence between Israeli and Palestinians in the
autumn of 2000, the struggle over Israel's Jewish character also had been
considered the most contentious issue within the Jewish-American diaspora, which has been grappling with its own identity. True, internal Jewish-American debates regarding the standards for gauging Jewish iden-

tity are mostly informed by the reality of Jewish life in the United States and are thus somewhat distant from internal Israeli debates. Yet, the American and Israeli contexts are closely interconnected in principle and in practice. Jewish-American positions on matters of politics and society in the United States, including on Judaism and the interests of the Jewish people, are often fashioned according to perceptions about Israel, U.S.-Israeli relations, and Israeli domestic and international behavior. Israeli politics and society, in turn, has been highly dependent on the government and the Jewish community of the United States and must take into consideration the views of the diaspora regarding Israel's disposition on matters of war and peace, as well as Israel's Jewish and democratic character.

Certainly the efforts of non-Orthodox denominations to influence the homeland's Jewish identity are not new.[13] Yet, until the 1980s their intervention in Israeli affairs was sporadic at best. In 1977, Charles Liebman wrote that "because Israel is a symbol, its particular policies are not very important to [non-Orthodox] American Jews . . . fall[ing] outside the boundaries of [their] legitimate activity." The Orthodox, however, are the only ones who "have a clear image of what Israel should be like and a sense of religious obligation to translate the image into specific policies."[14] Liebman could only envisage Jewish-American Orthodox interventions to restrain Israeli Zionist attempts to erode the state's "Jewish content." The assertion that Israeli Jewish content is more relevant to the diaspora Orthodoxy than to non-Orthodox denominations was thus built on the assumption that the latter's version of Judaism is loose and ephemeral.[15]

Regardless of the validity of this argument, this is certainly not the case today. Reform and Conservative Jews now increasingly embrace more traditional Jewish religious practices as a way of combating complete secularization and reversing the impact of interreligious marriage. A corollary of this indigenously American trend is the heightened attention toward Jewish identity in Israel. There are many answers to the question of why Reform and Conservative Jews in the United States, who have always considered the United States their chosen country, are so invested in shaping Jewish identity inside Israel at this juncture. Many emphasize the comfort of having a place to which one can always move should conditions in the United States become unfriendly. Periodic episodes of anti-Semitism are seen as reminders to older generations of Jewish-Americans of the precariousness of being a Jew in a Christian-majority culture. Others argue that it is not danger but rather the absence thereof that drives the current attention of Jewish-Americans to Israel. As they achieve full integration and great triumphs in all aspects of American life, American Jews, qua Jews, have become victims of their own success.[16] From the point of view of Jewish identity, some argue that the community faces a demographic peril as half of its members marry non-Jews, assimilate, or drift.[17]

In *Jewish Identity Survey, 2001*, a study of American Jewry, Egon Mayer et al. portrayed mutually reinforcing trends of increasing secularity, decreasing attachment to Jewish religious and communal institutions, decreasing commitment to and involvement with Israel, and a weakening sense of Jewish identity among large parts of American Jewry. Heightened divisions among American Jews over the nature and future of Jewish identity and affiliation were accompanied by increased assimilation in the forms of intermarriage and religious and philosophical syncretism, conversion, and indifference. The primary fault line was Jewish religious observance, a line pressed further into the ground by issues such as membership in other Jewish organizations, general social milieu, and attachment to Israel, with largely the same individuals falling on either side of the line.

Mayer described the ongoing exodus of Jews from organized Jewish life, shedding both the form and the substance of Jewish affiliation. Jews who became more secular found Jewish organizations less accommodating and less fulfilling. This process fed on itself, pushing these individuals further away not only from Jewish organizations, but from Jewish social attachments and other potential reinforcements of Jewish identity, eventually placing many altogether outside any kind of Jewish identity or affiliation. Among the ever-larger portion of American Jews who described themselves as secular but retained consciousness of Jewish identity, many searched for something substantive upon which to base this identity and develop effective vehicles for belonging and community, and did not find it in the larger Jewish community's existing frameworks. In the conclusion to Mayer's study, Jewish philanthropist Felix Posen writes that since so many American Jews do not identify with the main religious streams of Judaism, "Jewish secularism" must be given serious attention and new resources in order to become "a potent source of identification and motivation."[18]

Notwithstanding the debate regarding the content of "Jewish secularism"—especially outside the state of Israel—it is clear that with Jewish-American ethnicity (as a cultural trait) no longer enough to sustain Jewish existence in the United States, and with the fading of traditional Jewish neighborhoods, Jews in America have lost many of their distinctive ethnic markers. Not surprisingly, other survey data show that religion is the most distinctive attribute of most Jewish-Americans.[19] Today, even the most liberal streams in American Jewry acknowledge that "without the synagogue Jewish life in the U.S. cannot endure."[20] Reform Jews—as part of the movement's "worship revolution"—are now searching for new meaning in old religious rituals that were disposed of as part of their grandparents' desire to assimilate.[21] Likewise Conservative Jews also experienced renewed interest in ritual observance. A 1995 survey of Conservative synagogue members found that "younger Conservative Jewish adults are . . . more Jewishly active than their older counterparts, even when taking family life stage and presence of children into account." The younger Conservative Jews were also proved "more ritually active than older congregants despite having been raised by less observant Parents."[22]

Certainly, the memory of the Holocaust has become a major source of communal identity and mobilization and to a large extent is "a primary vehicle not only of invoking unity among Jews . . . but also of connection between the Jewish and non-Jewish communities."[23] However, given the fact that the Holocaust is gradually becoming what Daniel Levy and Natan Sznaider called a universalized, "cosmopolitan memory," even this memory is no longer sufficient in and of itself to foster and retain Jewish identity (especially as the generation of survivors leaves the historical stage). These trends further heighten the importance of religion in the ongoing formation of American-Jewish identity.

In the mid-1950s many Jews were satisfied with the legitimation and normalization of Judaism as part of a larger Americanized Judeo-Christian framework that downplayed religious differences with Christians, best articulated in Will Herberg's famous American "Tripartite Settlement,"[24] *Protestant-Catholic-Jew*. Yet a generation later, the resurgence of religious exclusivity, rather than the process of religious blending, was the desirable goal. The fact that Jews do not have to hide their religion, but rather celebrate it as part of their American identity, was made evident most strikingly by the landmark selection of modern Orthodox Jewish senator Joseph Lieberman as Al Gore's running mate in 2000. His candidacy symbolized, perhaps more than anything else, that accentuating one's Jewish religious life is, in itself, a part of normal American life. Even inside Israel, Lieberman's selection seemed to challenge some of the fundamental assumptions of modern Zionism regarding the alleged anomaly of diaspora life. It also presented many Israelis with an attractive model of reconciling religion and state.[25]

Among the major religions, Jewish theology is distinctive with its stress that religious membership is tied to a particular homeland, "the Land of Israel" (*Eretz Israel*). From biblical times, Jewish nationalism has been indistinguishable from religion as "God chose a particular people and promised them a particular land."[26] The fact that Jewish kinship is territorially related makes the character of the Jewish diaspora quite unique, since living outside the Land is theologically a sign of failing to fulfill God's plan. The vision of returning to the holy homeland is built into the very definition of all Jewish diasporic communities, at least symbolically. Thus, while most religions do not define themselves according to "political maps" and are not bound by membership in states, nations, or homelands, Judaism lends itself more to nationalism than to transnationalism.

Interestingly enough, even though traditional Zionism and many Israelis have long rejected the theological significance of the Land of Israel as the *holy homeland* (emphasizing instead the creation of the state as a political-secular undertaking to ensure a safe haven for Jews—like all other "normal" nations), the very existence of a Jewish state has great theological implications for many non-Jews (Christians and Muslims). Joseph Dan has written that secular "Israelis would do well to note the vast differences between their understanding of the state as secular, and the perception by others that it is a theological phenomenon *par excellence*."[27]

For fundamentally religious Jews, whose religious self precedes their other identities, the *halachic* decree of dwelling in the land of Israel implies that life in the United States is only a temporary sojourn, at least conceptually. Those religious Jews who consider exilic life (*galut*) as a punishment from God may suspend their move to Eretz Israel until the coming of the Messiah. In fact, at least until 1945, "most Orthodox Jewish authorities opposed Zionism as a blasphemous anticipation of the divine eschatological plan. And on this point they found common cause with most early (modernist) leaders of Reform Judaism—though the two groups would have shrunk with horror from any thought of commonality."[28] Yet the founding of Israel in 1948 presented all streams of American Jews with a constant dilemma of whether the modern nation-state of Israel and its policies, both internal and external, reflect their aspirations for a true Jewish state.

In the mid-1950s Rabbi Joseph B. Soloveitchik, representing the most important voice of centrist modern Orthodox Rabbis in the United States, urged members of his community to commit themselves fully to the project of secular Zionists in Israel. He argued that the unifying fate of the Jewish people—regardless of the degree of their religious observance, economic status, or place of residence—obliges religious Jews to have a feeling of solidarity, kinship, and responsibility for all secular Jews. Hence, when religious Jews are overlooking the critical importance in the creation of the State of Israel they ignore God's "knocking." Just as Soloveitchik called on Orthodox Jews in the diaspora to recognize and assist the new State of Israel, he also called upon secular Israelis to abandon Zionism's "nonsensical" idea of creating "'the new type of a Jew'... who has nothing in common with the diaspora Jew." He did not resort to messianic oratory, and as much as he believed that the creation of the State of Israel was a miracle, Judaism in his view is about free will; it requires rational understanding and action lest Jews squander the opportunity that the Almighty has presented them. Soloveitchik, who decried the failure of American Jews to utilize their resources during the Holocaust, reminded his Orthodox followers that the security and destiny of the new state of Israel was in their hands. Israel's very existence in his view was entangled with the fate of the diaspora.[29] Other religious Orthodox Zionists in the United States, like their counterparts in Israel, considered the creation of Israel as the "beginning of the flowering of Jewish redemption" (*geula*), a messianic doctrine that became the ideological hallmark of many American Orthodox after the Six-Day War.[30]

Indeed, a disproportionate number of Jewish-American immigrants to Israel are Orthodox.[31] A 1998 survey indicates that while 81 percent of Orthodox Jews in America visited Israel, only 38 percent of Reform Jews visited the country, and only 25 percent of Reform Jews think that a visit to Israel is important for maintaining their Jewish identity. Still, 91 percent of Conservative Jews and 73 percent of Reform Jews agree that "caring about Israel is a very important part of my being a Jew."[32] To be sure, the centrality of the state of Israel as the spiritual and cultural center of world Jewry is now recognized even by the Reform movement, which has undergone a dramatic shift from its early anti-Zionist position toward endorsing Zionism.[33] In its 1999 Pittsburgh Convention, the Reform Movement embraced "religious and cultural pluralism as an expression of the vitality of Jewish communal life in Israel and the Diaspora," affirming the unique qualities of living in Eretz Yisrael and encouraging aliyah (moving to Israel).[34]

Perhaps even more critical is the growing understanding of Reform and Conservative rabbis in the United States that their ability to develop and disseminate their creed of Judaism in the context of modernity and democracy inside Israel is the "ultimate test of Jewish authenticity for Progressive Judaism" in the diaspora. These sentiments were expressed by Rabbi Richard Hirsch, executive director of the World Union of Progressive Judaism, in his keynote address to the Twenty-ninth International Convention of the movement, held notably in Jerusalem in March 1999. Rabbi Hirsch also declared that "to support the movement in Israel is not philanthropy toward other Jews, such as is Diaspora support for universities, hospitals, yeshivot, and a host of other worthy Israeli causes. To support Progressive Judaism in Israel is inseparable from investing in liberal Judaism in the Diaspora."[35] Similarly, Dr. Ismar Schorsch, chancellor of the Jewish Theological Seminary of the American Conservative movement, has acknowledged that building a strong presence of the Conservative (Masorti) stream inside Israel is essential for "revitalizing the Conservative movement in North America."[36] Thus, the question of how to strengthen the ties between Jewish-Americans and Israel preoccupies the leadership of the more liberal Jewish-American religious streams who consider Israel to be indispensable to their Jewish identity in the United States.

The Israeli Kulturkampf and Jewish-Americans

In its first three decades the state of Israel was able to contain the strain between secularism and religion by turning the Zionist ideology and institutions into Israel's civil religion. To begin with, Israel was established as the state of all Jews. Israel's famous 1950 Law of Return is not only "the concrete expression of the prophetic vision of the 'ingathering of exiles,'"[37] but also a statutory expression of its commitment to its Jewish character. The state's legal system distinguishes between personal status laws, which are based on the religious Jewish legal code (*halacha*), and all other laws (criminal and civil), based on the Napoleonic codex and Western universalistic orientations. The state was set at the center of a belief system (*mamlachtiyut* or statism) that provided the base for an eclectic Zionist identity. It gave Jewish content to the national project by building on the ideas of a divinely chosen nation (*am nivchar*) or "light unto the nations" (or *lagoyim*).[38] The state often used religious symbols in order to build the national narrative, enhance nationalist conformity and collaboration among the nationalist religious community, and co-opt the newly arrived religious Mizrahim (or oriental Jews). Zionism, in turn, was slowly accepted by the nationalist religious community as a modern theology that perceived the establishment of the state as a divine intervention in Jewish history.[39]

In the last two decades and especially during the years of the Oslo

Peace Process, however, Zionism has been in decline, some argue under assault, inside Israel. This attrition was the result of a general perception that the Zionist vision had reached its triumphant realization—a secure sovereign state with a large Jewish majority. The decline of traditional Zionism was also a result of a confluence of factors in the rapidly changing context of Israeli politics and society. In the words of Peter Berkowitz, the forces of market capitalism and globalization pushed large segments of the Israeli public to embrace "hedonism over heroism and modern consumerism over piety."[40] These tendencies, coupled with growing public sentiment that peace with the Arabs was imminent, further exacerbated Jewish-Israeli disunity. Within this context, several ideological and political camps challenged the core values of mainstream Zionism. The ultra-Orthodox envisioned Israel as a Jewish state ruled by Orthodox precepts. This camp includes the ultra-Orthodox Ashkenazim of European origin and a growing voting bloc of Mizrahim represented by the Shas party, which "seeks to replace secular Zionism with religious Judaism as the hegemonic ideology in Israeli society and presents this as the remedy for both the socio-economic and the cultural grievances [of Mizrahim]."[41] The secular universalistic forces, on the other hand, advocate transforming Israel into a liberal and secular state for both its Jewish and Arab citizens. While the more extreme among the ultra-Orthodox veer toward Jewish theocracy, radicals in the secularist community see post-Zionism as an opportunity to "de-Judaize" the country. Israel's internal cultural debate has also been compounded by conflicting visions over peace with the Arabs and Palestinians and the future of the occupied territories. During the late 1990s these factors ruptured the alliance between religious and secular Zionists, culminating in fundamentalist nationalism and a growing blurring of the distinctions between religious Zionists and the ultra-Orthodox (*haredim*).[42]

For years, many believed that the internal Israeli Kulturkampf between the religious and secular communities was "fought out against the background of a general agreement on the value and importance of the Jewish tradition to Israel's cultural identity."[43] This was also the prevailing opinion among Jewish-Americans, many of whom adopted idealized images of Israel after its 1967 victory in the Six-Day War. Yet by early 2000, many in Israel and in the United States were no longer certain about the unassailable nature of Israel's Jewish-Zionist character, let alone satisfied with its conflicting directions—the insularity and perceived backwardness of Israeli ultra-Orthodoxy, or the weakening sense of Jewish identity among secular Israelis. Many now fear that Israeli religious forces will continue to gain power and erode Israel's liberal democracy, or alternatively, that the secularism of the West, which Israel has adopted as its own, will obliterate Israel's distinctly Jewish identity. For instance, Yehuda Nini, a professor of Jewish Studies at Tel Aviv University, has argued that the crisis of identity experienced by secular Israeli youth is so profound that "assimilation is a malaise no less chronic in Israel than in the Diaspora."[44] Yoram Hazony has charged that Israel's Zionist-Jewish foundations are undermined by the rise of a post-Zionist, post-Jewish educated elite in Israel society. He maintained that left-oriented Israeli scholars have penetrated the state's Education Ministry, rewriting school textbooks in an effort to undermine the founding vision of Israel and replace its Zionist and Jewish core values with more universal and democratic ones.[45] Many, however, were more apprehensive about the growing power of the haredi parties, which use their grip on the balance of power in Israel's political system to draw greatly on state resources for their own sectarian needs. While ultra-Orthodox leaders carry a lot of weight in Israel's domestic and foreign affairs, including matters of war and peace with the Arabs, their followers enjoyed draft deferment and military exemption while they study at state-subsized religious schools (*yeshivot*). Many secular Israelis and some religious Zionists railed against the fast-growing state-funded (yet outside the state-run education system) ultra-Orthodox schools that discredit the democratic values of the state. They believed that ultra-Orthodox students "are being trained to support an intolerant theocracy like Iran."[46]

Moreover, while religious Zionists and the ultra-Orthodox camp represent a minority of the Israeli Jewish population, albeit a growing one, their authorities have maintained a monopoly over marriage, burial, conversion, and other functions governing life in Israel. The exercise of this domination, and the strong political activism of Israeli ultra-Orthodox parties in the 1990s, bred broad resentment among nonreligious Israelis and caused a backlash against Judaism in general. Va'adat Shenhar, a committee appointed by the late education minister Zvulun Hammer to study the decline of Jewish identity among Israelis, found that the general decline of ideologies, the rise of consumerism and global markets, the politicization of religion, and the growing gap between religious and secular Jews, as well as debates over issues of peace with the Arabs (which over the years became imbued with religious significance), have all contributed to the declining attachment to Judaism among nonobservant Jews.[47] In the 1999 Israeli elections, one of the top issues galvanizing support for Prime Minister Ehud Barak and the newly established anti-

Orthodox party Shinui Party (*Change*) was opposition to religious coercion. In the 2003 elections Shinui became in the third largest party in the Knesset, and its platform calling for "fights against religious coercion and for a secular state with room for all opinions and beliefs" a rallying cry for many middle-class Israelis.[48] By the turn of the twenty-first century many polls in Israel rated the religious-secular cleavage as the country's most dangerous crisis—even above security concerns.[49]

Despite all of these developments, survey data also show that most Israelis continue to value their ties to their ancestral faith and in fact are eager to practice it with modern content. In other words, they are not necessarily fully secular, even if they label themselves that way.[50] The late Charles Liebman argued that most Israelis participate in Jewish religious rituals that are not fully in accordance with Jewish religious law (*halacah*) and in that way "have transformed [religious rituals] into the folkways of secular Jewishness." These Israelis tend to label themselves secular rather than traditional because of "the animus they feel toward the religious establishment and the religious parties."[51] Others argue that many Israeli Jews who are Sephardim (or Mizrahim) and who never experienced the pluralist reformation of the Ashkenazi world do not wish to abolish the Orthodox monopoly but rather to "reserve for themselves the informal right to pick and choose" while maintaining "the [Orthodox] formal religion to remain as is."[52] These are forces that militate against non-Orthodox Judaism in Israel but are not the result of ultra-Orthodox machinations or the secular backlash.[53] This argument, however, does not take into account the rapid changes in Israeli society over the last decade, above all, the large influx of about one million post-Soviet immigrants, about a quarter of whom are not Jewish by *halacha*. This wave of newcomers introduced a large bloc of nonreligious citizens into Israeli society who may be seeking non-Orthodox options.[54]

In this complex reality, the American Reform and Conservative movements have appeared in Israel as among the main groups trying to confront the religious establishment in the battleground over Israeli Jewish identity.[55] They have mainly targeted Israelis who have been exposed to Jewish alternatives in America and want similar religious choice at home and those who wish to register protest against the ultra-Orthodox political, legal, and religious stronghold. These movements also appeal to secular Israeli values, such as egalitarianism.[56] In other words, these movements are trying to provide a middle-ground Jewish option and put special emphasis on outreach programs for the new post-Soviet immigrants.[57] The movement toward pluralistic Judaism has grown inside

Israel, with the Reform and Conservatives establishing synagogue centers, educational programs, rabbinical schools, youth movements, and other outreach institutions. They attract a significant number of the new Russian immigrants whose secular upbringing made liberal Judaism a natural fit to their needs and orientation in the process of becoming Israeli citizens.[58] These movements are also instrumental in the legal struggles to alter the Orthodox monopoly over Jewish marriage and conversion, to loosen Orthodox domination of religious councils, and to allow burial in nondenominational cemeteries. These Jewish-American movements and their Israeli sister organizations have also played a role in the Israeli High Court ruling to allow women to hold religious services at the Western Wall, Judaism's holiest site. Finally, they led in redirecting diasporic funds from general fund-raising for Israel to educational institutions and social-political programs aimed at promoting tolerance, democracy, and religious pluralism.[59] This new pattern in financial flows has greatly affected the sums, structure, and destination within Israel of Jewish-American philanthropy.

Since the early 1990s, targeted American-Jewish giving to Israel has quadrupled reaching approximately 2 billion dollars in the year 2000.[60] The campaign for pluralist Judaism further made the Reform and Conservative movements the nemesis of much of Israel's religious establishment, which has, at various times, denounced them as nonreligious, antireligious, "enemies of Judaism and the Jewish State," and even "more dangerous to the Jewish nation than the Holocaust." The last statement, made in 1999 by Israel's Sephardi Chief Rabbi Bakshi-Doron, was described by leaders of the Reform movement in Israel as an "incitement to bloodshed and civil war."[61] Ultra-Orthodox leaders also charged that these movements represent a foreign American phenomenon.

As they have become more cognizant of the centrality of Israel to their own Jewish-American identity, liberal American Jews have decided to engage directly in a struggle to redefine Israel's identity in their own image. The assumption of many Jewish-Americans, wrote Jack Wertheimer, provost of the Jewish Theological Seminary of America, is that the diaspora "has much to teach its benighted Israeli cousins. Living in a heterogeneous environment, American Jews . . . have learned the blessings of diversity, and accept the legitimacy of many different forms of religious Jewish expression. Moreover, thanks to constitutional guarantees of church/state separation, American Judaism is not demeaned by the kinds of electoral horse-trading to which Israeli religious parties inevitably must stoop. In short, American Jews and American Judaism have grown in an atmosphere of pluralism and tolerance, and Israeli Jews would do well to learn from their example."[62]

The Controversy over "Who Is a Jew?"

The involvement of Conservative and Reform Jewish-Americans in Israeli affairs was rejuvenated in 1988 when the religious parties moved to redefine who is a Jew in a manner that invalidated Reform and Conservative rabbis in the United States. Subsequently, leaders of the vast majority of American organized Jewry declared "open revolt against Israel."[63] It was the first time that the bitter hostility between American non-Orthodox leaders and the New York–based Lubavitch Hasidic movement—led by the late Rabbi Menachem Mendel Schneerson—was injected into the Israeli arena with such ferocity. The Lubavitchers' ardor and money ignited Israeli religious zealousness and the move to change Israel's legal definition of who is a Jew.[64] It left an indelible mark on the future direction of Israeli politics and society. Dr. Ismar Schorsch commented:

> This is not an Israeli affair. This is a personal affair of the Lubavitcher Rebbe. He is trying to use the Law of Return in order to discomfit Conservative and Reform Judaism. His concern is not the purity of immigrants to Israel, but rather the strength of Conservative and Reform in America. This is an American affair which the Lubavitcher Rebbe is forcing upon Israel. . . . Israel is the battlefield; but the war is in America. . . . If the State of Israel declares that [our] conversion is no conversion, that means that [our] rabbis are no rabbis. This is the instrument through which the Lubavitcher Rebbe proposes to declare that Conservative and Reform Judaism in America are not authentic Judaism.[65]

Such debates signaled the rise in diasporic intervention in Israeli domestic and foreign affairs and brought into the open the divergence between diaspora hawks and doves regarding the Oslo Peace Process.[66] Diaspora activists fueled the sharp divide within Israel over the peace process, even to the point of American ultra-Orthodox rabbis issuing rulings that sanctioned Israeli soldiers' insubordination and the assassination of Prime Minister Rabin in 1995.

Although the initial impetus for political battle over the legitimacy of non-Orthodox Judaism came from the diaspora, these issues took on a life of their own in Israel, raised again under the Netanyahu government

(1996–99), which comprised an unprecedented number of religious party representatives. In 1997 the Israeli religious establishment sought once again to enact a conversion law "designed to formalize and institutional-ize the prevailing norm, according to which the only acceptable conver-sions in Israel would be those performed by Orthodox rabbinical author-ities," and "delegitimize Reform and Conservative rabbis."[67] This brought Israeli-diaspora relations to their lowest point. Although the conversion law was eventually suspended, the storm left a lasting mark on Israel-diaspora relations. It eroded further the posture of automatic Jew-ish-American support of Israel in U.S. foreign policy. Thus, with the increasing involvement of Jewish-Americans the Israeli Kulturkampf took on an ever more complex international dimension.

Confronting the religious establishment inside Israel with outright secularism—which denies Israel's Jewish character as a sine qua non of the state's identity—seems unrealistic even to secularized and staunchly antireligious sectors of Israeli society. Thus when leading Israeli writers, like Amos Oz, A. B. Yehoshua, Yehuda Amichai, and David Grossman criticized what they saw as the ultra-Orthodox attack on Israeli liberal-democratic institutions, they called on Israelis to join the Reform and Conservative movements in order to "save Judaism from the enemies of democracy" and to "generate a new dynamic which will renew Israel's spiritual and cultural landscape."[68] A. B. Yehoshua added that "to stand with the Reform and Conservative movements is to defend ourselves."[69] The idea that American Judaism can give Israel "the greatest gift . . . a sense of pluralism in Jewish expression,"[70] has been gaining momentum among the liberal segments of American Jewry, with a growing foothold inside Israel.[71] Capping these trends, in 1999 Prime Minister Barak appointed Israel's first Minister for Diaspora Affairs. When in November of that year the new diaspora minister Melchior addressed the Jewish-American General Assembly, he said that "the future of the Jewish people requires a new definition of the partnership between all Jews and finding common ground on the question of Jewish pluralism."[72]

In sum, when ultra-Orthodox and more liberal Jewish denominations in the United States and in Israel clash over the central question of who is a Jew, they are fighting not only to decide the character of the modern Jewish homeland but also over the right to claim and determine religious and national identity for Jews wherever they reside. It was at this juncture that a semantic change began to appear in the discourse over Israeli-dias-pora relations with terms such as the negative *Galut* (exile) and the more neutral *tfutzot* (diaspora) being replaced by references to partnership with *ha'am hayehudi* (the Jewish people). This new approach was also behind the unprecedented financial backing ($70 million) that the Israeli government provided to the Birthright Israel program. This program was initiated by diasporic philanthropists and is also supported by North American Jewry's communal institutions as an outreach effort to young people in the diaspora "who have not been drawn into existing Jewish frameworks and may therefore soon be lost to the Jewish people."[73]

Jewish-American Identity and Its Israeli Component

Given the complex ties between Israel and American Jewry that developed over the last two decades, it should be recalled that Israel was not always the main focus of American Jewish life. Although Zionism captured the imagination of many Jews in America, until World War II major Jewish groups—Reform, Orthodox, and Socialists—were very hesitant or hostile regarding the idea of Jewish nationalism. Moreover, even American Zionists rejected the idea that life in America is exilic or temporary; they held a new vision of a dual Jewish existence in two promised homelands that coexist and nurture each other. Ezra Mendelsohn observed that from the start American Zionism was "similar to other varieties of ethnic nationalism in America." It did not encourage American Jews to speak Hebrew or to return to the homeland and, like other mobilized diasporas in the United States, it always stressed that support for Jewish nationalism was "in no way conflicting with [the Zionists'] intense Americanism at home, just as Americans of Irish origin who fought to oust England from Ireland were perfectly good Americans."[74]

To be sure, the divisions among American Jews over the legitimacy and necessity of the Zionist experiment in Palestine largely ended after the Holocaust and especially with the establishment of the state of Israel.[75] Even after the state was established the diaspora focused mainly on integrating itself and European Jewish newcomers into American society and on eradicating post-Holocaust American anti-Semitism. The three major Jewish defense groups, the Anti-Defamation League, the American Jewish Committee, and the American Jewish Congress, struggled against racial and ethnic stereotypes, in ways that helped establish universalistic liberalism as Jewish-Americans' postwar ethnic identity. This emphasis on integration also did not leave much room to cope with the trauma of the Holocaust.

Even with the very real emotional attachment they felt for Israel, Jewish-Americans feared that political expressions of support for the new state would bring charges of dual loyalty that could not be allowed. Indeed, diaspora leaders forced Israel to recognize that for American Jews America is the promised land. A document negotiated between Israel's first prime minister Ben-Gurion and Jacob Blaustein, then president of the American Jewish Committee, declared in 1950, "The Jews in the United States, as a community and as individuals, have only one political attachment and that is to the United States. . . . They owe no political allegiance to Israel."[76]

Ben-Gurion's brand of Zionism largely ignored Jewish-American contributions to Israel's War of Independence and relegated diasporic Zionist efforts, "no matter how . . . helpful they might be to the Jewish State, . . . [to] lower status in the hierarchy of Jewish values."[77] In turn, Jewish-Americans believed that, unlike other Jewish centers in the world, their experience was not going to recede into insignificance but would continue to develop alongside the newly established state. Nevertheless the definitions of this duality varied according to ideological camp. Regarding religious identity, from the beginning of the century until the 1950s, Jewish-Americans were generally removed from regular religious observance and synagogue life. Only with the postwar move to suburbia did synagogues begin to grow and proliferate, and Jewish community institutions to thrive. As religion took a more central place in American public life, Jews in suburban America began to enter mainstream American society. The social radicalism of the second generation of descendants of Jewish immigrants did not find favor among the third that came of age at this time. This new generation, following the pattern of their non-Jewish neighbors, expressed a greater interest in the religious element of their identity, but in a distinctly American way. Synagogue services and organizational structures borrowed heavily from Protestant practices, with the creation of Sunday schools, sisterhoods, and so forth.

Altogether, the return to religious worship, based in large part on a search for roots and authenticity that could in other circumstances have denoted a retreat into cultural isolationism, became a clear signal of Jewish acculturation and integration into the broader society, which adopted religious practices informed by American values. American Judaism at this juncture had little to do with Israel, a stance that was reinforced by the often hostile policy of the Eisenhower administration toward the homeland.[78] Even further, organized Jewish lobbying for Israel did not come into its own until the early 1960s. The growing legitimacy of ethnicity in American public life in the 1960s led to the growing politicization of U.S. Jews and brought to the fore the diasporic component of their identity. The openness of American society and the assertion of identity that came with it had several important influences on the community, leading to changes among American Jews that would soon have significant political repercussions. On the one hand, Jewish intermarriage rates, which had held steady at 4 to 6 percent for half a century, rose dramatically from 1965, reaching 30 percent in 1974 and more than 50 percent by the mid-1980s.[79] On the other hand, differences of many kinds became more acceptable in American society, in ways that enabled younger Jews to claim their distinctiveness in a bolder manner than their parents' generation had done. This was also the period when Jewish day schools throughout the United States began to proliferate, including the Conservative and Reform movements, whose leaders gradually subscribed to the Orthodox view "that only through day school education can Judaism survive [in the United States]."[80] The effects of general social change were also reflected in the push for gender desegregation, leading Jewish women to challenge traditional practices and claim roles as cantors and rabbis. At the same time Jewish Orthodoxy also gained confidence, "in sharp contrast to the timidity that often characterized the movement in the first two thirds of this century."[81] Its younger representatives were no longer hesitant to express opposition to liberal Judaism, including the separation of synagogue and state, "the hallmark of American Jewry."[82]

This activism found a new outlet in the energy and emotions that the Eichmann trial and the 1967 war released among Jewish-Americans, which were channeled into the establishment of pro-Israeli organizations and the reorganization of traditional Jewish-American institutions with greater emphasis on the Israeli dimension. Israel's victory also helped American Jews to finally begin the process of reckoning with the Holocaust. "Their psychologically empowering discovery . . . [that there would be] no annihilation of the Jews at this time, not in the face of superior Jewish armed forces" was so cathartic that they were finally able to confront this existential trauma. The diaspora's ability to embrace both the Holocaust and Israel was augmented by America's domestic developments as "Jews ceased to be (sort of) race (somewhat) apart, and became (white) Americans—not as mere assimilationist but with vehement reference to Israel and to the Holocaust."[83] Israel grew more dependent on American support, and assumption of a strategic alliance with the United States made Jewish-Americans more important to the maintenance of Jewish existence in the homeland and gave them a strong and clear purpose around which to lobby and organize. They underwent "a kind of a mass conversion to Zionism, and the UJA, through Israel, evolved into 'America's Jewish religion.'"[84] The new role of Israel provided Conservative and Reform Jewish-Americans more secular alternatives to Orthodox categories of Judaism. For Reform Jews in particular, this was a significant departure from their earlier opposition to Zionism, and part of their recognition that their fate as diaspora Jews was intimately—and legitimately—intertwined with that of the state of Israel. These developments also raised questions as to the political implications of their faith.

The 1967 war was also significant for ethnic relations within the United States. The war and its aftermath were major causes of a fundamental political and social realignment among groups that had previously fought as a united front in favor of civil rights and the general advancement of minorities. Many Jewish-Americans distanced themselves from their previous partners in the desegregation movement and the American Left. Israel bashing, especially among radical black activists and the New Left, was generally perceived by Jewish-Americans as a barely disguised form of anti-Semitism.[85] The shock of the 1973 Yom Kippur War heightened Jewish sensitivity to the continued insecurity of Jews. A significant and highly visible minority of Jewish-Americans and Jewish organizations began to move to the right politically, a phenomenon that had been virtually unimaginable ten or twenty years before. One indication of the move rightward was the Jewish approach to the Jackson-Vanik Amendment, which linked the issue of trade with the Soviet Union to Soviet willingness to permit Jewish emigration and that ran counter to the spirit of détente. The effort to free Soviet Jews gave American anti-communism "a new moral argument," and it increased Jewish-American clout in U.S. foreign policy. This higher profile was enhanced by Jewish-American campaigns against the Arab economic boycott of Israel and against the anti-Zionist propaganda prevalent among third world and communist countries that culminated in the 1975 UN vote equating Zionism with racism.[86]

The new diaspora-Israeli alliance pushed aside the Israeli demands from Jewish-Americans to immigrate. The dilemma of Israel's democratic character and its contentious treatment of the Palestinian issue was minimized when safeguarding Israel's existence was at stake. From the late 1970s, however, with the rise to power of the Likud Party and the growing divisions within Israel regarding peace, diasporic political positions became more diverse. These divisions were encouraged by Israeli efforts to establish Jewish-American counterparts in the United States that as "Friends of . . ." raised funds and lobbied to support their political agenda in Israel, in effect expanding their constituencies to include non-voters in the diaspora. It was at this juncture that liberal Jewish-Americans established the New Israel Fund to promote a liberal agenda for Israeli politics and society. This organization represented an early departure from the traditional patterns of Jewish-American giving to the UJA toward nonstate institutional frameworks.

Although the internal diasporic rift was largely kept quiet, it surfaced whenever the American government collided with Israel's Likud-led government. This was the case with the 1982 Reagan plan, more dramatically with the issue of loan guarantees under the George H. W. Bush administration in 1991 and 1992, and throughout this period with the controversial subject of settlements in the occupied territories. Yet, when criticism of Israel came from sources traditionally, or even categorically, seen as hostile to Israel or to Jews in general, American Jews were generally reluctant to accede. In an environment of broadly based and harsh criticism by the United States, other governments, the media, and other institutions, most American Jewish spokespeople declined to give what they saw as aid and comfort to enemies of Jews and of Israel.[87] By the late 1980s, as the question of Israel's moral standing became increasingly disputed, many Jewish-Americans felt that Israeli affairs might jeopardize their own standing in America. The 1985 Pollard Affair, in which an American Jewish intelligence analyst was convicted of spying for Israel, was deeply disturbing to Jewish-Americans. They were shocked to discover how Israel's actions could quickly expose them to charges of double loyalty. Israel's controversial relationship with South Africa's apartheid regime also increased the tensions between Israel and the diaspora, by exacerbating tensions between Jews and Blacks in the United States.[88] With the first Palestinian intifada, the diversification and erosion of Jewish-American support for Israel became evident.[89]

By 1990, the deep penetration of Israel into Jewish-American life and organizational structures raised concerns about Israeli meddling in and manipulation of Jewish-American affairs.[90] From an Israeli foreign policy view, in 1990 it seemed that an "Israel-centric perspective" in mobilizing the diaspora reached a dangerous level when AIPAC and other Jewish organizations felt so empowered that they began to adopt an independent foreign policy agenda in the Middle East.[91] Remarking on the Israeli government's pressure on American Jewry to stand behind the homeland, even against the U.S. government's official position, David Vital has written that "Israel and its affairs tend to continuously rob [Jewish-Americans] of their long sought for and so very recently acquired peace of mind."[92]

The Hopes and Doubts of Peace

The dismantling of the friend/foe pattern of the Cold War was reflected in a blurring of similar boundaries in the Middle East and in changing Israel-diaspora dynamics. The majority of American Jews welcomed the 1993 Oslo Peace Accord, but right-wing and Orthodox groups in the United States expressed outright hostility.[93] After Oslo, many Jewish-American organizations began to ask how they would recruit politically in the era of peace and what would compel them to remain Jews if the danger to Israel receded. Some sounded the alarm that "the declining needs of Israel will contribute to the steady decline of Jewish giving, weakening American Jewish institutions and accelerating the rate of [Jewish] assimilation."[94] Other voices began admonishing the diaspora for making Judaism in the United States ephemeral due to its overwhelming concentration on the Jewish state. Arthur Hertzberg wrote that with peace in the Middle East, Israel would no longer remain Jewish-Americans' "secular religion," and the diaspora must reshape its identity and institutions to meet domestic American challenges.[95]

Diaspora groups that opposed the peace process financed a public relations campaign against the accords, gave financial support to the Jewish settler movement, and established American affiliates of key right-wing Israeli parties to financially support their political campaign against Rabin and his Labor Party successors, Shimon Peres and Ehud Barak.[96] The divergent positions on the Israeli-Palestinian peace process basically paralleled the rift between Jewish-American religious denominations. A 1995 public opinion survey revealed that while 77 percent of Reform and 74 percent of Conservative Jews supported the Rabin government's handling of the peace negotiations with the Arabs, 64 percent of Orthodox Jews opposed it. A large majority of the Orthodox also opposed the idea of dismantling any Jewish settlements in the West Bank.[97]

When in 1995 right-wing diasporic groups attempted to forestall the Oslo Process by encouraging Congress to adopt initiatives that could undermine Israeli-Arab negotiations, Thomas Friedman described their actions as attempts to subvert the Israeli democratic process by Jewish-American groups that "could only thrive if they have an enemy, someone to fight. They have no positive vision to offer American Jews on the central question of American Jewish identity or the fate of Israel-diaspora relations in this new era."[98]

By the year 2000, many Orthodox Jewish-Americans expressed disappointment with the pronounced secularist shift in Israeli society, which for them was reinforced by the widespread willingness to give up the West Bank and parts of East Jerusalem. Even modern Orthodox—who uphold halachic theology but also allow for Western-democratic norms and values in their daily life, and espouse the Zionist vision without its messianic elements—became disillusioned with what they saw as a liberal post-Zionist reluctance to preserve the Jewishness of Israel. Norman Lamm, president of Yeshiva University and an important voice of modern Orthodoxy in the United States, drew a direct parallel between the "demographic and cultural catastrophe" brought on American Jewry by the lax practices of Reform and (less so) Conservative Judaism, and the deleterious impact of Israel's post-Zionists on Israel's loss of its Jewish character.[99]

Ironically, just at the time when it seemed that in Israel moderate Orthodox forces were on the verge of losing the Israeli Kulturkampf to both secularists and post-Zionists on the left and extreme religious nationalists and the ultra-Orthodox on the right, America embraced a modern Orthodox candidate for the vice presidency. These developments prompted some Orthodox leaders inside the United States to contemplate how to better build the future of their vibrant community by developing an "improved" brand of a modern Jew on American soil rather than directing their energies toward the biblical homeland. Even more ironically, such rethinking came at a time when non-Orthodox Jewish-Americans work harder than ever before to expand their message into Israeli society.

Throughout the Oslo Peace Process leaders of the American Jewish community acted as unofficial emissaries in the efforts to open new diplomatic channels to countries that had no diplomatic relations with Israel, to lift the Arab boycott, to reward Arab and Islamic states that normalized relations with the Jewish state, and to encourage others to do the same.[100] Many Reform and Conservative Jews promoted a Palestinian-Israeli rapprochement because they viewed the Israeli occupation of the West Bank and Gaza as belying the liberal political principles they championed in the United States and that, they argued, were the foundation of Israel's natural and close alliance with the United States. These movements saw the era of peace as an opportunity to disseminate their American views of a multifaceted Jewish identity inside Israel and to bring their vision of Jewish pluralism to the Israeli public, which was already more eager for greater openness. Yet the fact that Reform Judaism in the United States, and its extension in Israel, allied itself with the Israeli peace camp (i.e., the Israeli left) and ascribed much importance to its positions on peace with

the Palestinians as part of its religious creed alienated some of its potential constituents among the Russian immigrants. Dimitri Slivniak, an
astute observer of Russian immigrants' life in Israel, argues that this liberal tradition represents "a different cultural and social environment, not
ours"—and expresses American-inspired "politically correct" positions.
This American liberalism on the Arab-Israeli conflict was inconsistent
with the views of many Russian immigrants. These attitudes are unat-
tractive to post-Soviet Jews who are staunchly liberal in their religious
orientations and in their belief in the market economy, but have a more
conservative, right-wing outlook on security and cultural matters more in
tune with American neoconservatives.[101]

By the year 2000 the diverse American Orthodox camp was divided
between two poles: the moderates who considered religious imposition
inside Israel as "ideologically dubious and pragmatically unwise"[102] and
the more ardent group that declared the old alliance with secular Zionism
as defunct. Some in the latter camp even began to question the centrality
of Israel to their Jewish theology to the point of embracing the prena-
tionalist haredi approach. This spectrum of views is visible in the Orthodox Union, the leading Orthodox organization in the United States. In
1996, the organization attempted to strengthen its own vision of Jewish
identity in Israel by creating a branch of the American National Conference of Synagogue Youth, aimed at "combating the trends of American-
ization, secularization, and alienation." This organization also targeted
semireligious youth and Russian immigrants in secular Israeli cities.

When Security Overshadows Identity

By the year 2000, the Jewish Kulturkampf, both within and outside Israel,
reshaped the relationship between Israel and the diaspora in several ways.
First, the peace process and the widespread notion of increasing "nor-
mality" widened the gulf between Jewish universalists and Jewish partic-
ularists. As identities were pushed to the fore, the splits within Israel
regarding the direction of peace negotiations further divided American
Jews over their vision for U.S. Middle East policy.[103] When in the summer of 2000 Prime Minister Barak negotiated with Palestinian leader
Arafat at Camp David, Jewish-American leaders issued conflicting mes-
sages both supporting and opposing the Israeli government's position.
The issues that divided Israel became resonant within the diaspora, and a
new symbiosis between diasporic organizations and domestic Israeli
social and political formations solidified, which served the Jewish identity

interests of groups both inside and outside Israel. Conversely, many Israeli groups actively recruited Jewish allies in the diaspora to buttress their domestic political and social agendas and, consequently, pushed diaspora voices to the center of the Israeli Kulturkampf with particular emphasis on the question of religious pluralism. A third development was a growing assessment within the diaspora that Israel remained a very important factor for their own identity in the United States and that they had a vested interest in the evolution of the Israeli polity—a development that reflected their own worldview on religious pluralism, security issues, and sociopolitical affairs.

With the notion that "Israel is no longer waging an existential battle for its survival . . . against an external enemy," a 2000 Jewish Agency for Israel study chronicles the vast proliferation of largely diaspora-supported voluntary enterprises that have become so visible in the struggle to shape Israeli-Jewish identity.[104] In sum, the core of support for Israel remains, and there has not been a reduction of interest in Israeli affairs. On the contrary, a desire for reinvigoration and intensification of the Jewish-American–Israeli relationship surfaced on both sides, albeit marked by a comprehensive transformation of kinship affinity.

The crushing failure of the Oslo Peace Process and the waves of violence that ensued dramatically shifted the focus from identity back to existential security. To some extent, and reminiscent of the shock of the 1967 war, almost overnight both the internal and international Jewish Kulturkampf ceased as the community reunified and re-created solidarity to face the new threat. When the Barak government appeared to be willing to compromise Jewish sovereignty in Jerusalem, some observers expressed their concern "that a hand-over of the Temple Mount and parts of Jerusalem threatens to undermine the Jewish identity of American Jews and tear away the already delicate fabric of their relationship with Israel."[105] Indeed, many in the diaspora were adamant that the Temple Mount was the inheritance of all Jews and must be discussed within the wider Jewish community rather than solely by the Israeli government. Their position was reinforced when Arafat made Jerusalem into a Muslim-Jewish battle. Malcolm Hoenlein, the executive vice chairman of the Conference of Presidents, stated, "Israel has a right to make decisions that affect its security. All Jews have a right to discuss it, but it's up to the government of Israel. The Temple Mount is a different issue. It belongs to all Jews, it is the inheritance of all Jews, and all Jews have vested interests in it."[106] Even within the Conservative movement, there was vocal disagreement over the issue of Jerusalem, with American members refusing to accept the idea of their left-leaning counterparts in Israel that a compromise over the Temple Mount was only a political matter rather than a core religious identity one.[107]

With Middle East violence rising, the urgent Israeli need for unity with the Jewish people at such a time of duress made the American diaspora an intimate partner in the articulation of the new challenges of Jewish identity and security. This new sense of Jewish unity was further magnified when Jews around the world closed ranks in the face of new manifestations of anti-Semitism, which were reaching levels not seen since the end of World War II, and renewed attempts to equate Zionism with racism at the UN conference on racism in Durban in September 2001. As one diaspora observer said, "Jews can call themselves liberal, conservative, Reconstructionist, Reform, it doesn't matter. When Israel is in danger, a different alarm system goes off."[108]

When the newly elected prime minister, Ariel Sharon, appeared before AIPAC in March 2001, he announced that he considers himself "first and foremost as a Jew" and that he saw himself as having been given a mandate to unify not only Israel but Jews worldwide. In what sounded like a dramatic departure from Ben-Gurion's Israelocentrism and the overarching Zionist vision that those who do not fight here should not have a voice on Israeli security matters, he declared that "the future of Israel is not just a matter of Israelis who live there. Israel belongs to the entire Jewish people. And Israel would not be what it is today if it were not for the efforts of all Jews worldwide."[109] At this juncture, renewed Jewish solidarity heightened issues concerning the costs of kinship loyalty. Visits to Israel at times of duress and terrorism were presented to the diaspora as litmus tests of their Jewish loyalty. Combined with the legacy of the Israeli Kulturkampf, the new dilemmas of loyalty created some paradoxical situations when ultra-Orthodox anti-Zionists attempted to capitalize on the hesitance of American Reform Jews to visit the threatened homeland by using Zionist rhetoric of loyalty to the Israeli state (in which they refuse military service).

Moreover, the return to the Jewish security dilemma had long been based on events in Israel that spilled over into the diaspora. However, the events of September 11, 2001, and the emergence of violent terrorist threats on U.S. soil brought the security dilemma home to American Jews and made the American-Israeli nexus of Jewish security closer than ever before. Widespread Arab and Muslim defamation of Jews as perpetrators behind the attacks further amplified this new sense of threat and solidarity.[110] Even younger, highly assimilated American Jews were awakened to the reemergence of the Jewish security dilemma and to the subtle inter-connections between anti-Americanism and anti-Semitism. One young Jewish-American writer, who was suddenly reminded of his own father's flight from Nazism, wrote in the *New York Times* magazine, "Arab governments have transformed Israel into an outpost of malevolent world Jewry, viewing Israelis and Jews as interchangeable emblems of cosmic evil."[111] In this time of peril, the debates over identity were once again trumped by Jewish existential questions.

Just a few days before the eruption of the second intifada, when the newly elected Israeli president spoke before a large gathering of Jewish educators from Israel and the diaspora, he announced that Jewish education and identity outside Israel "could at best last two or three generations." These words angered Jewish-American leaders, who decried his ignorance about Jewish diasporic life, and even Israeli commentators attacked the president for his "foolish outbursts." The New York–based Jewish weekly *The Forward* wrote in a lead editorial that President Moshe Katzav's speech was scandalous. When pressured by the media, the president amended his statement and declared that he believed that diaspora Jews "have the right to live abroad." A leading Israeli journalist observed that "what the Jews of the Diaspora were willing to hear (even as they clenched their teeth) from someone like [Israel's founding prime minister David] Ben-Gurion forty years ago, they are not prepared to put up with from someone like President Katzav."[112] When security once again thrust itself to the center of Jewish concern, the Israeli leaders' attitudes changed dramatically.[113] Sallai Meridor, the head of the Jewish Agency for Israel and the World Zionist organization, announced that "Jewish solidarity with Israel contributes greatly to the sense of security of Israelis. Israel's deterrence in the eyes of the Arab world is enhanced when Jewish-Americans present a unified front behind her."[114]

The question of Jewish identity inside and outside Israel took on a completely different dimension in the face of indiscriminate daily terror. The bitter Kulturkampf fell by the wayside as an overriding sense of existential threat that crossed all Jewish divides emerged. Following an attack on an ultra-Orthodox neighborhood by a Palestinian suicide bomber, prominent Israeli journalist Nahum Barnea wrote:

The terror does not distinguish between Zionism and ultra-Orthodox, between those who have served in the army and black-clad yeshiva students, between man and woman, between adult and child. Israelis stand as equals before it. This brutal equality does not erase the causes of the secular-ultra Orthodox struggle, but it obliges both sides to reduce their tones.[115]

Barnea was correct. Without a doubt, a security crisis always overshadows identity issues. At the height of the suicide bombing attacks inside Israel, the Israeli supreme court affirmed Reform and Conservative conversions. Yet internal Jewish shock waves were marginalized and Orthodox outcry muted. Although the Rabbinical Council of America—the largest association of Orthodox rabbis in the United States—declared that the court's "myopic decision . . . will be tragic for all of Israel" it kept its voice low: "Jews around the world have closed ranks. . . . People are more concerned right now about the physical existence of Israelis than about social issues in Israel, . . . and Israel has more goodwill and sympathy from all quarters [including Orthodox]," explained the director of public policy for the Union of Orthodox Congregations of America.[116] American Reform leaders reciprocated. A few weeks later, when Rabbi Eric Yoffie, head of the Reform Movement in America, convened the annual meeting of the Reform leadership in the war zone of Jerusalem, he addressed Knesset members, stating, "This is a time of crisis, a time of terror attacks, a time for unity. This is not the time for a religious crisis over conversion. People are getting killed because of the security situation, not the religious situation."[117]

By Way of Conclusion

The Jewish condition is fundamentally different today than a century ago. It is no longer characterized by deep divisions between and within proponents and opponents of Jewish sovereignty. Ezra Mendelsohn is correct when he writes that the simplicity of Jewish politics today derives from the fact that nationalism has triumphed over all other diasporic solutions. The antimodern ultra-Orthodox, the Jewish Left and the cultural Bundists, the liberal assimilationists and the Jewish cosmopolitans, the local nationalists and anti-Zionist Reform integrationists—all believed (until World War II) that the "Jewish question" must find its solution in the lands of the dispersion. Yet in the post-1948 era all aspects of Jewish life—above all, Jewish politics—are tied to "the growing hegemony of Israel." In Jewish politics, as in the politics of so many groups in the twentieth century, the nation-state has enjoyed great triumph, even if it is not entirely victorious. The cosmopolitan, culturally and religiously divided Jewish people is united today in support of the Hebrew-speaking

Jewish nation-state where an ever-growing number of Jews actually live, and where many more visit in order to gain inspiration.[118]

Despite the growing hegemony of Israel for Jewish identity and consciousness worldwide, this influence is far from being total. At the beginning of the twenty-first century the Jewish world remains bifurcated between Israel and the United States with Jewish populations of approximately five and a half million in each center. Given this reality all other diaspora centers are secondary or marginal in negotiating Jewish identity. However, the situation of American Jews is somewhat anomalous. Their external environment is rarely hostile—and never overtly so. The comfortable and influential status they have achieved in their country is arguably as consequential for world Jewry as the resumption of Jewish sovereignty in Israel. To begin with, the prosperity of Jewish-Americans has enabled them to assume a world leadership role by providing smaller Jewish communities elsewhere with everything from educational funding and leadership training to political intercession on behalf of Jewish human rights. Yet, the same prosperity that enables them to assist external Jewish communities is not without its own considerable inconveniences. More precisely, the perception abroad of that prosperity and its attendant benefits leads to considerable inconveniences for the Jewish communities that enjoy its largesse. The perceptions of excessive Jewish power in America have been especially acute in recent years when characteristically shrill and hysterical voices attribute to American Jews authorship of U.S. foreign policy in many domains. Though the impact of Israel and American Jewry on the two to three million Jews residing in other countries is often direct and powerful, there is no formal mechanism for consultation among these communities. As a result, communication and cooperation is often ad hoc and haphazard. The question of Jewish identity—religious, ethnic, or national—remains entangled with the question of Jewish power and security in Israel and the United States. Other Jews may continue to face peril and other challenges related to identity and security in their countries of domicile, but the two large centers dominate their voices or even speak on their behalf.

As we have seen, Jewish security concerns always trump issues of Jewish identity. Nevertheless, the two concerns will remain intimately and uniquely intertwined and are never completely detached, because of the nexus between land and religious identity for Jewish kinship. Moreover, the physical territorial shape of the homeland greatly determines Jewish-Israeli and diaspora identity, a fact that further entangled the diaspora, particularly the religious community with the homeland. This "fate," "an existence of necessity," in the words of Rabbi Joseph Soloveitchik, remains the constant and unchanging predicament of the Jewish people. The events in 2005 once again revealed the diaspora-homeland Jewish identity nexus. With the Palestinian intifada in some retreat, tensions surrounding Israel's withdrawal from Gaza and northern Samaria once again heightened the culture war on religion and democracy between secular Zionism and Orthodox nationalists. Religious denunciations against those who gave and obeyed orders to evict settlers as Jewish traitors, including physical attacks on army officers by religious extremists, reminded many of the violent days leading to Rabin's assassination in 1995. The debate over whether the homeland territory is a base for Jewish security or must be treated as a sanctified religious patrimony led to a dramatic showdown between the well-organized Israeli state apparatus and the large and fully mobilized national-religious camp. Revered Orthodox rabbis called on their followers—especially among Israel Defense Force (IDF) soldiers—to disobey orders: "Should they carry out their commanders' orders to evacuate the settlements in Gaza despite what they see as God's commands and their rabbis' call to oppose evacuation?"[19] With an alarming number of religious soldiers announcing their intention to disobey orders, IDF chief of staff Dan Halutz threatened to shut religious-Zionist Hesder yeshivas, where students combine religious study with military service.

Surprisingly, the internal schism of Israeli society so exacerbated by the Gaza withdrawal did not emerge as such a divisive issue among diaspora Jewry in the United States. Even more revealing was the careful response of Orthodox rabbis there. While many expressed deep sympathy and even abetted their Orthodox Israeli kin in their political struggle, they generally refrained from employing violent rhetoric against the Israeli government or religious threats reminiscent of the behavior exhibited by some religious diaspora nationalists prior to Rabin's assassination. In fact, this careful diaspora posture showed concerns mainly for the settler community's civil liberties and religious rights as they protest their evacuation. This plea was fundamentally divergent from the arguments made by nationalist opposition in Israel, which had long crossed the boundary of legality in challenging the mandate of all Israeli governments to return territories to Palestinian hands. On the eve of the Gaza withdrawal, leaders of the Union of Orthodox Jewish Congregations of America (the largest Jewish-American Orthodox umbrella organization) wrote an open letter to Daniel Ayalon, Israel's U.S. ambassador.

The Orthodox Union has acknowledged that questions of Israeli foreign policy and domestic security are best left to the citizens of Israel and the State of Israel's democratically elected government. We have maintained this position despite our strong reservations regarding aspects of the disengagement plan and its effect upon the very fabric of Israeli society . . .

The Orthodox Union has fought for more than 100 years to protect the rights of world Jewry and has opposed religious discrimination in all of its forms, wherever it may arise. We certainly can not accept any justification for the discrimination against religious Jews that police and security forces appear to be pursuing in Israel in the implementation of the government disengagement policies. . . . Actions [by the Israeli government toward the settlers and their religious supporters] . . . represent religious discrimination and bigotry that should not be tolerated in any country. It is heartrending and distressing beyond words for this to be happening in the Jewish state, for which we pray each and every day.[120]

Even Orthodox nationalists among U.S. Jewry must take American notions of tolerance and religious pluralism into account when it comes to exporting their religious ideas or participating in Jewish debates about identity. To be sure, the interactions between American Jews and their homelands has long been premised on the idea that Americans' ties abroad would serve America's interests and perpetuate American ideals. U.S.-based diasporas will typically try to emphasize that there is no conflict of interest between their American identity and their ties to their kin states and cultures.[121] For example, Hindu Indian-Americans who are major advocates of the religious nationalist Hindutva try to link their dream of a greater Hindu state in India to anti-Muslim sentiment in the United States. Moreover, when selling their vision to American politicians they present it not as religious nationalism but a version of pluralist Hinduism.[122] In the case of diaspora Jewry, these declared American principles are not only a product of intra-Jewish theological debates among various denominations but are also informed by larger American controversies about the role of religion in public life and foreign policy. In this process, intersectarian coalitions may externalize tensions generated by religious diversity in the United States and the so-called church-state schism into Israel, bringing American-born controversies to play an important role thousands of miles away.

Certainly, differences in denomination, theological orientation, levels of religious observance, and frequency of attendance at religious services have been the hallmark of American religious plurality. This inter- and intradenominational diversity is also associated with specific views on personal morality, cultural, environmental, social, and political matters, and even U.S. foreign affairs. For example, members of the American Presbyterian Church have clashed (even) with Jewish liberal groups, eventually initiating "a process of phased selective divestment in multinational corporations operating in Israel." Christian fundamentalists, by contrast, have been staunch supporters of the Israeli settler movement and have struck coalitions with American Jewish Orthodox-conservative groups (to the chagrin of liberal Jews and Jewish Reform organizations). Christian evangelists who espouse the eschatological doctrine of dispensationalism have tied the Jewish rebirth in the state of Israel and Israel's return to its biblical patrimony in the West Bank after 1967 to the belief that certain events must take place before the onset of Armageddon, or the end of the world.[123] In July 2004, the Presbyterian Assembly voted by large margins to condemn Israel's construction of a security wall across the West Bank and to disavow "Christian Zionism" as a legitimate theological stance. It also directed "the denomination's Middle East and Interfaith Relations offices to develop resources on differences between fundamental Zionism and Reformed theology."[124] In short, Christian-American differences sometimes impact the Jewish diaspora to protect Israel's standings or may even extend the Jewish diaspora with additional Christian pro-Israeli voices and a rising prominence of the "Judeo-Christian" tradition in the United States.

Finally, as we have seen, the very notion of a cohesive transnational community is complicated because in international affairs a state can, in practice, represent only the people living within its boundaries. But in reality, neither the diaspora nor the homeland community, both of which are internally divided, dominates in constituting and communicating the kinship interest. In fact, a degree of flexibility can be preserved because of the distance between the homeland and the diaspora; they each can, to a degree, put their own spin on the national narrative and live out their shared identity in their own way. The degree to which the one influences the other is related to the kin community's collective history, its members' core identity, and the relative strength that the homeland and the diaspora can exercise vis-à-vis one another through monetary flows, cultural and religious productions, community leadership, or political clout in the international arena. To be sure, the power of diasporas and their perceived influence in the international arena may be amplified by the weakness of the homeland's government and by their own capacities as independent actors. The role of American Jewry in world affairs is enlarged by uncertainty and instability in the Israeli political arena and by the Israeli government's international constraints. Moreover, the diaspora's influence extends beyond the reputation merited by its accomplishments. It encompasses the psychological factor of the notion, current in many parts of the world, of overwhelming "Jewish power" in the United States. Altogether, sufficient areas of overlap exist between kin communities in the homeland and the diaspora despite differences of emphasis in local identity and in the overall communal self-understanding. For years, this was the case in the vibrancy and pride of American Judaism, whereas the traditional Zionist-Israeli version of the Jewish collective identity insisted that only in the Jewish state can Judaism survive. Now, even these distinctive visions are starting to be reconsidered.

From the background of the changes that this chapter has analyzed to the events since the year 2000 that prompted the switch from the Jewish Kulturkampf to Jewish security, we have witnessed a new kinship vision emerging. This vision seems to affirm the old American Zionist formula in which the Jewish-American community is not to be subsumed into or subordinated to the Israeli homeland. Rather, the two communities are to live side by side in a symbiotic relationship of mutual influences. As early as 1914, when future Supreme Court Justice Brandeis assumed leadership of the American Zionist organization, he said: "To be good Americans, we must be better Jews, and to be better Jews we must become Zionists."[125] Whereas previously Israeli Zionism demanded a privileged Israeli voice in defining Jewish interests and identity, now not only does the diaspora largely determine its own way of life in America, but it has also demanded and gradually gained access to and voice in Israeli Jewish affairs. This new Zionist vision of reciprocity strengthens both pillars of world Jewry today in America and Israel, while simultaneously encouraging their kinship solidarity. Thus, against the thesis regarding the growing separation between Israel and the diaspora, on the contrary, one sees a new affirmation, intensification, and redefinition of Jewish kinship.

My analysis of how Jews continue to negotiate their identities in transnational ways has implications beyond this case study. Nowadays, when technological innovation and greater tolerance in host lands remove the spatial and temporal barriers that once separated diasporas from their countries of origin, kinship ties across frontiers are an inevitable feature of international relations, with important impacts on the construction and reconstruction of national identities and policies. The evolving relations between Israel and Jewish-Americans shed light on the manner in which other diasporas, primarily in the United States, can participate directly and indirectly in shaping national policies and identities in international relations.

FOUR

The Role of Diasporas in Conflict Perpetuation or Resolution

MANY VIOLENT CONFLICTS and their resolution in the world today pertain not only to security matters but also to the definition of ethnic and national communities.[1] Beyond issues of sovereign boundaries and territorial security, these conflicts also directly affect the lives and well-being of diaspora communities in far-off lands that share ethnic ties with the people engaged in the conflict. Hence, the resolution of such violent conflicts often requires addressing an audience beyond the immediate geographic boundaries of the conflict's arena.

The diaspora's role in homeland conflict perpetuation and conflict resolution can be so powerful that homeland leaders ignore diaspora preferences at their own peril. In confronting the kin state's conflict, the diaspora attempts to promote its own view of the ethnic community's identity and interests, a view that is not always congruent with the view of the homeland authorities. As we have seen in previous chapters, diasporas are important players in the economics and politics of their countries of origin as well as in the production and articulation of their homeland's national identity. Yet despite the growing recognition of their role as transnational players, few studies have focused on their specific impact on conflict resolution (or peace processes) that involve their homelands. Those that do tend to view diasporas mostly as detrimental to such processes, often failing to appreciate a diaspora's potential to advance peace negotiations. Many also overlook the complexities concerning the negotiation of identities between homelands and diasporas in such processes. In fact, some of the narratives that are prevalent among diaspora communities may challenge the dominant ideology at home. In other cases the multiple forms of nationalisms and kinship identities that emerge in the diaspora can play a positive role in checking and counter-ing the vicissitudes of the homeland's nationalism. This dynamic is par-ticularly, but not uniquely, evident in the Armenian and Jewish diasporas. Their behavior and its effects on Armenian-Azeri and Palestinian-Israeli peace efforts in the last decade show that conflict resolution in communal conflicts is often not just a two-level, but "a three-level game of peace-making."[2] The diaspora becomes a key constituency of concern for homeland leaders, their homeland's adversaries, the governments of their host states, and, through their international diplomatic activities, for other states as well.[3]

The following discussion of diasporas and conflict perpetuation and resolution does not concentrate on refugees and exiles who represent, in a sense, personified consequences of a violent conflict. Nor does it con-cern "stateless" diasporas or irredentist and secessionist groups that reside in a "near abroad" and wish to reconfigure the boundaries of exist-ing states to include their current places of residence within their desired homelands. Such communities tend to view themselves (or are viewed by their kin states) as "kidnapped victims" and thus have an inherent and direct stake in a particular outcome of their homeland's conflict.[4] The focus, instead, is on far-removed diasporas that are well established and organized in their countries of domicile and who have embraced life out-side their ancestral homeland. These groups are removed from the arena of the conflict and are generally not making territorial or communal claims on their own behalf. Rather, homeland-related conflicts have only an indirect impact on them. As such, these types of groups reflect the important phenomenon of *transnational communal politics*, defined both by the states in which these communities reside and by the ethnicity of the group in question.

Based on a theoretical perspective that is rooted in the constructivist insight that the identities and interests of states are both flexible and mutually constitutive, several propositions about the identities and inter-ests that engage diasporas in homeland communal conflicts are notewor-thy. The first of these propositions addresses the general role of identity and diasporas in international affairs. This in turn leads to an examination of diasporas as "third-level" players in the peace negotiations determin-ing the fate of their homelands.[5] Finally, four interrelated concerns of group identity and interest that affect diasporic attitudes and activism toward peace negotiations in their homeland regions require further attention. In particular, the discussion focuses on identity and interest issues either "over there" (i.e., in the real—or symbolic—homeland) or "over here" (i.e., inside the host country), including the difficulties of maintaining the identity of both the people and the homeland, the competition for leadership of the transnational community, the struggle to defend organizational or bureaucratic interests, and the challenges of preserving social or political status in the host state.

Diasporas in International Relations and the Question of Identity

Diaspora communities identify themselves, and are identified by others, as part of the homeland national community. This notion that homeland and diaspora constitute one people is especially strong for relatively weak, new, or reconstituted states. In the case of new and weak states, the national identity was often "held in trust" by the diaspora during the years of foreign domination.[6] Diasporic communities may personify the national community even after the (re)establishment of an independent nation-state. They may embody the experience of calamity and suffering stemming from dispossession and the loss of the homeland, while also becoming the standard-bearers for the ideals of recovery and restoration.

A community's view of itself as a people or a nation is not static but shifts with time and circumstance.[7] The "national interest" shifts along with national and kinship identity. As Peter Katzenstein points out, "definitions of identity that distinguish between self and other imply definitions of threat and interest that have strong effects on national security policies."[8] With regard to Armenia, Ronald Suny writes, "National histories may be investigated, not so much to discover the 'real' story behind . . . the Armenian-Azeri hostility in Karabakh . . . but rather . . . to assess [how] particular conceptualizations of nationhood contribute to notions of national interest and threats to national security."[9] Indeed, the historical narrative of the Jewish people as preordained to "dwell apart" (*am levadad yishkon*), coupled with the Holocaust creed of "Never Again," have shaped Israel's sense of "national security exceptionalism."[10]

Of course, the very notion of a unified people that stretches across frontiers is complicated, since in international relations, a state can, in principle, represent only the people living within its boundaries. In reality, neither the diaspora nor the homeland community ultimately dominates the process of constituting and communicating national identity. Indeed, a certain degree of flexibility can be preserved because of the distance between homeland and diaspora; each can, to a degree, put its own spin on the national narrative and live out their shared identity in its own way. The degree to which one influences the other depends on their relative strength, which is determined by, among other things, monetary flows, cultural productions, community leadership, and transnational political parties. Sufficient areas of overlap exist for homeland-diaspora ties to be quite close despite differences of emphasis in the ethnonational narrative. This is evident, for example, in the vibrancy and pride of American Judaism, whereas the traditional Israeli-Zionist version of Jewish history insists that only in the Jewish state can authentic Judaism survive, sheltered from the pressures of assimilation and the onslaught of anti-Semitism that endangers Jews in the rest of the world.[11]

While kinship identity can be negotiated between homeland and diaspora, the structure of modern international relations gives the prerogative of constituting, elaborating, and implementing the national interest to the state. Indeed, states may consider their diasporic kin as part of their national security equation under the premise of mutual responsibility. Israel, for example, declares itself, by law, responsible for the well-being of all Jews around the world. It also regards the Jewish diaspora, and especially Jewish-Americans, as one of Israel's strategic assets.[12] The new state of Armenia has made similar claims. Such attitudes in the homeland, however, can create resentment, engender the fear of dual loyalty, and even strengthen calls for greater participation on the part of the diaspora in homeland politics. Armenian-American scholar Khachig Tololyan, for example, complained that, in Armenia, "They want service and money from diasporans, not thoughts or opinions."[13] All in all, governments may construct the national interest with the explicit intent of protecting the whole kin community, both diaspora and homeland. Yet in practice, struggles often erupt between homeland and diaspora groups over the definition of the nation and therefore over the proper balance between the interests of the homeland and those of the people.

Because many diasporas demonstrate an impressive capacity for independent action with important international ramifications, peace negotiations must be viewed as a political activity that engages more parties than the usual "domestic" and "diplomatic" categories. The notion that international negotiations are a two-level game rather than merely a government-to-government interaction was originally developed by Robert Putnam in the late 1980s. In Putnam's view, state leaders balance two competing spheres at once in an international negotiation; they must satisfy both domestic political constituencies and also meet the negotiating counterpart's minimum demands.[14]

The analysis of the Armenian, Jewish, and other cases suggests that, when active diasporas exist, they cannot be viewed simply as a domestic constituency within their host state but must also be recognized as an independent actor in the conflict resolution process. These diasporas appear to have made peace negotiations into a three-level game for their homelands' leaders. Those leaders who tried to limit the negotiations to a two-level framework have suffered. Host states and other third parties realize the independent role of diasporas as political actors in homeland conflicts and try to influence them accordingly.

Jeffrey Knopf recognized the necessity of expanding the two-level game concept when analyzing bilateral security negotiations, such as the talks between the United States and the Soviet Union on the Intermediate Range Nuclear Forces Treaty. He develops the two-level game framework into a "three-and-three" framework, encompassing transgovernmental, transnational, and "cross-level" interactions between combinations of government leaders and domestic constituencies. His analysis shows that using three levels rather than two enables the analyst to explain outcomes not predicted by unitary-actor approaches to international relations.[15] Knopf's "transboundary connections" are particularly relevant to the analysis of ethnic conflicts, where relevant constituencies naturally extend beyond state borders. Indeed, diasporas act as more than just domestic constituencies within their countries of domicile. They also function as an important "domestic" constituency for homeland political leaders and, moreover, as trans-state players, acting on behalf of their entire people in interactions with third-party states and international organizations.

Diaspora Activities in Pursuit of National Security

The connection between a sense of endangerment to the homeland and the sense of diasporic peril may be definite or more psychological. The diasporic connection with events at home may be largely social and psychological, through the diasporans' identification with their homeland's aspirations and struggles. Homeland conflicts can also affect diasporas more directly: economically, socially in terms of their self-image and how their host society views them, and even through physical threats directed against them by those groups engaged in the conflict against their homeland kin. Indeed, whether "stateless"—aspiring to establish an independent sovereign state in a claimed homeland—or "state-based"—with kin communities already forming a majority in their own established nation-state—diasporas are affected by homeland conflicts even if they live far from the arena of violence.[16] These ties and the psychological identification of diasporas with their kin states explain the high stakes they perceive in homeland conflicts, and they lead diasporas to search for an active role in the continuation or resolution of such conflicts. The type and degree of their activities are determined by their political and social status, their host society's and host government's views of the conflict, the political and social character of their kin state, and the diaspora leaders' perception of how conflict resolution affects the people's identity and future.

The national interests articulated by the homeland government with respect to the resolution of a violent conflict with a neighboring state or an internal ethnic minority can have a significant impact on the identity of the transnational community. Disputes erupt between diasporic elements and homeland authorities not only over the definition of nationhood but also over the conceptualization of the homeland's territorial boundaries, often a critical component both in conflict perpetuation and conflict resolution.

For example, consider a state that gives up its claim to a piece of historically significant territory in order to achieve peaceful relations with a neighboring state. Diaspora and homeland citizens often have different attitudes toward the implications such policies have for ethnic and national identity. For many homeland citizens, territory serves multiple functions: it provides sustenance, living space, security, as well as a geographical focus for national identity. If giving up a certain territory, even one of significant symbolic value, would improve security and living conditions, a homeland citizen *might* find the trade-off worthwhile. By contrast, for the diaspora, oftentimes a territory's symbolic functions outweigh its security value. A territory's practical value (and, indeed, the practical value of peace with a former rival) is not directly relevant to the diaspora's daily experience. In such situations, altering the geographic configuration of the homeland state for the sake of peace may be more disturbing to some diaspora elements than to some segments of the homeland community. In precisely this vein, a rupture opened in 1999–2000 between many Jewish-Americans and Israeli prime minister Ehud Barak over his acceptance of a U.S. peace plan that called for giving the Palestinians sovereignty over the Temple Mount. Several Israeli analysts of the Jewish-American diaspora expressed their concern "that a hand-over of the Temple Mount and parts of Jerusalem threatens to undermine the Jewish identity of American Jews and tear away at the already delicate fabric of their relationship with Israel."[17] Malcolm

Hoenlein, executive vice chairman of the Conference of Presidents of Major American Jewish Organizations, declared:

> In future years, all of us will have to answer to all our children and grandchildren when they ask us why we did not do more to protect their heritage and safeguard Har Habayit [the Temple Mount]. . . . Israel has a right to make decisions that affect its security. All Jews have a right to discuss it, but it's up to the government of Israel. The Temple Mount is a different issue. It belongs to all Jews, it is the inheritance of all Jews, and all Jews have a vested interest in it.[18]

Indeed with the collapse of Oslo and the rise of Ariel Sharon to power, Hoenlein's position became the official position of the Israeli government. In his February 20, 2003, message to the Conference of Presidents, Prime Minister Sharon declared that although he believes that American Jews should not determine what should be Israel's final boundaries because "you do not live here," when it comes to "the struggle for Jerusalem" the diaspora voice is as important and legitimate as the voice of Israeli Jews.

> [W]hen it comes to Jerusalem, it is an entirely different thing. . . . Jerusalem is yours no less than it is ours. When it comes to that, then you have to participate in this struggle, and you have to raise your voices. . . . We here in Israel are only custodians. We are keeping the holiest place of the Jewish people. We are custodians. It belongs to you no less than to ourselves. . . . All of us together— us here, and you there—we are guardians of Jerusalem for future generations, and therefore, it is your responsibility no less than ours.[19]

Certainly, there is no consensus among Jewish-Americans or Israelis regarding the concession on Jerusalem.[20] Yet, overarching tendencies do characterize the two groups. Different priorities, functions, and meanings assigned to the homeland territory by the diaspora versus the homeland citizenry can lead to tremendous tensions over peace policies. This is also the case for the interaction between the Armenian homeland and diaspora.[21]

When the conflict is hot and the homeland is under severe threat, diaspora concerns about the homeland's existential survival are paramount, and divergent opinions may be subsumed under a broader show of support. But when the possibility of peace arises, homeland-diaspora debates and power struggles reemerge. This can also happen in reverse order. In the summer of 2000, as the Camp David peace summit took place, Jewish-Americans demonstrated publicly both for and against the peace process.[22] But once violent clashes between Israelis and Palestinians began in September 2000, and especially following a series of deadly suicide bombing attacks inside Israel, Jewish organizations closed ranks to demonstrate their unified support for Israel.[23] When peace negotiations are a real option, differences in the diaspora's and the homeland's conceptions of the nation imply different conceptions of the national interest, and thus distinct views on policy toward the ongoing conflict.

The homeland political elite may have an ambivalent view of how much it should take diaspora concerns into account in formulating domestic and international policies, particularly those that relate to ongoing conflicts. To a large degree, homeland leaders and publics feel that their direct stake in the outcome of their conflict with their neighbors should trump any diaspora preferences. On the other hand, they often have come to rely on the diaspora's political clout and financial assistance, at home and internationally. As Elihu Saltpeter noted, "'The children of Diaspora Jews will not have to fight if war breaks out here' is a view that doesn't hold much water since Israelis do expect American Jews to intervene on Israel's behalf in their own political system."[24]

The homeland-diaspora nexus is such that on some occasions the diaspora may feel threatened by homeland decisions; in others, the homeland may feel that diaspora preferences threaten national goals. In 1992, for example, a Labor-led Israeli government took office shortly after AIPAC had gone to the mat with the Bush administration to support settlement-building activities in the West Bank and Gaza. The new prime minister, Yitzhak Rabin, flew almost immediately to the United States to confront the AIPAC board, telling them that he rejected their traditionally heavy involvement in Israel's bilateral relations with the U.S. government, and that he would prefer to handle those relations himself.[25]

In this homeland-diaspora tug-of-war to define the national and the people's interest, many voices inside and outside the state feed off one another. Indeed, an increasingly important aspect of kinship politics is the transnational coalition. The diaspora-led Armenian Dashnak is an early example, once serving as the leadership organization of Armenians worldwide and quickly establishing itself as a political party within Armenia when the new state was formed. The Young Israel movement is a more recent example. This grouping of nationalist Orthodox synagogues in North America and Israel and a spin-off of the U.S. organization, the National Council of Young Israel, serves (among other things) as a means of mobilizing religious nationalist opinion both in the diaspora and in Israel against territorial concessions to the Palestinians.

Nevertheless, the motivation and interests in the two centers of domicile are, for many segments of the community, fundamentally different in light of their different circumstances. Being removed from the arena of violence, those diaspora segments that are fully integrated into their host societies may feel more desire to settle a long-standing violent dispute than the homeland government, especially if the homeland's policies conflict with values adopted by the diaspora in their country of domicile, and if their host state is pressing for a settlement. Reform Jews in the United States, for example, promoted a Palestinian-Israeli rapprochement in part because they viewed the Israeli occupation of the West Bank and Gaza as belying the liberal political principles that underlay their identity as Jewish-Americans and which, they argued, were the foundation of Israel's natural and close alliance with the United States. By contrast, religious Zionists in the United States, whose identity as an ethnic group in American society is much less important to them than their religious identity, opposed the peace accords because they required Israel to relinquish land that the religious community considered part of the biblical patrimony and a necessary vehicle to fulfill Israel's redemptive function.

The largest mainstream Armenian organization, the Armenian Assembly, is far more supportive of conflict resolution in Karabakh than the deeply nationalist Dashnak.[26] Whether diaspora members are fixated on the wrongs of the past or are ready to consider new prospects of change has much to do with their host state's surroundings and the shifts of generations. Ethnic diasporas in the United States have often absorbed a great deal of America's multicultural ethos and liberal social values, and indeed sometimes try to export those values back to their homeland. This tends to make diasporas see their position as seconding peace efforts when they are supported by the U.S. government.

Types of Diasporic Support

Diasporic support of the homeland during conflicts can be critical to the homeland's well-being and its very existence. Diasporas provide a lifeline of resources and weapons, serve as a source of recruits, act as a propaganda platform, and lobby to influence host governments and other international players.[27] Shedding blood for the homeland is not commonly associated with far-removed diasporas, whose activists are often perceived as "standing on principle" from afar while their homeland kin pay the physical price. Yet there are many cases of direct participation by diaspora members in homeland violent conflicts, including active participation in the kin-state military or homeland insurgencies. In recent years diaspora members of the Kosovar Albanians, Croats, and Sri Lankan Tamils have returned to participate in the respective struggles of their homelands. According to the Independent International Commission on Kosovo, "It was the Kosovar Albanians in the diaspora who became the most radicalized part of the Kosovar Albanian community and were to create the KLA."[28] Byman et al. note that "some of the most significant diasporas of today, like the Indians and Sri Lankan Tamils, have begun to exercise unprecedented clout in the affairs of their home countries, akin to the Jewish diaspora in the U.S.," and that "the more activist elements among these larger immigrant communities . . . have more rapid and visible means of calling attention to issues of interest in their home countries than ever before thanks to the communication and information technology revolution."[29] One scholar who analyzed the specific impact of the Internet and pro-Eelam Web sites with respect to the Sri Lankan Tamil diaspora observed that these sites "preserve the form of the nation as territory for the LTTE and those who want to believe in its mission" and that

> this works for all those nationals of Tamil Eelam who click onto <eelam.com> from New York, Oslo, Sydney, or Amsterdam, who have no wish to return to Eelam, no wish to live there, but who must believe in it if they are to keep living where they are. . . . For them, Eelam is real; it is lived—not as a place but as an image. And for them, eelam.com exists at the intersection of cyberspace and Eelam, at the intersection of an extraordinary technology of representation and the imagi-nation.[30]

The relations between Israel and diaspora Jewry remain the paradigmatic case of such interactions. When Israel's vulnerability once again became the central theme of Jewish existence after the breakdown of the Oslo Process, a large majority of Israeli Jews said that they considered diasporic demonstrations on Israel's behalf essential to their physical and psychological well-being.[31] Yet even though Israelis have come to rely on the diaspora in times of peril, the diaspora itself is never monolithic and will not automatically support homeland official policies. In the Armenian case, diaspora money was instrumental in mobilizing Armenian public opinion against President Ter-Petrossian and his peace efforts with Azerbaijan and Turkey, ultimately forcing his resignation. In Israel, the religious-nationalist campaign against Prime Minister Yitzhak Rabin (1994–95) was largely financed by diaspora sources. In late 2000, Prime Minister Ehud Barak lost diaspora (and Israeli) support over his agreement to a U.S. peace proposal—in the face of a Palestinian terror campaign—that would have yielded Israeli sovereignty over religiously significant areas of Jerusalem to the Palestinians. Most recently, in November 2005 the Israeli daily *Ha'aretz* reported that left-wing American Jewish leaders encouraged U.S. secretary of state Condoleezza Rice to intervene aggressively in the Israeli-Palestinian dispute over the Gaza border crossings, "telling her this would gain the support of American Jews, they urged her to take a tough line against Israel, especially on issues such as a settlement freeze and dismantling illegal settlement outposts."[32] Abraham Foxman, director of the Anti-Defamation League, questioned the wisdom of such diasporic involvement, maintaining that it was more common for diaspora liberal or left-leaning organizations— such as Israel Policy Forum, Americans for Peace Now, and sometimes the Reform Movement—to lobby the administration to exert pressure on Israel. As we have seen, however, all sides of the diaspora political-ideational spectrum feel they can oppose the Israeli government in the name of Jewish and Israel's well-being and all in pursuit of a "true" peace. This leads us to the important question of "who speaks on behalf of the Jews" and what distinguished "peace spoilers" from "peace harbingers."

Who Speaks on Behalf of the People?

The debate (inside and outside the homeland) about whether diasporic segments "have the right" to publicly oppose an official position of the homeland's elected government—in favor or against a war or a peace deal with its external enemies—is always contentious. Benedict Anderson opines that while diasporas "find it tempting to play identity politics" with respect to their home states, "this citizen-less participation is inevitably non-responsible—our hero will not have to answer for, or pay the price of, the long-distance politics he undertakes."[33] Many claim that those who do not reside inside the homeland and who do not serve in the army should stay out of the homeland's high politics. When it comes to Israel and American Jewry, diasporic politics (left and right) tend to reflect Israeli internal divisions on foreign policy and potential peace deals with the Arabs. The question of whether American Jewry should reflexively support Israel's officially articulated policy or have the right to publicly criticize Israeli official policy often splits the diaspora and intensifies division between its activists and their counterparts inside Israel who often recruit them.

Since the 1980s, political divisions within Israel and among Jewish-Americans on peace with Arabs grew wider. In the 1990s the government of Yitzhak Rabin, while enjoying support for the Oslo Peace Accord among most Jewish-Americans, also became the target of venomous opposition from more conservative sectors of the diaspora. In addition to outright hostility directed at government officials, diaspora groups that opposed the peace process financed a public relations campaign against the accords, gave financial support to the Jewish settler movement in the occupied territories, and established U.S. affiliates of key right-wing Israeli parties to support their political campaigns against Rabin and his Labor Party successors.[34] When a similar split reappeared after Ariel Sharon's decision to pull out from settlements in Gaza, rabbi Dr. David Luchins, a prominent leader of America's Jewish Orthodox community—which usually holds right-wing positions on yielding territory in peace deals with Palestinians—condemned those in his camp who rallied in New York against Sharon. His criticism was based not only on his conviction that diaspora members do not have the right to be players but only an audience in the homeland's politics, but also on his concern that when a Jew criticizes Israel for its policies the outside world cannot understand the nuance of criticism based on affinity and concern for the homeland well-being. Comparing Israeli politics to a baseball game and Israeli citizens to the teams, he said, "American Jewish Zionists have box seats, and we have the right and obligation to support our team. But we are not playing. Only members of the team, even those who are benched, have the right to take part in the team meetings. We fans talk strategy, but the only ones with the right to decide matters are the team members."[35]

This position, however, is not shared by many other diaspora activists, left and right. Even more interesting, homeland decision makers tend to implicate diaspora members in their decisions on peace negotiations and even endow the diaspora with an authoritative voice. For example, the Jewish-American diplomat Dennis Ross, the former chief negotiator for the U.S. Middle East Peace Team who now chairs the Institute for Jewish Policy Planning, founded by the Jewish Agency, recently called on Prime Minister Ariel Sharon and the State of Israel to grant diaspora Jewry an official consulting status when it comes to Israel foreign policy that affects the entire Jewish people.[36] This vision is a far cry from the vision of Israel's founder David Ben-Gurion, who always stressed the centrality of the state over the "temporary" existence of the diaspora. Yet Ross's message is now endorsed at least rhetorically by the Israeli government itself. Thus, when Ariel Sharon addressed Jewish leaders in New York shortly after becoming prime minister in 2001, he told them that if Israel weakens or disappears their comfortable lives as American Jews would not be the same. He added that diaspora Jews should raise their voice in defense of Jerusalem since "the future of Israel [and Jerusalem] is not just a matter for Israelis who live there: Israel belongs to the entire Jewish people. And Israel would not be what it is today if it were not for the efforts of all Jews worldwide."[37]

In the case of Jews and Israel the concept of a collective security dilemma—and the corollary idea of mutual responsibility (*kol Israel arevim ze baze*)—extending beyond the Jewish state boundaries is well established. It was recently reinforced once again by concomitant waves of Middle East violence and anti-Semitism. For many Jews inside and outside Israel, the terror and anti-Semitic attacks of the last few years and their global aftermath of uncertainty, insecurity, and shifting alliances merely confirmed that Jews were in the most uncomfortable of binds. The developments of recent years represented a truly global crisis for many Jews. In the case of American Jewry, their deep involvement in Israeli security constantly leads to charges of undue Jewish influence on U.S. foreign policy beyond Israel specifically. Many allege that the diaspora led by so-called Jewish neoconservative leaders has distorted U.S. policy to serve primarily Israeli security interests and not necessarily the national interest of the United States. These charges emerged immediately after September 11 and grew more insistent during the lead-up to the war in Iraq in 2003.

Two assumptions are at the root of widespread apprehension regarding Jewish influence on U.S. foreign policy. The first assumption is that Jewish opinion is cohesive enough to find expression in a specific opinion or policy; the second is that neoconservatism is essentially Jewish, or at least that its origins and purposes are more Jewish than anything else. Closely examining these assumptions, one quickly finds that Jewish opinion is so diverse, Jewish influence so multivalent and contradictory, and neoconservatism so fundamentally liberal democratic as to render highly dubious any talk of a neoconservative U.S foreign policy as an expression of Jewish opinion. Nevertheless, mainstream American media felt compelled in recent years to discuss neoconservative Jewish influence, even if they defensively concluded that the diversity of American Jewish voices makes such a "Jewish" perspective chimerical. Yet, the very fact that they problematize the issue shows not only how deeply ingrained the fears of Jewish power are but also inadvertently gives credence to those charges. This point was manifested in a *Washington Post* article regarding the fear of an anti-Semitic backlash in light of allegations of Jewish influence in the Iraq war. It observed that Jewish-Americans are "deeply divided over the wisdom of invading Iraq [and that] . . . Jewish groups have taken a broad range of positions. On the left, Rabbi Michael Lerner, head of the San Francisco–based *Tikkun* community, called this week for nonviolent civil disobedience if war breaks out. On the right, the Union of Orthodox Jewish Congregations declared in October that it supports the use of force. The far larger, centrist groups representing the bulk of Reform and Conservative Jews have straddled the fence, endorsing military action only if the United States exhausts all diplomatic alternatives." Yet the article goes on to analyze Jewish neoconservative influence in the White House including Wolfowitz, Feith, Abrams, and Perle.[38]

Peace Spoilers or Peace Harbingers?

The term *peace spoiler* must not be regarded as self-evident. Certainly it implies an attempt to thwart the achievement of peacemaking at all cost, yet it perhaps should also include those who enter peace processes without genuinely seeking such results or even those who prematurely seek peace at all costs notwithstanding the evidence that by engaging in the process of peace they may in fact exacerbate the conflict. In turn it becomes imperative that the success of a peace process depends upon effective mechanisms to manage spoilers. Early research relating to peace spoilers centers around the work of Stedman who defines them as "leaders and parties who believe that peace emerging from negotiations threatens their power, worldview, and interests, and use violence to undermine attempts to achieve it."[39] With reference to diasporas, it is more meaningful that the act of spoiling be viewed along a continuum that ranges from high levels of support (when diasporas act as catalysts) to extreme levels of hostility (when diasporas act as spoilers) toward a negotiating process or settlement.

It has been suggested that when compared with their homeland kin, diasporas are more hard-line nationalistic and more maximalist in homeland-related conflicts. Writing in 1860, English politician-historian Lord Acton observed that "exile is the nursery of nationality," and that nationality arose from exile when men could no longer easily dream of returning to the nourishing bosom that had given them birth.[40] Certainly, many political exiles and their diasporic constituencies have historically played an integral part and often led in the struggle for political independence in their claimed homelands. They have influenced the shaping of new nation-states that were born out of wars (notably exiles during World War I) or the nature of postwar governments in already established states (as in the case of Iraq after the downfall of Saddam Hussein). Their success has been often ensured by their alliance with foreign victors.

Political exiles who have struggled while abroad to return to their native land are only one segment of a diaspora. Yet even those who reside away from the (real or historic) homeland on a permanent basis are often driven toward deep involvement in homeland international affairs and particularly wars. Motivated by ethnic affinity, communities abroad feel a genuine sympathy for the struggles of their brethren elsewhere. Diaspora members may feel a sense of guilt that they are safe while those left behind are enmeshed in bloody conflict. In some cases evidence suggests that "diaspora harbor grievance for much longer than resident populations," and since they "do not themselves suffer any of the costs of conflict, [they] have a greater incentive to seek vengeance than the resident populations."[41] Also being much wealthier than resident populations in their kin countries, diasporas are much better able to finance conflict. From the point of view of international stability, Collier warned recently that "the global effort to curb civil wars should focus on reducing the viability—rather than just the rationale—of rebellion." To do so, he added, "governments of rich nations should keep the behavior of diaspora organizations in their borders within legitimate bounds."[42] Collier also argued that both governments in postconflict countries and the international community should develop strategies for reducing the damage done by diasporas in postconflict societies, in order to reduce the risk of conflict repetition. Such strategies might focus upon co-optation, persuasion, and penalties.[43]

Yet just as far-off diasporas play important roles in supporting violent conflicts involving their homeland states, they may also play a critical role in conflict resolution. For years Irish-American organizations flooded Ireland with money for weapons as well as lobbying within the United States. Led by the Irish Northern Aid Committee (NORAID) with thousands of members and numerous branches throughout the United States, the Irish-American diaspora gave the Provisional Irish Republic Army (IRA) millions of dollars for weapons. In the early 1990s new Irish-American organizations began pushing their kin in Northern Ireland to search for a peaceful solution (while successfully lobbying the White House to get involved in the Northern Irish cause).

> The shifting views of the diaspora encouraged the IRA leaders to embrace a new direction. This shift in turn reinforced the more peaceful strains among the diaspora. As the IRA began to abandon the armed struggle in the 1990s, it created a new group to raise money in the place of the [militant] NORAID . . . [that] was unwelcome after the ceasefire, as the IRA sought to have its representatives work directly with U.S. political leaders.[44]

During the years of the Oslo Peace Process, many Jewish-American groups also acted as unofficial emissaries in the efforts to open new diplomatic channels to countries that had no diplomatic relations with Israel. They lobbied to lift the Arab boycott, to reward Arab and Islamic states that normalized relations with the Jewish state, and to encourage others to do the same.[45] These missions were not always undertaken with the prior approval of the Israeli government; indeed, at times both the Jewish and the Armenian diasporas have undertaken international political initiatives that conflicted with the desires of their homeland governments. The clearest examples in the Jewish case during the 1990s were the activities of diasporic elements to push the U.S. government to move its embassy from Tel Aviv to Jerusalem to the chagrin of Israeli officials. Indeed, American Jews who opposed the Rabin government's concessions to the PLO went as far as questioning the Israeli government's loyalty to the Jewish people.

In the Armenian case, the homeland government does not officially oppose diaspora efforts to win international recognition of the Armenian genocide, but it often finds that these efforts complicate its bilateral relations. For instance, the Armenian government had very little to do with the Armenian-American lobbying groups that successfully pushed for a ban on U.S. aid to Azerbaijan (known as Section 907 of the Freedom Support Act), which has now withstood a decade of State Department efforts to have it overturned. Diasporic activities may also help set the ideological parameters of a homeland conflict and the requirements for a termination of hostilities.[46] Armenians in the United States and France, for example, are responsible for instilling into the current Armenian-Azeri conflict an echo of the Armenian genocide. Ultimately, the genocide also became the central "chosen trauma" of the Armenian state.[47] It was increasingly invoked when Turkey extended its support to Azerbaijan, another Turkic country. Turkish moves to support Azerbaijan in the

Karabakh conflict were seen by the diaspora "as the logical continuation of a long-term policy to keep Armenia helpless and vulnerable . . . [that] at a convenient moment it can, perhaps, seize upon an excuse to eliminate the little that was left of the historic Armenian territories."[48]

Host states, particularly Western democracies, take into account the interests and political power of diaspora communities in formulating policies toward homeland conflicts. For example, regardless of France's official reluctance to consider itself a host country for immigrants or a breeding ground for ethnic identity, it cannot escape the U.S. style of manifestation of diasporic politics.[49] U.S. interest in the conflicts in Northern Ireland, Cyprus, between Armenia and Azerbaijan, India and Pakistan, and between Israel and its Arab neighbors are all heavily influenced by the strength of well-organized ethnic diasporas in U.S. politics. Because of U.S. leadership in encouraging conflict resolution in these regions, homeland governments rely on diasporic aid to influence foreign policy in congenial directions. U.S. decision makers, for their part, try to commission diaspora leaders to promote U.S. interests in the homeland and U.S. preferences for the way the homeland's violent conflicts are resolved. In India, the Indian-American community is currently seen as enhancing Indian foreign policy and security goals as well as contributing toward its economic development. The Government of India's *High Level Committee Report on the Indian Diaspora* states: "A section of financially powerful and politically well connected Indo-Americans has emerged during the last decade. They have effectively mobilized on issues ranging from the nuclear tests in 1998 to Kargil, played a crucial role in generating a favorable climate of opinion in Congress and defeating anti-India legislation there, and lobbied effectively on other issues of concern to the Indian community. They have also demonstrated willingness to contribute financially to Indian causes, such as relief for the Orissa cyclone and the Latur and Gujarat earthquakes, higher technical education and innumerable charitable causes." The report continues, "For the first time, India has a constituency in the US with real influence and status. The Indian community in the United States constitutes an invaluable asset in strengthening India's relationship with the world's only superpower."[50]

Even the adversaries of kin states recognize and try to confront or work with diasporic forces involved in the homeland conflict. After the defeat of the labor government in Israel's 1996 elections, the PLO reached out to liberal Jews in the United States to try to sustain the progress of Palestinian autonomy in the West Bank and Gaza. However, the efforts of Palestinians and other Arab officials to use Jewish-Americans as a lever on the U.S. executive branch, Congress, or the Israeli government were undermined when Arafat lost all credibility as a result of the collapse of the Oslo Peace Process. Azeri officials, for their part, name the Armenian-American lobby in Washington as the primary obstacle to peace in the Caucasus and to developing U.S.-Azeri relations.[51] Azerbaijan has cultivated the Jewish organizations in Washington as allies to counterbalance Armenian lobbying efforts. The Turkish mission in Washington also devotes immense resources to combating the Armenian diaspora's lobbying efforts.[52]

Determinants of Diaspora Attitudes toward Conflict Resolution in the Homeland

A diasporic community's attitude toward potential peace deals involving its kin state stems from the interrelated concerns of identity and interest inside and outside the homeland. Five main concerns can be identified that influence diasporic postures toward conflict resolution efforts in their homeland, including a concern to maintain their ethnic identity as they conceive of it; competition with the homeland for leadership of the transnational community; organizational or bureaucratic interests stemming from diasporic organizations; and the diaspora's other political interests and goals in its host state. A final countervailing consideration in judging diasporic attitudes on conflict resolution and peace settlements is economics, in particular the prospects that peace agreements may hold for the protection of diasporic assets and investments in their homeland.

Maintaining Identity

The ethnic identity of a diaspora group is made up of elements that are shared with their kin in the homeland (historical, social, and cultural ideals) as well as other elements that are unique to the diaspora and derive from its separate experiences. The diaspora's identity is also affected by the degree to which its leaders (and members) are actively engaged in domestic affairs in the homeland. All the symbols of homeland sovereignty—a currency, stamps, the military, a flag, and the like—are ingredients that may reinforce the identity of the diaspora kin just as they cultivate and sustain the national identity of the homeland's citizens. The "wholeness" or inviolability of the homeland's territory is also a key marker of the nation's well-being for the diaspora. Thus, an interstate conflict or internal separatist movement generally becomes a major ingredient in diasporic identity.

A threat to the homeland's survival from conflict serves as an important mobilizing force for diasporic communities, enabling them to build institutions, raise funds, and promote activism among community members who might otherwise allow their ethnic identity to fade to the level of mere folkways. This is especially true for diasporas who are part of the rich and accommodating tapestry of U.S. multiculturalism. Zvi Gitelman argues that the open nature of U.S. society has led the Jewish diaspora, similar to many other ethnic Americans, to lose much of the content of their ethnocultural and religious identity and create instead "a highly individualized ethnic [Jewish] identity." This dynamic "further erodes commonality of experience, the 'mutual understandings and interpretations' that are the substance of 'thin' Jewish content."[53] The fate of the homeland's violent conflict can thus play an important role in the diaspora community's ability to maintain and nourish its own ethnic identity.

Since the threat to the homeland is a powerful tool to mobilize diaspora community members to fund diaspora organizations and engage in political activity in the host state, peace itself can threaten diasporic identity. After the signing of the Oslo Agreement in September 1993, Arthur Hertzberg wrote that, with peace in the Middle East, Israel would no longer remain Jewish-America's "secular religion," and the diaspora would have to reshape its identity and institutions to meet domestic U.S. challenges.[54] Indeed, during the Oslo Process, many diasporic organizations began to ask what their source of political recruitment would be in the era of peace and what would compel them to remain Jews if the danger to Israel receded.[55] It was in this context that some sounded the alarm that "the declining needs of Israel will contribute to the steady decline of Jewish giving, weakening American Jewish institutions and accelerating the rate of [Jewish] assimilation."[56]

The eruption of mass violence in the Middle East in the fall of 2000 deeply affected the thinking and organizational efforts of the majority of Jewish-Americans that had generally become accustomed to think and act in a "peace" mode. Jewish-American organizations that had spent the better part of the 1990s learning to focus on domestic challenges and searching for new roles in the changed political environment produced by the Oslo Accords quickly reverted to their pre-Oslo programming and rallied to Israel's side as the extent of the danger to Israel became clear. After nearly a year of violence, Mort Zuckerman, chairman of the Conference of Presidents of Major Jewish Organizations, commented that "one of the things Arafat has accomplished is a greater degree of unity among Jews in Israel and [the United States]. There is a wider degree of support and unanimity within this community than has existed in a long time."[57] This new posture of Jewish unity has also generated a significant resurgence of Jewish donations to ensure Israeli security and economic viability.

Moreover, if a homeland government chooses to pursue reconciliation with a historical enemy, diaspora communities may feel that their identity as historical victims of that enemy is under threat. To the extent that an Armenian rapprochement with Turkey requires deemphasizing the genocide issue, for example, it threatens the identity of diaspora Armenians. As Khachig Tololyan and Krikor Beledian aptly remark, "The diaspora . . . has the Genocide as its point of departure. It clings to the memory of the Catastrophe; the more distant the memory becomes, the more the diaspora seems to write about it."[58] If the Armenian state, the international embodiment of "Armenianness," decides to lower the genocide on the list of national priorities, it is by implication devaluing diaspora Armenians as part of the transnational Armenian community.

Contesting the Leadership of the Transnational Ethnic Community

In transnational ethnic communities, the very notion of the national interest is often contested: diasporas may believe that national politics should take their preferences and situation into account, while homeland elites may wish to vest national politics entirely within the institutions of the nation-state. The leadership of the diasporic Armenian Dashnak Party rejects any distinction between native Armenians and diasporans as "insulting," while former Armenian president Ter-Petrossian saw Armenia and the diaspora as "two different polities."[59] The Dashnak and the Armenian government in this period struggled mightily over who represented Armenian interests in settling the conflict in Nagorno-Karabakh.

Indeed, the Armenian-American diaspora is perhaps the example par excellence of homeland-diaspora rivalries over leadership and national interest because of the diaspora's overwhelming role in sustaining Armenian national identity during the years of Soviet rule. As noted before, for a long time, the Armenian national cause was upheld by the diaspora, specifically by the Dashnak Party, which served as a sort of "government-in-exile."[60] The Armenian diaspora, especially its highly mobilized U.S.-based community, has always been dedicated to homeland affairs, often serving as a critical lifeline for Armenian security and welfare needs. By the mid-1990s, "contributions to Armenian relief from the Armenian [diaspora] community amounted to $50 million to $75 million a year."[61] Razmik Panossian has written that, since the time of Armenia's independence from Soviet rule in 1991, "*sending financial and material aid to Armenia has become [the] operative paradigm of homeland-diaspora relations*" (italics in original).[62] The government of Ter-Petrossian sought to control the diaspora fund-raising efforts under a government-controlled Armenia Fund—allegedly to "keep politics out" of the process of the building of the country but actually to neutralize the influence of traditional diaspora parties. While the more moderate diaspora parties generally lent unqualified support to the Armenian government, the Dashnak bloc and the Armenian Revolutionary Federation assumed an opposition role.[63] The Dashnak, with its pan-Armenian orientation and long-established prominence in carrying the torch of Armenian nationalism, challenged the home regime's monopoly in defining Armenia's national interests vis-à-vis Nagorno-Karabakh, its relations with Turkey, its religious and cultural practices, its national mythology (particularly with regard to the Armenian genocide), and even the very notion of Armenianness.

The emergence of the independent state of Armenia itself challenged the status of the diaspora within the transnational Armenian community, and the new state brought a new set of interests to the discussion of Armenian foreign relations. The diaspora leadership has little reason to consider repairing relations with Turkey, for example, but the weak Armenian state has strong incentives to do so. Turkey has been forced by circumstance to recognize the harm diasporic activism can wreak on its bilateral relations with Armenia, the United States, France, and other states where diaspora activists have managed to put the genocide issue on the national political agenda. Yet the Turkish government held Armenia's present leadership responsible for the ongoing recognition campaign. At the same time, Turkey has been trying to use direct negotiations with the Armenian government over the genocide issue to de-fang the Armenian diaspora's capacity for independent action. In 2001, Turkey announced that it had "opened a direct diplomatic channel" with Yerevan to discuss the genocide issue.[64]

The U.S. government has also found Armenian diaspora activism to be a confounding factor in its foreign policy. When the U.S. House of Representatives neared passage of a nonbinding resolution recognizing the genocide, Turkey threatened to halt U.S. military flights from the

Incirlik air base that were used to enforce the northern no-fly zone over Iraq.[65] Likewise, after the French National Assembly unanimously passed a law recognizing the massacres as genocide in January 2001, Turkey curtailed its relations with France, a fellow NATO member and a prominent member of the European Union. In similar and ironic fashion, the Azeri and Turkish governments have both improved ties with Israel in part as a way of compensating for their lack of a strong diaspora in the United States. By cozying up to Israel, they have tried to win the support of Jewish diaspora organizations on Capitol Hill and fracture the Jewish groups' previously close ties with their Armenian counterparts. The Azeri ambassador to Washington said: "We understood that we needed to make friends in this country. We knew how strong Jewish groups are. They have asked us about the condition of Jews in our country. I helped them to go to Azerbaijan and open Jewish schools. They came back with [a] good understanding [of the conflict]."[66] Thus, the son of the Azeri president announced in 1999 that "we now have a lobby in the United States and that is the Jewish community."[67]

Organizational and Bureaucratic Interests in Homeland Conflicts

Diasporas may have organizational or political interests in their host countries that are affected by the homeland conflict or its potential resolution. Settlement of a homeland conflict may threaten long-cherished political institutions in the diaspora community. Some have argued that if the Arab-Israeli conflict were resolved peacefully, the American-Israel Public Affairs Committee (AIPAC) would likely see its mission greatly diminished, along with its membership, its funding, and its level of attention from elected officials in Washington.[68]

The diaspora's support and influence may initially be called upon both by the homeland government and by the host state's government as each seeks to influence the other's policies in a congenial direction. However, once a conflict is settled, the high-level meetings and phone calls may abate, and diasporic community leaders find that both their internal communal prestige and their external levers of influence degrade as a result. In addition, the struggle between different diasporic camps over homeland peace policies may become an extension of their broader competition for position and power among their ethnic constituents and within host state politics. Within the Jewish-American and Armenian-American communities, multiple organizations compete for time and attention on

Capitol Hill and other corridors of power. They likewise try to link themselves to political allies in the homeland so as to increase their prestige there.

Concerns about Political and Social Status in the Host Society

In many cases, the policies of homeland authorities with respect to their ongoing violent conflicts may also impinge on diaspora communities' political or social status in their host society. When kin states violate norms that are valued by the host state (such as, for the United States, democracy or human rights), diasporas are often implicated or held accountable morally and politically. The U.S. government and perhaps even the U.S. public may expect diaspora leaders to persuade or pressure their homeland government to alter its policies in a more congenial direction. Israel's democratic system of government has certainly made proud ethnic identification and activism easier for Jewish-Americans. On the other hand, to the extent that the young state of Armenia fails to combat corruption and consolidate its democracy, this makes diaspora lobbying work more difficult and threatens the strength and degree of U.S. support for Armenia. It also limits the degree of financial support the Armenian-American diaspora is willing to provide.[69]

The homeland's policies toward violent conflict can also impinge on the diaspora's ability to achieve cherished political goals as well as affect its status. This is especially true when the homeland government rejects U.S. policy preferences in dealing with the conflict or a potential peace process. The violence sponsored by Palestinian nationalist and Islamic movements during many years, and Arab states' endorsement of that violence, severely hampered the ability of Arab-Americans and Muslim-Americans to ingratiate themselves with America's elected leaders. Finally, homeland conflicts and peace efforts can confront diaspora leaders with a dilemma of dual loyalties and torn allegiances. When the George H. W. Bush administration threatened to withhold loan guarantees to Israel unless Israel agreed not to spend the money in the occupied West Bank and Gaza in 1991, Jewish-American advocacy organizations were forced to choose between their good relations with the U.S. foreign policy establishment and their loyal support of Israeli policies in its conflict with the Palestinians. Most chose to support Israeli policy at the cost of incurring the wrath of their U.S. partners. But after the bilateral U.S.-Israeli confrontation was resolved and the loan guarantees were put into place, many of those same organizations joined the effort to pressure the Israeli government to adopt a different attitude toward settlement activity in the West Bank and Gaza.

Economic Interests in the Homeland

Just as they invest in helping their kin in homeland conflicts, diaspora members often find economic opportunities and advantages in their kin states, especially those emerging out of long years of backwardness and adversity. Thus they may be motivated to take part in efforts to resolve conflict and to sustain postconflict reconstruction, as happened with Irish Americans for a New Irish Agenda (ANIA). While the Irish members of ANIA helped in facilitating the Good Friday Agreement and served as "stakeholders serving their homeland, which had been torn apart by violence. . . . Their motivations were not completely altruistic . . . [as a] peaceful Ireland would also open the door to lucrative investments."[70] In the cases of Eritrea, Bosnia, and Sri Lanka, some studies report that diasporic economic links and investments helped to herald peace processes. And yet, with the money they send home, diasporas can also increase the risk of renewed conflict in the years immediately following an upheaval.

Conclusions

The survey and analysis provided here allude to a very mixed picture regarding the impact of diasporas on conflict resolution and the role they play as peace spoilers or catalysts. A few observations would be pertinent. In the resolution of interstate conflicts (with or without a distinct minority dimension) kin states must address both domestic and far removed constituencies that may promote or hinder a political settlement. During negotiations with external enemies, political debates that take place within the nation-state often include diasporic constituencies that are geographically removed from the homeland and yet have a strong voice and interest in the conflict and its outcome. The diaspora activists who are *outside the state but inside the people* have weight on the international scene because of their stature, means, institutions, and connections. Moreover, the fact that third parties that are not ostensibly connected to the conflict may see diaspora activists as potential allies in advancing their own causes further enhances the diaspora's stature. Such visibility and prominence also come at a price. If the conflict flares up, the diaspora may be seen as culpable.

The interaction between diaspora and homeland constituencies (pre-

or poststatehood) in conflict resolution is dynamic. Diasporas are not merely agents fulfilling the orders of their homeland leadership. More often they are architects and initiators of policy, especially, but not exclusively, in intrastate conflicts when a minority is seeking secession or irredentism. Sometimes both parties to an international conflict have diasporic constituencies that may play a positive role, as facilitator, or a negative role, raising obstacles to dialogue. Diaspora leaders on both sides may also open a channel of negotiations. The diasporas' propensity to serve as facilitators or spoilers of negotiations both depends on and affects the homeland governments' (or nonstate aspirants') readiness to compromise or continue the conflict. Homeland governments that are permeable to diasporic influence always have to calculate to what extent the diaspora will support or oppose its policies. In some cases, the diaspora is not just the homeland's tail but may dominate the wagging. The understanding that diasporas are important players in the conflict brings third parties to address them and their interests.

The diaspora's own identity issues with regard to the homeland and their countries of residence shape their understandings of the conflict. These understandings fluctuate in accordance with their concern for current and pragmatic agendas or the saliency of history and memory in their communal identity. Some may argue that the diaspora has the luxury of dwelling in the past, while at home, governments and people must occupy themselves with issues of day-to-day existence. Yet others maintain that the diaspora's faithfulness to issues of kinship identity reminds the homeland of its historical obligations to preserve certain values that are crucial to the nation's raison d'être. In applying their own identity concerns to the homeland's policy, diaspora elements may consider how the homeland may be a source of pride abroad, or alternatively, how it may become a source of embarrassment. This observation is valid regardless of the individual's position about the conflict and regardless of his investment in his kinship identity.

Finally, emphasizing one or the other trend of diasporic involvement as spoilers or catalysts in conflict resolution is too simplistic. Whether diaspora spoil or whether they act as catalysts in supporting peace processes remains a more complex issue that is closely tied to the representation and leadership of the homeland. The extent to which diaspora members are empowered over the homeland voices is a function of many elements of the host state, home state, economics, and the viability of organization, all of which have an impact upon the direction of diasporic influences. It is evident that a diaspora's role in homeland conflict perpetuation and conflict resolution can be so powerful that homeland leaders would ignore diaspora preferences at their own peril. Moreover, one must consider seriously the view that a diaspora and its leaders are not just careless nationalists. In fact they may be better placed to view the conflict in the homeland precisely because of their remoteness and being outside the range of fire. This argument considers diasporic voices as more realistic and therefore at times less willing to accept "false" compromises. In the latter case their alleged spoiling is in fact an eye-opener, saving their kin in the homeland from themselves—a view that was expressed by key Jewish leaders in the United States who opposed Oslo because of the risks involved. All in all, the larger the diaspora and more diverse its perspectives, the greater is the likelihood that its members produce conflicting views that mirror debates in the homeland rather than dictate them.

FIVE

Diasporas and International Relations Theory

A RECENT STUDY by the World Bank concluded that "by far the strongest effect of war on the risk of subsequent war works through diasporas. After five years of post-conflict peace, *the risk of renewed conflict is around six times higher in the societies with the largest diasporas in America* than with those without American diasporas. Presumably this effect works through the financial contributions of diasporas to rebel organizations" (emphasis added).[1] This is perhaps the strongest quantitative indication of the influence of diasporas on the international scene, but it is far from being the only influence. Media reports and numerous academic studies point to the influence of diasporas on international behavior in many cases, such as the Kosovar Albanians, Armenians, Chinese, Croats, Cubans, Indians, Iranians, Irish, Jews, Palestinians, Sikhs, and the Tamils. These and other diasporas have influenced world affairs in numerous ways, passive and active, constructive and destructive. The final chapter focuses on one aspect of such influence: *diasporas as independent actors who actively influence homeland (ancestral or kin state) foreign policies.*

As we have seen throughout this book, diasporas' impact is being felt as part of the process of migration and the problem of refugees. Furthermore, as national minorities, diasporas serve as political conduits for conflict and intervention. Diasporas may become the pretext for state-sponsored irredentism—the effort by a homeland government to "recover" territory populated by ethnic kin in a nearby state. Theoretically, diasporas challenge traditional state institutions of citizenship and loyalty by resting at the nexus of domestic and international politics.[2] Above all, they are regarded as a force in identity formation. Since diasporas reside outside the state but claim a legitimate stake in it, they defy the conventional meaning of the state. They are therefore defined as the paradigmatic Other of the nation-state, as challengers of its traditional boundaries, as transnational transporters of cultures, and as manifestations of deterritorialized communities.[3]

Diasporas also operate as ethnic lobbies in liberal hostlands and as advocates of a multicultural foreign policy.[4] They campaign to democratize authoritarian homeland regimes[5] and are a force in the global economy assisting and changing the character of homelands' economies.[6] More generally, diasporas are increasingly able to promote transnational ties, to act as bridges or mediators between their home and host societies, and to transmit the values of pluralism and democracy as well as the "entrepreneurial spirit and skills that their home countries so sorely lack."[7] Yet, diasporic influence is not always constructive. Diasporic activists may be a major source of violence and instability in their homeland. As actors in conflict, just as diasporas can be advocates of peace processes, so too can they also be spoilers. Diasporas often support homeland struggles against neighboring states, or kin communities' struggles to obtain statehood. Their help may be critical to nation building and state consolidation in the homelands, making the views of the diaspora regarding national conflict a weighty factor in the deliberations of homeland leaders. Diasporas may also constitute actors in what Samuel Huntington termed the "clash of civilizations" and may even broaden the conflict by importing it to hostlands or by dealing in international crime and terrorism.[8] Given their importance, and since they are a permanent feature in the imperfect nation-state system,[9] diasporas now receive growing attention from decision makers around the world. So too the study of diasporas nowadays constitutes a growing intellectual industry, with numerous academic conferences and writings devoted to the subject.[10] Yet, despite the increasing recognition of their importance in international affairs, international relations (IR) theory has not adequately incorporated this phenomenon. This chapter seeks to fill that void. How can IR theories help to better understand diasporic activities, and how can the study of diasporic international activities enrich existing IR approaches?

I argue that diasporic activities can be understood better by setting their study in the theoretical space shared by constructivism and liberalism. Because of their unique status, diasporas—geographically outside the state but identity-wise perceived by themselves, the homeland, or others as "inside the people"—attach great importance to kinship identity. Given their international location, diasporas are aptly suited to manipulate international images and thus to focus attention on the issue of identity. Once triggered, this dynamic can be used to influence foreign policy decision making. This is done by engaging in the domestic politics of the homeland. Diasporas exert influence on homelands when the latter are "weak" (in the permeable sense of the word), tilting the balance of power in favor of the former. To varying degrees, both constructivism and liberalism acknowledge the impact of both identity and domestic interaction on international behavior. Constructivism seeks to account for actors' identities, motives, and preferences, while liberalism deals largely with explaining their actions once the preferences are settled.

Beyond emphasizing the contribution of constructivism and liberalism to the understanding of diasporic activities, I also offer ways in which the study of diasporic activities can enrich both approaches. Diasporas are among the most prominent actors that link international and domestic spheres of politics; their identity-based motivation should therefore be an integral part of the constructivist effort to explain the construction of national identities. Furthermore, despite their international location, diasporic activities and influence in the homeland, expand the meaning of the term *domestic politics* to include not only politics *inside the state* but also *inside the people*. For the liberal approach, this is a "new fact," in the Lakatosian sense. Both approaches can and should use the diasporic perspective to deepen the explanations of the phenomena on which they focus.

The first section offers typologies of diasporic international roles and interests. I choose to focus on the role I consider theoretically most interesting: *diasporas as independent actors exerting influence on homeland foreign policies*. Next, I incorporate the diaspora factor into IR theory, placing it at the meeting point between the constructivist emphasis on identity, which explains the motives of diasporas, and the liberal focus on domestic politics, which explains their venue of influence. The following section theorizes about factors affecting success or failure of diasporic attempts to affect homeland foreign policies. The Armenian case study is then presented. The conclusion offers a comparison of the Jewish and Armenian cases and recommendations for further research.

Throughout the chapter examples are mainly drawn from the Jewish-Israeli interaction. As noted earlier this case may be seen as a fully developed paradigm of relations between diasporas and their homelands, portions of which often reflect other diaspora-homeland experiences that do not (perhaps, as yet) exhibit the same level of evolution. This, of course, does not indicate that other cases are qualitatively different but rather that they manifest only part of the full range of the paradigmatic diaspora-homeland nexus. Moreover, the case of the Jewish-Israeli interaction is often singled out by other diasporas and their kin states as a model to be emulated. It is instructive to apply our theoretical insight by delving into Armenia's relations with its diaspora. This case study offers a within-case variance in diasporic impact on homeland foreign policy. The comparison with the Jewish-Israeli case also reflects the variation in the impact of diasporas on homelands' foreign policy.

Although the two cases share similarities in terms of relations between the homeland and the diaspora, their respective abilities to affect homeland foreign policy diverge significantly. This difference derives from four main elements: *permeability* of the homeland (state, government, and society); *perception* of the diaspora by the homeland (and vice versa); the *balance of power* between the two; and the *cohesion* of diaspora voices regarding homeland foreign policy.

Diasporic Roles and Interests

In all my works I have defined diaspora as a people with a common origin who reside, more or less on a permanent basis, outside the borders of their ethnoreligious homeland, whether that homeland is real or symbolic, independent or under foreign control. Diaspora members identify themselves and/or are identified by others, inside and outside their homeland, as part of the homeland's national community, and as such are often called upon to participate, or are entangled, in homeland-related affairs.[11] Members of mobilized diasporas may be divided into three categories: core members, passive members, and silent members. Core members are the organizing elites, intensely active in diasporic affairs and in a position to appeal for mobilization of the larger diaspora. Passive members are likely to be available for mobilization when the active leadership calls upon them. Silent members are a larger pool of people who are generally uninvolved in diasporic affairs but who may mobilize in times of crisis. Diasporas are mostly part of the "imagined community," to use Benedict Anderson's expression, often existing only in the minds of diasporic political activists, as well as of home or host governments.[12]

Diasporic Roles

Following Milton Esman's early typology, I collapse his seven classes of diasporic activity into two major types—active and passive—which then create three role types of diasporas in the international arena.[13]

First, diasporas can be passive actors. Diasporas are passive actors when they are interjected into international relations not by their own doing. There are three well-known reasons for this as well as a fourth highly important but less recognized one. First, a diaspora may be in need of foreign help vis-à-vis its hostland. For example, Israeli foreign policy has placed a high priority on saving Jews individually and as groups, expending great resources to free Jews in Syria, the USSR, Argentina, Romania, Ethiopia, and elsewhere. Yet this has always been done in the context of the Zionist vision of the ingathering of the exiles, of ultimately uniting the nation inside the state, and not of perpetuating Jewish communities in their foreign domiciles. In a second scenario, homelands may aspire to represent their people, including those residing outside the state, regardless of the inclination of diasporic members to be represented. While at times authentic, these claims may also be aimed at reinforcing ties between an empowered kin abroad and a needy homeland, or at gaining leverage on internal and/or external affairs of weak neighbors. To illustrate, an important factor in assessing the policies of the Russian Federation toward the newly independent non-Russian successor states is the position of the ethnic Russian diasporas in the "near abroad."¹⁴ A third kind of passive circumstance is when diasporas cannot control their status as perceived members of a remote homeland, and they thus become implicated in the homeland's international affairs. The terror attacks allegedly perpetrated by the Hezbollah with Iranian backing against the Jewish community in Argentina in 1994, within the context of the conflict in Lebanon, is a case in point.

A fourth, mostly unrecognized passive diasporic role is perhaps best characterized as political-cultural or even symbolic. The German-Jewish reality today is in many ways a microcosm of the larger web of political influences and processes operating in the international system that helps us to disentangle domestic politics and identity-building processes from geopolitical considerations, multilateral and bilateral interactions, civilizational clashes, and the politics of Diaspora and kinship affinity. The Jewish community in Germany sits at the nexus of the German and Jewish questions: qua Jews, the community is a constant reminder of the past and the challenges of the future. The very idea of a Jewish community in "the land of the perpetrators" still seems unthinkable for many; yet reality has prevailed, with the German Jewish community constituting the fastest growing Jewish community outside Israel. In some people's minds, this reality marks the beginning of a renaissance of Jewish life and culture in Germany with the potential of reinvigorating European Jewry once again. Joschka Fischer, the former German foreign minister, expressed the view of many when he said that the rebuilding of the Jewish community in Germany represented the country's second chance and remained a standard by which Germany would continue to be judged. Most important, the symbolism and the historical memory attached to the reality of Jewish existence within Germany today is a critical dimension and a common link to the transatlantic alliance and the way Germany defines its role in the Middle East. In other words, the meaning assigned to Jewish life in Germany by a variety of international actors has consequences for the conduct of international politics. The point is that the German-Jewish community has not actively chosen this role, but this role is entrusted to it because of the importance assigned to the Holocaust and Jewish issue in the postwar German state and beyond (especially in the American-Jewish community, which often sees itself as a guardian of and a voice for Jewish kinship).[15] Under all these circumstances, diasporas play a passive role. The active actors are the homelands and/or other states and groups. Academic analysis of these cases belongs to the standard IR scholarship dealing with foreign policy and international behavior; I shall not deal with this role type in this chapter.

Second, diasporas can be active actors, influencing the foreign policies of their hostlands. Diasporas, especially those in democratic-liberal societies, often organize as interest groups in order to influence the foreign policies of their hostlands vis-à-vis their homelands. This phenomenon is best exemplified in the United States, where, it has been argued, the power of various ethnic lobbies has brought about a fragmentation of American foreign policy.[16] When addressing the relations between ethnic American lobbies and American national interest, Tony Smith has warned against the narrow policy agenda of diasporas that undermine the nation's "common good."[17] Samuel Huntington also views diaspora influence on the foreign policy of the host state negatively, citing instances where diasporas supporting their home governments against the United States become sources of spies to gather information for their homeland governments and serve as a corruptible influence in the American electoral process. He claims that, as with commercial interests, American national interest is increasingly being eroded as a result of U.S. foreign policy being driven by ethnic interests.[18] Others, however, challenge the view that ethnic lobbies and transnational ties threaten the coherence of U.S. foreign policy or endanger its national security. They see ethnic lobbies as part of American pluralism or as counterweights to traditional political elites.[19] Again, there is an extensive body of literature on this topic (albeit apparently focused almost exclusively on the American case); I shall not deal with this role type either.[20]

Third, diasporas can actively influence the foreign policies of their homelands. Diasporas that achieve economic and political power can affect directly the foreign policies of their homelands. Diasporas may be the source for recruits, funding, or arms for violent activities on behalf of their kin states, and can thus play a crucial role in homelands' decisions to continue fighting or to adopt accommodating policies. Diasporas also exert direct influence through political proxies at home (e.g., Armenian or Taiwanese parties). Above all, they may achieve leverage at home by economic means, through investments in national projects or through political contributions. Diasporic political contributions have influenced electoral results in many countries including Israel.[21]

This chapter focuses solely on this role type of diaspora, as actively influencing the foreign policies of homelands. I do so because this role type is the least theoretically developed of the three. I posit diasporic activity as the independent variable and foreign policies of homelands as the dependent variable.

Diasporic Interests

As groups ostensibly external to the state, what interest(s) do diasporas have in the foreign policies of their homelands? As we saw in chapter 4, there are four main motivations for wishing to exert influence on the homeland. These motives are not mutually exclusive and are often intertwined. The motives may be focused outside the hostland (first two types), or inside the hostland (last two types).

First, diasporas might view the homeland's foreign policy as having an impact on the interests of "the people" (the entire kin community inside and outside the homeland). The diaspora must interface with the homeland government over a number of issues and concerns: a definition of identity—what Martin Buber called a "vocation of uniqueness," feelings of solidarity and kinship (e.g., the struggle over the right to immigration for Soviet Jews in the early 1970s), maintenance of memory (e.g., Armenians and the genocide memory), or financial considerations (e.g., policies regarding repayment of Holocaust debts). It is the first possibility—interest in a definition of the people's identity—on which I offer a theoretical twist to the constructivist approach. Identity does not always determine interests, as constructivism posits,[22] but sometimes identity *is* the interest. For some diasporas, the people's identity is not the starting point to be captured in order to influence interests, practices, and policies; identity is both the starting and the end point. In such cases, the only interest is to assert through the homeland's foreign policy a preferred version of kinship and national identity.

In August 2002, Britain's chief rabbi Jonathan Sacks questioned Israeli activities in the occupied territories that he considered incompatible with Judaism. Yet because Sacks's words were uttered at a time when anti-Semitism was rising, and Israel and Jewish security worldwide were perceived to be under assault, the chief rabbi was quickly castigated by other Jewish leaders for disloyalty and self-abasement. It did not help his case with his critics that these remarks were made in an interview with the *Guardian*, a newspaper noted for the virulently anti-Israel—and some have even alleged anti-Semitic—positions expressed in its pages (at the time that Sacks made his comments, the paper was serializing his latest book). British National Zionist Council co-chair Eric Graus stated, "We are worried that this will be used by the Arabs as an indication that there is a split and that their acts of violence and terrorism are working and that it will encourage more violence."[23] Rabbi David Rosen, a former chief rabbi of Ireland, expressed similar concerns. *Guardian* columnists staunchly defended Sacks's comments and his moral authority, even as Sacks himself worked feverishly to distance himself from certain impressions his remarks had created, particularly the sense among some Jews that what he had done reeked of disloyalty and self-abasement. A *Jerusalem Post* editorial calling for Sacks's resignation expressed another dimension of this position—disgust at the arrogance and pretentiousness of diaspora Jews living a safe distance from the daily dangers Israelis face, agonizing and moralizing about Israeli behavior as though they had something to teach Israelis about moral reflection and the pursuit of justice.[24]

Second, diasporas may have a strong stake in the ways the homeland's foreign policy affects the homeland's future (as separate from the people). Obviously, the interests of the homeland, its existence, well-being, and international alliances are ultimately the concern of its government, and thus diasporas are mostly reactive in this domain. Yet, diasporas perceive certain policies as enhancing or endangering the homeland's security. This is important for diasporas, either in real terms (i.e., the homeland as a place they can always move to, should conditions in hostlands become unfriendly, or for less existential reasons), or in terms of their vision of the homeland's mythical standing (i.e., as a place that helps them sustain their fading ethnic identity in an assimilating environment).[25] Diasporas may therefore try to alter such policies in order to address their concerns.

This, of course, is a product of the diasporic vision of its own ideational and associational links with the homeland, namely, the centrality of these links to the diaspora's national and ethnic identity.[26]

Some have argued that the Jewish-American diaspora should not interfere with Israel's security policy, because its members do not pay in blood for such critical decisions, and because diasporic criticism may provide both comfort for Israel's enemies and cover for political pressure on Israel. Others, however, may see their voices as essential "to save Israel from itself." In fact, such voices—on the left and the right—may be solicited by Israeli political leaders as they debate among themselves critical issues of national security and state boundaries. It is sometimes even the case that homeland leaders define the issue in terms of kinship rather than in terms of the security of the state and its inhabitants, and thus invite diasporic endorsement or criticism of state policy.[27]

Third, diasporas might view the homeland's foreign policy as affecting the interests of a specific community. These interests may be almost existential or "merely" material. In the former case, they include the viability, security, image and standing, and self-perception of the diaspora in the hostland. In such cases, diasporic activists may try to alter the homeland's policy to fit with their own priorities (e.g., Jewish-American pressure on Israel to sever its ties with the apartheid regime in South Africa). In the case of material interests, the community may even claim to represent the people's interests, including those kin members who are residing in the homeland (e.g., the American Jewish Congress campaign to recover the money of Holocaust victims from Swiss banks). In such a case, the community adopts a "foreign policy" of its own, going so far as to pressure the homeland not to interfere.

Finally, diasporas might view the homeland's foreign policy as affecting the narrow bureaucratic interests of their organizations. Since diasporic organizations are largely focused on homeland-related affairs, a homeland policy that undermines the worth of the diaspora as an asset to the homeland may threaten diasporic organizations' raison d'être. Should the Arab-Israeli conflict be resolved peacefully, for example, AIPAC is likely to see its mission greatly diminished, along with its membership, its funding, and the level of attention it receives from elected officials in Washington.[28]

Diasporas are motivated, then, by four types of interests. "Over there," away from the hostland, they may be motivated by the people's or the homeland's interests. "Over here," in the hostland, they may be motivated by communal or by organizational interests. In any case, all these

motives are based on a perception of shared identity and may lead diasporas to try to exert influence on the homeland's foreign policies. How
can this phenomenon be incorporated into IR theory?

Diasporas and IR Theory

I focus on how diasporas strive to influence the foreign policies of their
homelands through the political process in the homeland. The theoretical space to locate this phenomenon is where constructivism, with its
emphasis on identity, meets liberalism, with its focus on domestic politics. The existence of this shared theoretical space should come as no sur-
prise, since the two theoretical approaches share assumptions and claims.
On one hand, the liberal approach includes an ideational strand that
assumes states' preferences are "identity-based."[29] On the other hand, the
constructivist approach claims that identities and therefore interests are
determined by social interaction in which domestic actors also participate.[30] Furthermore, both constructivism and liberalism share concern
for states' preferences, perceive states as embedded in a larger social context, and acknowledge the importance of a wide variety of nonstate
actors.[31] Given that diasporas are mainly identity-motivated, that they
exert influence on homelands mainly through domestic politics, that they
are part of a larger international society, and that they are nonstate actors,
this shared theoretical space is a sound basis for the incorporation of diasporas into IR theory.

Constructivism and Identity

Unlike the traditional "rational" approaches, constructivism views the
state as a social actor. States are not assumed to be solely goal-driven
rational actors, seeking utility maximization and governed by the "logic
of consequences." States are rather also rule-driven role players, seeking
identity expression, and governed by the "logic of appropriateness."[32]
Constructivism thus opens up two black boxes. First, interests are not
assumed to be exogenous and constant, but endogenous and varying; the
national interest is a variable influenced mainly by national identity.
Furthermore, identity itself is also debracketed, because it too is a variable shaped by international and domestic forces.[33] In order to understand the dependent variable (international behavior or foreign policy
decision making), one must look beyond the intervening variable (inter-

ests), and focus on the independent variable (identity) and the way it is molded.

What is the nature of this variable, "national identity"? At its most basic level, as Alexander Wendt points out, it is a personal or corporate identity: "a consciousness and memory of the Self as a separate locus of thought and activity . . . a joint narrative of the Self as a corporate actor."[34] Yet, as Roxanne Doty observes, the identity is actually not of the nation but of the people, "who constitute the inside of nations and to whom national identities are attached."[35] This observation is relevant to our discussion, since I posit diasporas as part of the people beyond the scope of the nation-state.

As Doty notes, "constructing the identity of a people is a continual and never-completed project."[36] Identity is continuously molded through ecological processes (relations between actors and their environment), social processes (relations between the actors themselves), and internal processes (internal characteristics of the actors).[37] Within the social and internal processes, the construction of identity "occurs through discursive practices that attempt to fix meanings that enable the differentiation to be made between the inside and the outside [of the people]."[38] Yet, this discourse should not be understood in academic terms. As Katzenstein has observed, "The process of construction is typically explicitly political and pits conflicting actors against each other."[39] This political process, therefore, is a conflict over the power to determine national identity and thus also policy outcomes in the domestic and international arenas. In constructivist terms, however, power is not merely materially based or resources oriented, but is mainly "the authority to determine the shared meanings that constitute the identities, interests, and practices of states."[40] Thus, the social and internal forces that shape national identity are those actors that gain leverage over this authority.

Within the context of international relations, of the people/nation vis-à-vis others, William Bloom identifies a process of "national identity dynamic: the tendency among the individuals who [identify with the nation] . . . to defend and to enhance the shared national identity." This, of course, is part and parcel of the general political conflict over the determination of national identity. Therefore, "it is a permanent feature of all domestic politics that there be competition to appropriate the national identity dynamic."[41] By appropriating the dynamic, an actor gains not only the authority to determine national identity but also to direct state policies toward being compatible, or seemingly compatible, with the predominant identity. How do diasporas figure into this dynamic?

Doty has observed that "unitary claims to a national identity permit the convergence of the state and the people. However, the convergence is never totally fixed." This is so because groups outside the people become part of the state (minorities), and groups inside the people leave or dwell outside the state or their symbolic homeland (diasporas). Both groups however "are constantly raising questions as to who should be considered on the 'inside,' that is, the 'people.'"[42] Indeed, the Jewish-Israeli case is the quintessential expression of divided and overlapping identities and loyalties. Arab Israelis have often been perceived as *nochachim nifkadim*—those present physically but absent from (membership in) the national community, while diaspora Jews are seen as *nifkadim nochachim*—those absent physically from the state but part of the national community by virtue of Israel's Jewish character and its Law of Return.[43] Since national identity is both a variable and a resource, it stands to reason that various groups attach varying importance to it. A resource is usually more valued by those lacking in it. In this case, diasporas attach more importance to national identity, since their identity status is problematic. Furthermore, in terms of foreign policy, "the national identity dynamic can be triggered by international images manipulated by the government *or* by other actors."[44] Once triggered, it may be used in order to influence foreign policy decision making. Diasporas, given their international location, are aptly suited to be precisely these "other actors." Thus, constructivism helps us to better understand identity-based diasporic international activities.

Diasporas have both the motive and the opportunity to exert influence on the identity construction process, especially in its foreign policy facet. Constructivists dealing with this political process should factor in diasporas as actors highly motivated and able to engage in the competition over identity construction. This is the manner in which the study of diasporas enriches the constructivist approach, and it should be part of constructivism's response to Yosef Lapid's justified critique that "IR's fascination with sovereign statehood has greatly decreased its ability to confront issues of ethnic nationhood and political otherhood."[45] Factoring in diasporic input should be done even though it is difficult to classify diasporas as purely domestic actors. But then, as Peter Katzenstein puts it, "often social environments that affect state identity link international and domestic environments in a way that defies the reification of distinct domestic and international spheres of politics."[46] Indeed, diasporas defy this reification by engaging in the domestic politics of homelands.

Liberalism and Domestic Politics

Liberalism rejects the conventional assumptions that states are both the primary actors in international affairs and that they are unitary. Instead, it posits that the primary actors in international politics are individuals and private groups who struggle to promote different interests. The state, then, is not an independent actor but rather a representative of the transient coalition that captured it. Consequentially, states do not automatically seek fixed interests (security or power or prosperity, as neorealism and institutionalism claim), but rather pursue particular interests preferred by the specific coalition currently in power.[47]

According to the liberal approach, the degree of influence that domestic actors may exert on foreign policy depends on the strength of relations between the state (political institutions) and its society (social organizations). The weaker the former and the stronger the latter, the more influence various groups will exert on governmental policies. In this context, a "weak" state is a state highly permeable to societal influences on its decision-making process, the United States and its inviting constitutional process being a quintessential example. Matthew Evangelista highlights the connection between this approach and constructivism, asserting that the "interaction between a country's domestic structure and the historically derived normative understandings embodied in its society," that is, between domestic politics and identity construction, is of particular importance.[48]

Diasporas either interject themselves or are interjected into this political process, and should be viewed as one of many domestic interest groups. *Domestic* here does not carry the conventional meaning as opposed to international. More often than not, diasporas are considered by the homelands as domestic actors even though they are outside the nation-state, because they are (as noted earlier) inside the people. This is the manner in which the study of diasporas enriches the liberal approach; it expands the meaning of the key term *domestic*. On the other hand, by applying liberal insights about the dynamics of domestic politics (in this and in the next section), liberalism helps us to better understand the influence of diasporas on homelands.

Diasporas thus enjoy a privileged status of exerting influence as an interest group in both the homeland and the hostland, often affecting the homeland *because of* influence in the hostland (as analyzed in the next section).[49] In any case, as interest groups, diasporas may use whatever clout they can in order to advance their interests. Like other interest groups, they use their financial resources, especially since members of diasporas are usually richer than their counterparts at home. Aside from exerting indirect influence through donations to various "civil society" projects, they exert more direct influence through political contributions to parties or candidates of their choice. In many cases, their financial input is perceived as justifying a political voice. Jewish diasporic donors often maintain, and some Israelis agree, that their voices should not be ignored by Israel while their wealth is solicited.

In the use of financial clout, diasporas are similar to other interest groups. However, unlike conventional interest groups, they can also use their diplomatic value as interest groups in the hostlands. Diasporas also differ from other interest groups in the electoral realm. Since they are not physically present in the homeland, this has always naturally meant that they do not enjoy direct electoral influence. That, however, is changing. Taking notice of the growing financial and political clout of their diasporas, homelands are courting them by creating ministries or departments for diasporic affairs and—more important—by allowing dual citizenship, thus encouraging expatriate voting rights. This tendency serves to highlight the domestic politics aspect of diasporic activity.

Yet, beyond seeking to advance their interests, diasporas have an additional role in the domestic political process. From a liberal perspective, Helen Milner posits an ongoing polyarchic struggle between the executive, the legislature, and interest groups over power and preferences. She highlights the critical role that information plays in this process. Ceteris paribus, the executive enjoys an advantage of access to information over the legislature. However, in the domestic political process, interest groups are not just pressure groups; they are also information providers for the legislature. In this role, they act as signalers, "alerting political actors to the consequences of various policies."[50] Just as diasporas, given their international location, are aptly suited to trigger a national identity dynamic by manipulating international images (as mentioned earlier), so are they also important as providers of information on the international impact of foreign policy. American Jews were very influential in changing Israeli policy toward South Africa in the mid-1980s. Their motivation was fueled by concerns over here and over there.[51]

Diasporas are interest groups participating in the domestic political process of the homeland. As such, they seek to advance their identity-based interests, both directly through lobbying and indirectly by providing information to the institutional actors. Furthermore, given their international location, they are singularly (among interest groups) important to the homeland government as tools of influence vis-à-vis foreign governments. Analyzing this relationship between diasporas and homeland governments will explicate the potential efficacy of diasporic activity.

Factors Affecting the Efficacy of Diasporic Activity

In order for a diaspora to exert influence on a homeland's foreign policy, there should exist motive, opportunity, and means (i.e., a diaspora should both want to exert influence and have the capacity to do so). This capacity depends on the ability to organize members of the kin community as an influential group (which depends in part on the nature of the hostland regime) and on the receptivity of the homeland's political system to diasporic influence. Thus, the factors affecting the efficacy of diasporic influence include the degree of diasporic motivation, the social-political nature of both the hostland and the homeland, and the balance of power between the diaspora and the homeland. All these factors are interconnected.

Degree of Motivation

The identity-based motivation element is not dichotomous: different diasporas have, across time and issues, varying degrees of motivation to influence their homeland's foreign policy. Furthermore, within each diaspora there might be significant differentiation between groups, usually varying according to their position vis-à-vis the identity issue. Diasporic activists may be motivated by "over there" interests (of the people and/or of the homeland), or by "over here" interests (of their community and/or of their organization).

A number of factors may counter potential motivation to influence the homeland. One is the problem—or perception thereof—of dual loyalty. For example, during the 1956 Suez campaign, American-Israeli relations deteriorated due to President Eisenhower's demand that Israel withdraw its forces from the Sinai Peninsula. Nahum Goldman, president of the World Jewish Congress, warned Prime Minister Ben-Gurion not to expect Jewish-Americans to mobilize support against the administration. Another factor may be related to cultural impediments. Diasporic Chinese, for example, are culturally bound by a tradition of strict noninterference in affairs of others. Yet a third factor can be labeled frustration, though it encompasses also anger, fatigue, or contempt. Thus, the degree of motivation depends mainly on the interaction between the basic identity-motivating element and the experience the community has with the receptivity of the homeland. If engagement in a homeland's foreign policy is perceived by diasporas as identity-reinforcing and by the homeland as legitimate, then diasporas will be motivated to exert influence on the issue. These factors depend, of course, on the nature of the hostland and the homeland.

Nature of the Hostland

The basic nature of the hostland regime determines the ability of a diaspora to organize influence; indeed it determines the ability to organize at all. Generally, in nondemocratic regimes, civil society organizations are at least discouraged if not prohibited. Civil society groups that claim to organize on behalf of a diaspora, an outsider group within the hostland, tend to be doubly discouraged because they are perceived as being inimical to national unity. There might be cases in which such regimes would seek to exploit a diaspora in order to advance its own foreign policy interests (e.g., the Iraqi government and the Iranian exile community during the 1980s). Such cases, however, fall outside the purview of this essay, because these diasporas are not independent actors.[52]

Beyond this direct effect of the regime's nature, the hostland affects the ability of a diaspora to exert influence on its homeland also indirectly. By the way the state allows the community to exert influence on itself, it affects the worth of the diaspora as a foreign policy asset in the eyes of the homeland (discussed later). A diaspora in a permeably weak state, such as the United States, can exert influence on the state's foreign policy toward the homeland. The diaspora is perceived as an asset and is therefore better empowered to exert influence on the homeland. All this assumes that the hostland's foreign policy is important to the homeland; a hypothetical Jewish community in Kenya, even if as influential in the hostland as the American one is, would not have held much importance to Israel.[53]

Nature of the Homeland

The same "weakness" element important in the hostland comes into play also in the homeland, albeit not necessarily in the same manner. As in the hostland, policy-making is susceptible to diasporic influence the more democratically permeable the homeland is. Yet, this is not the only manner in which a state may be weak. Since in this context weakness means permeability, a weak state is not only one that is too democratic, but also one that is permeable because it is weak in terms of ideological, material, and institutional resources. This is the case with failing states.[54] In such states, not necessarily fully democratic (e.g., Armenia) governments need support in order to survive, and powerful diasporas may render this support—for a price. Thus, weak states, whether democratic or not, invite diasporic influence.

There is another side to the dual loyalty coin. A homeland may perceive a diaspora as a legitimate part of the people and still reject its interventions in sensitive or crucial matters, particularly those relating to ongoing conflicts. Homeland leaders and publics may feel that their direct stake in the outcome of a conflict with their neighbors should trump any diasporic preferences. For example, it has been said often by Jews, both in Israel and in the United States, that since Jewish-Americans do not serve in the Israeli army, they should not try to influence Israel's policy in national security matters. As mentioned earlier, this receptivity element naturally also affects the degree of diasporic motivation.

Strength Relations between Diaspora and Homeland

Since I focus on the influence of diasporas on homelands, the strength relations are actually the degree to which the homeland needs the diasporic resources. This need is measured mostly through financial resources that diasporas can invest in their homelands and/or through political support they can mobilize in their hostlands. Given the poor Armenian economy, Armenian diasporas in the West are a critical financial asset to Armenia. Given Israel's diplomatic isolation, the Jewish community in the United States is a crucial political and diplomatic asset.[55] Yet need is not everything. In order to exert effective influence on homeland foreign policy, a diaspora must be united in its position on the issue. Different groups within the community might have diverging (if not opposing) views about the appropriate direction of a homeland's foreign policy. This is usually due to the aforementioned distinction between an "over there" orientation and an "over here" one. To the extent the community is divided, its influence weakens, or it might be applied in different directions. Thus, if the homeland is in need of diasporic support, and if the diaspora is united about the direction the homeland's foreign policy should take, then the ability of the diaspora to influence that direction is enhanced.

All these factors affecting the efficacy of diasporic influence interact in the following manner: Given a democratic hostland, the opportunity for organizing and exerting diasporic influence is present. The weaker the homeland is, both in terms of need for diasporic assets and in terms of permeability to societal pressures, and the more cohesive the diaspora is (in terms of its organized voice and determination to affect policy), the greater influence the community will exert on the homeland. In a nutshell, and quite intuitively, if the strength relations between the diaspora and the homeland favor the former, then the diaspora will be better able to influence the homeland's foreign policy.

Thus, on the basis of the aforementioned set of assumptions shared by both the constructivist and liberal approaches, I offer the following theory. For diasporic influence to be exerted on homeland foreign policy, two antecedent conditions must be present: a democratic hostland and an identity-based motive. Given these two, the influence of a diaspora on the foreign policy of its homeland is determined by the balance of power between the community and the homeland. This balance, in turn, is determined by three factors: the strength or weakness of the homeland (materially, ideologically, and in terms of permeability); the degree of cohesion in the diaspora regarding homeland foreign policy; and the degree to which the diaspora is perceived as an asset or as a liability by the homeland. To test these hypotheses I delve into the Armenian case. As noted previously, this example offers a within-case variance in diasporic impact on homeland foreign policy. It also comes close to reflecting the wide range of paradigmatic diaspora-homeland nexus.

Both antecedent conditions are clearly met in the Armenian case, given that the Armenian diaspora in Western democratic states is large and well organized, and that it has long been identity-driven. Because the new Armenian state is weak and permeable, because the diaspora is generally united on kinship matters, and because it came to be perceived as an asset by the homeland, I expect the diaspora to have considerable influence on Armenian foreign policy. As became evident since the restoration of Armenian statehood in 1991, a complex and difficult interaction developed between Armenians inside and outside the state regarding the most basic questions of how Armenian identity should affect foreign policy. This was especially so regarding the conflict over Nagorno-Karabakh (an Armenian-populated enclave within Azerbaijan) and regarding Armenia's relations with Turkey. Who has the right to legitimate and authoritative representation of the Armenian people? Over what group of people does the authority of the newly independent Armenian state extend, and for what purpose or national mission?

Regarding foreign policy, should diasporic Armenians constrain the actions of the Armenian state? In what direction should diasporic identity preferences—over here versus over there—influence the content of foreign policy?

The Armenian Case

National calamities, traumas, and struggles for national restoration inform Armenian consciousness and politics in the twentieth century. The experience that has most centrally defined recent Armenian history is the genocide of 1915, in which about 1.5 million of the 2 million Armenian subjects of the Ottoman Empire perished in massacres and forced deportations, orchestrated by the Turks. In their genocidal approach to achieve "national homogenization," Turkish authorities created the modern Armenian diaspora, as the surviving half million Armenians were forced into exile.[56]

Following the genocide and the collapse of the first Armenian Republic in 1920 and throughout the Soviet era (three-fourths of the world's surviving Armenians lived in the USSR) Armenian diasporic leadership was generally split between the conservative bourgeoisie (whose wealth and political ambition were left intact) and militant intellectuals, urban workers, and former peasant soldiers represented by the Dashnak Party. The Dashnaks dominated the elected government of the first Armenian Republic before surrendering to the Red Army and fleeing abroad, first to Persia and ultimately to France. While in exile Dashnak's leadership claimed to be the sole legitimate representative of the Armenian nation and retained an independent exile government that occasionally resorted to acts of violence and terrorism. The aim was to remind the world that "the Genocide was still an issue, that Armenian territories would be reclaimed someday, and that exiles still had one of the characteristics of government, armed forces, however puny."[57]

Within the Soviet Union a semiautonomous Armenian Soviet Socialist Republic (ASSR) was created on one-sixth of the territory of historic Armenia. With time, the ASSR developed into the most homogeneous of all the Soviet republics. With the city of Yerevan emerging as Armenians' "cultural center of national identity," ASSR leaders claimed to speak for the "authentic homeland" and the Armenian people as a whole. This claim was not readily accepted by segments of the diaspora, especially by Dashnaks who rejected the Soviet Armenian regime. Yet, even the Dashnaks had to accept the fact that Soviet Armenia was a homeland base, however truncated, and they had to adjust themselves to Moscow's domination. The exiled Dashnaks also faced the strong desire of other genocide survivors to keep the Armenian people unified despite their divisions and dispersion.[58] Soviet propaganda manipulated the ASSR as the source of Armenian national pride and peoplehood, in mobilizing diasporic financial assistance.[59] Recognizing that Armenian independence was a distant dream and that diasporic life would be long-lasting, diaspora activists shifted to an emphasis on identity retention (focusing primarily on the memory of the genocide) over here (in the diaspora) at the expense of national aspirations over there (in the ASSR). Assimilation and the fading memory of the genocide were seen as the "white massacre," while "knowing Armenian and some rudimentary facts about Armenian history became the [new] license to [diasporic] leadership."[60]

By the late 1970s, the diaspora and Soviet Armenia achieved a modus vivendi in their relations. With communism in the ASSR becoming more tolerable to the diaspora (in part because after 1965 the Soviets allowed commemorations of the genocide), and with a new generation of diasporic Armenians demanding greater militancy in the struggle for genocide recognition, the Dashnaks shelved their anti-Soviet orientation and entered a new phase in their national crusade. Armenian terrorism (primarily against Turkish targets) won international attention for the Dashnaks' cause and helped to rally the diaspora to demand international recognition of the genocide, albeit mostly via diplomatic efforts.[61] One scholar notes that "the true audience of Armenian terrorism [was not Turkey and its NATO allies but] the Armenian Diaspora, whose fraying culture is constituted to a remarkable degree by old stories."[62]

In the two largest Western centers of Armenian diaspora—the United States (more than a million) and France (roughly a half million)—activists focused their efforts on keeping and spreading the memory of the genocide, in the face of Turkey's refusal to take responsibility for the atrocities or even to admit they ever happened. Since 80 percent of diasporic Armenians were descendants of genocide survivors, the memory of this atrocity became the most important vehicle to transmit a cross-generational sense of kinship, solidarity, and identity. The Armenian Church also provided an institutional structure for group cohesiveness and ethnic mobilization. Tens of millions of dollars were raised to sustain Armenian day schools, churches, and other institutions in their efforts to nourish a viable diaspora. Millions were also channeled to family members in the ASSR, especially during the 1988 Armenian earthquake.

Diasporic mobilization intensified and took a critical turn with the achievement of Armenian independence in 1991. The new state was facing serious international challenges, most immediately the conflict over Karabakh and the nature of relations with Turkey. These issues quickly became the main focus of diasporic politics. A collision was brewing between President Levon Ter-Petrossian and the Dashnaks, who quickly established themselves inside the homeland as a transnational, pan-Armenian organization that viewed itself as the guardian of Armenian identity.

While the genocide was the most central issue to the diaspora's identity and its organizational agenda, it was less important to the homeland community, which for the most part had escaped the trauma. Moreover, while virtually no diasporic Armenians in the West were from Karabakh, they were very conscious of the historical memory of losing lands and lives to Turkish nationalists throughout eastern Anatolia between 1915 and 1923, and they therefore insisted that no more Armenian land be lost.[63] Thus, Ter-Petrossian earned the ire of the diaspora when he formulated a foreign policy that refused to recognize the self-declared independence of Karabakh, rejected calls for its annexation, and defined the conflict as one between local Armenians and the government of Azerbaijan. Even more controversial was his policy of downplaying the genocide as a central issue in establishing relations with Turkey. His so-called realist-pragmatist policy meant that "the steps of the Armenian people must be proportionate to the degree of [their] strength." This reasoning dictated that "the Armenian genocide should be left off Armenia's political agenda." The president also advocated "normal" relations with Turkey instead of so-called dreams based on "radical interpretations of the past." He even posed the rhetorical question: "Let's say that all states and the United Nations were to recognize that they slaughtered us; what then?" Ter-Petrossian maintained that, if Armenia wished to achieve political democracy and real independence from Russia, it should open up to Turkey. It was in his opinion an illusion that Russia could ensure the security of Armenia.[64]

Ter-Petrossian argued that the diaspora should not intervene in Armenian politics. Yet, he eagerly pursued diasporic funding to build his state-controlled Hayastan All-Armenian Fund and solicited diasporic lobbying efforts in hostland states. One observer wrote that diaspora activists resented the fact that they had become little more than a sugar daddy for the Armenian government.[65] Indeed, the Armenian Fund became the mechanism through which Ter-Petrossian sought "to tap and direct the resources of the diaspora." This policy intended to depoliticize the notion of "outside the state but inside the people" by blocking and circumventing the impact of transnational diasporic parties. In Ter-Petrossian's own words, "the concept of national political parties which exist and function outside their country is unnatural."[66] Since 1991, the diaspora has joined the domestic political scene. In addition to the Dashnaks' Armenian Revolutionary Federation (ARF), both the ADL-Ramkavar and the SDH were imported from the diaspora.

All parties were slow to build grassroots support and were initially marginal in the face of Ter-Petrossian's popularity and strong presidency. At the outset, the president made gestures toward the diaspora by appointing some of its members to senior positions—including the U.S.-born Raffi Hovannisian as foreign minister. After a short diaspora-homeland rapprochement, the Dashnaks became Ter-Petrossian's most ardent opposition as they challenged his state-sanctioned legitimacy to determine the core issues of Armenian identity, memory, and aspirations. After the Dashnaks precipitated agitated debates over fundamental foreign policy issues (Karabakh, the genocide, and relations with Turkey) Ter-Petrossian responded by outlawing their party as a "foreign organization controlled from abroad." Many Dashnak activists were arrested and expelled, to the chagrin of other diasporic forces that were ready to lend Ter-Petrossian their support.

The Dashnaks, in turn, responded aggressively. They funded newspapers, media campaigns, and demonstrations inside and outside Armenia that vilified the president as treasonous. They also capitalized on the government's domestic failures, such as the collapse in GDP in the early 1990s, runaway inflation, growing poverty, corruption, and lack of democratic accountability. In the face of massive migration out of Armenia, the president was accused of propagating antinational policies that were emptying the newly independent homeland. Ter-Petrossian was also discredited for his opposition to the diaspora's initiative for dual citizenship. His credibility was particularly damaged when Turkey refused to establish relations with Armenia, despite his willingness to forgo Turkish recognition of its culpability for the genocide. He even lost standing among diasporic sympathizers for underestimating the risk of another genocide without fundamental changes in the policies of Turkey and Azerbaijan.[67] In the face of these domestic, international, and intrakin failures, Ter-Petrossian was ultimately forced to resign in 1998. By many accounts, the diaspora was highly instrumental in his removal.[68]

Clearly, Ter-Petrossian's policy of soliciting financial and diplomatic resources from the diaspora while striving to neutralize diasporic voices on international matters exacerbated his relations with the hard-nosed Dashnaks. While initially strengthening his position, Ter-Petrossian's efforts to suppress these influences eventually proved costly. The strong state that he envisioned failed because it had become increasingly dependent on diasporic support and thus more permeable to the preferences of overseas Armenians. Indeed, since independence, Armenia's economy experienced a rapid collapse in GDP and in national currency and became one of the poorest countries in the world.[69] This economic catastrophe increased Armenian dependence on its diaspora and changed the balance of power between the two.

In contrast to the Armenian state, the diaspora is strong and well organized. It counts many affluent members who contribute money to homeland causes. The diaspora also boasts an elaborate lobbying network in the United States and in Western Europe, which secures diplomatic sympathies toward the homeland. The American-based diaspora has been Armenia's major source of support throughout the country's conflict over Karabakh. The mobilized diaspora in key states (California, Massachusetts, and New Jersey) continues to guarantee Armenia substantial American foreign aid and is the key factor in persuading Congress to pass and sustain a ban on any foreign aid to Azerbaijan.[70] In fact, only due to diasporic inflow of humanitarian aid, remittances, and private transfers, and diasporic success in extracting disproportionately large amounts of U.S. assistance to Armenia, could the homeland stay afloat.[71] Ter-Petrossian's domestic failures, compounded by his inability to elicit a positive Turkish response to his overtures, highlighted Armenia's dependence on diasporic support at the very time he persecuted the Dashnaks. The resulting conundrum eventually led to his downfall.

The newly installed president, Robert Kocharian, quickly recognized the power of the diaspora in defining Armenia's national goals. Moreover, he emphasized the pursuit of genocide recognition as an integral part of Armenia's foreign policy agenda. Ronald Suny has written,

> Almost immediately the new government reverted to a more traditional nationalism, one more congenial to the diaspora. . . . Armenia . . . reemphasized the genocide issue, always a source of pain and emotion for Armenians and a powerful wedge between Armenia and Turkey. As a consequence, a profoundly risky attempt to reorient the national discourse ultimately failed before intractable obstacles both domestic and foreign. . . . The power and coherence of the Armenian national identity, the popular projection of the

images of genocide onto the Karabakh conflict, and the closing off of the Turkish option all contributed to the fall of a once-popular national leader, whose move beyond the limit of Armenian identity choices and national discourse did not bring the expected political payoff.[72]

The critical role played by diasporic Armenians in shaping Armenian national identity and consequently the state's foreign policy manifests itself most powerfully regarding the possibility of a peace settlement with Azerbaijan. This influence exemplifies how powerfully diasporas affect national images of states. Indeed, Armenian diasporic groups have been in the forefront of presenting the case for recognition of the genocide to the Western media, academic community, and governments. Its international location allows the diaspora to influence public opinion regarding Armenian identity. Diasporic lobbies have also succeeded in pushing European parliaments and American legislators to pass genocide resolutions despite Turkey's denials, protests, and diplomatic efforts to thwart such pronouncements.[73]

As much as Kocharian recognizes the critical role of the diaspora, he has found himself squeezed between the potential advantage of improving relations with Turkey and the diasporic veto power. Moreover, as much as Kocharian contemplates the idea of striking a deal with Turkey (that gives attention to the genocide in a way that ultimately removes the issue from the political realm), he fully understands that without the high profile that the genocide gives the Armenians, his country may not receive the international attention for which it still yearns. Kocharian perceives the diaspora both as an international asset and as a powerful domestic lobby. Undoubtedly many homeland Armenians are likely to welcome a "new realism" in foreign policy, even though they may resent the fact that their ongoing suffering is not felt by the diaspora.[74] To some extent one can argue that, in the mind of the diaspora, Armenia as a homeland has served more as a notion, perhaps a mythical vision, rather than as a concrete sovereign state. This diasporic vision, so entangled with the memories of the genocide, has been inserted into the weak Armenian state to such a degree that it now overwhelms foreign policy decisions.

Conclusions

This chapter focused on the role of diasporas as independent actors exerting influence on their homelands' foreign policies. Within IR scholarship, I placed the diasporic factor in the theoretical space shared by constructivism (with its emphasis on identity) and liberalism (with its focus on domestic politics). Given their unique status, diasporas attach significant importance to kinship identity. Given their international location, diasporas are aptly suited to manipulate international images and thus to trigger a "national identity dynamic," as the Armenian diaspora has done with their image as genocide victims. Once triggered, this dynamic can be used to influence homeland foreign policy decision making. This is done by engaging in the domestic politics of the homeland, something that diasporas can do because, while being outside the state, they are still perceived as inside the people. Diasporas exert influence on homelands when the latter are weak, tilting the balance of in favor of the former.

In both the Jewish and Armenian cases, the homeland regards the diaspora as an integral part of the kin community and strives to cultivate its support. Both diasporas consider their ties to the homeland critical to their identity and mobilization in their countries of domicile, and place the homeland at the top of their kinship agenda. Both diasporas, particularly in the U.S. context, are strong (materially and politically), well-organized, and successful in lobbying American elected officials to support their respective homelands. Yet, the two diasporas diverge greatly when it comes to influencing their homelands' foreign policies. This divergence stems from the relative strengths of the homelands vis-à-vis the diasporas, which affect and contribute to the greater or lesser permeability of the homeland to diasporic influences.

From the time of Israel's establishment, the country, its leaders, and the diaspora all considered the homeland community as the vanguard of the Jewish people, even though American Jews were "the uncle in America" and Israel was the "the poor relative whose very existence was uncertain."[75] Israeli authorities were mostly viewed as having the moral legitimacy both to make life-and-death decisions for the state, and also to a large degree to speak on behalf of the Jewish people as a whole, as long as Israeli leaders refrain from interfering in the internal affairs of American Jews. As Israel's democracy flourished, integrated other Jewish communities, triumphed over its enemies, and thrived economically, the homeland increased its standing in the homeland-diaspora relationship. The Six-Day War in particular embellished the status of Israel in the eyes of the diaspora resulting in the Israelization of its agenda. Even though Israel is a weak state—in the sense of permeability to societal influences—its susceptibility to diasporic influence on foreign policy was limited by the fact that it was ideologically strong. Since the late 1970s the diversification and erosion of automatic diasporic support for Israeli foreign and domestic policies became evident. Growing divisions within Israel regarding peace with the Arabs and Palestinians were mirrored by a similar fracturing within the diaspora. These internal diasporic divisions on homeland foreign policy further undermined the possibility of Jewish-American influence on Israeli foreign policy.

By contrast, diasporic Armenians still consider themselves the vanguard of the nation, and they lack an ideological foundation for supporting Armenia as there is with Zionism.[76] Most critically, the state of Armenia is much too weak politically, economically, and culturally to assert its own leadership of the transnational Armenian community. Armenia's endemic corruption and its culture of violence, which drove so many Armenians to migrate, weaken the state's claim to speak in the name of the Armenian people as a whole, and they make Armenia significantly more permeable to diasporic influences. Finally when it comes to Armenian foreign policy, the Dashnaks have dominated all other diasporic voices. The Armenian diaspora was a crucial factor in replacing Ter-Petrossian with Kocharian, causing an intentional shift in Armenian foreign policy toward a more militant anti-Turkish line.

Beyond emphasizing the theoretical space shared by constructivism and liberalism, I have offered ways in which the study of diasporic international activities can enrich both approaches. Diasporas are among the most prominent actors that link international and domestic spheres of politics. Their identity-based motivation should be an integral part of the constructivist effort to explain the formation of national identities. Furthermore, diasporic activities and influence in the homeland, despite their international location, expand the meaning of the term *domestic politics* to include constituencies not only inside the state but also inside the people. Both approaches can and should use the diasporic perspective to deepen the explanations of the phenomena on which they focus.

In the third section, I theorized about factors affecting the efficacy of diasporic activity, that is, what determines diasporic success in influencing homelands' foreign policies. For further research, the next step would be to shift from process to content. In what direction do diasporas try to push their homelands' foreign policies? Can a generalization be made on this point? Are diasporas generally more militant than their homelands? Does the fear of being cut off and losing identity push diasporas to advocate more ideational and less compromising homeland policies, in order to gain a sense of belonging?[77]

At this stage of the research, it is difficult to answer this question. On one hand, theoretically, the answer would be that it depends on the identity focus of the diaspora. Communities focused on national identity as the tie to the people at large and/or to the homeland would push for a policy that accentuates national particularism at best, and national aggrandizement at worst. Communities focused on kinship identity as part of an effort to integrate within hostland society would push for an accommodating policy, in line with the norms of the liberal society in which they live. On the other hand, empirically, the paradigmatic case of Jewish-Americans does not necessarily support this preliminary hypothesis. True, Orthodox Jews are less inclined to integrate fully into American society and were generally anti-Oslo; liberal secular Jews, striving for complete integration, were pro-Oslo. Yet it would not be accurate to claim that liberal Jews are more moderate *because* they are focused on over here. They prefer moderate Israeli policy not only because it helps sustain their preferred image but also because they truly believe that it is the best approach for the state of Israel.

Altogether, more empirical studies should be conducted in order to provide a valid generally applicable answer to the question of the direction in which diasporas push. As migration flows accelerate, and as diasporas increase both in numbers and in political access to their homelands, answering this question is all the more important in order to understand future directions of homeland foreign policies.

Appendix: A Note on
Kinship and the Law

In the current tense discussions both in Israel and in the Jewish diaspora concerning the new wave of anti-Semitism, politicians and commentators alike have overlooked the legal dimension of kinship responsibility (in the sense of *kol Yisrael arevim ze laze*) that exists in the Israeli penal code. Section 13 of this code, enacted in 1994, enshrines in law an express Israeli commitment to the diaspora-homeland security nexus.

Section 13, part of a wider reform of the code, granted Israeli courts jurisdiction over what is termed "extra-territorial crimes," that is, crimes committed outside Israel. Section 13 is unique in the way that it relates to what is defined in its title as "crimes against the state or against the Jewish People." It states that:

> Israeli criminal law will also apply to offenses committed outside Israeli territory against: 1. The life of an Israeli citizen, Israeli resident or public servant, his body, his health, his freedom, or his property, because he is one of the above. 2. The life of a Jew, his body, his health, or his property, because he is a Jew, or the property of a Jewish institution, because it is Jewish.

In this section, Israel defined in explicit terms the connection between the diaspora and the State of Israel as the state of the Jewish people. Clearly, this connection was already affirmed and defined in the Law of Return, which established that "every Jew is entitled to make aliyah to

---

This appendix was first published (with Zeev Sega) as an essay in *Ha'aretz*, September 6, 2002.

Israel." It is also clear that the Law of Return and the corresponding Israeli commitment to the Jewish people are the elements that often defined the Israeli national interest as a "Jewish interest." Over the years, this interest compelled state action to save Jewish communities in distress and bring them to Israel. Israel's military ties and arms transfer policies were also influenced, among other things, by the desire to guarantee the well-being and civil rights of diaspora communities, and they were used "as quid pro quo for permission to emigrate." By enacting the section on the "Security of the Jews," the State of Israel expressed its commitment to protect all Jews regardless of their citizenship and their countries of domicile, as if they were citizens of the state and as if the crimes committed against them were committed within Israel's state borders.

In order to assess the far-reaching significance of the inclusion of the "Security of the Jews" clause in the penal code, we must understand the territorial principle of the law prior to the amendment of the penal code. In principle, criminal law is applied territorially. This means that the authority of a state to implement criminal sanctions is applied to a geographic/physical space over which the state has sovereignty. Within its sovereign domain, the state should exercise, in principle, a monopoly over the means of violence, and only its official institutions should determine criminal behavior.

"Extraterritorial" Connections

The scope of the law is based therefore on the fundamental requirements of state's sovereignty. Obviously, criminal law derives from the right of the sovereign to use force in order to enforce these laws. Since the sovereignty of other states also derives from their own claim to legitimate monopoly over the means of violence and inheres in their enforcement within their own borders, it is not possible to implement criminal sanctions established by one country in another's territory.

This territorial limitation to the application of criminal law has a number of "extraterritorial" exceptions, which are based on different linkages or connections arising from the special character of a specific crime or from the personal links of the perpetrator or the victim of the crime.

The universal connection is a connection that gives every state, qua state, judicial jurisdiction over crimes committed against international law. A grave violation of international law is by definition extraterritorial and constitutes a violation of the sovereignty of all states as one, harming as it does the very basis of civil society, as it exists. The classic example now is genocide. In the past, piracy was the prime example of a crime that was granted universal jurisdiction due to its extraterritorial character. The universal connection in essence provides authority to every state to apply its own criminal laws against an offender, while he/she is in that state's domain.

The Protective Connection. When a crime endangers the very existence of states' sovereignty, their security, or economic well-being, states are entitled to protect themselves. This means that when a certain violation jeopardizes the very basis of the state's fighting capability or its regular administration, the state is entitled to apply its criminal norms in order to protect itself, even though the violation occurred outside the state's borders. The justification for this application of criminal norms outside state boundaries lies in the great danger to the state's authority and order. This danger can be so severe that it sometimes justifies violation of another state's sovereignty.

The Passive Personal Connection. According to this (weaker) principle, a state may apply its criminal laws to those who harm its citizens or residents when they are outside its territorial bounds. This principle rests on the state's obligation to protect its citizens even when they are outside its sovereign domain. It is also based on the personal (kin) connection to the state. This connection is termed passive because it relates to victims who are "passive" relative to the damage caused to them.

The Active Personal Connection. According to this principle, a state is allowed to invoke extraterritorial jurisdiction and apply its own criminal norms to crimes committed outside the country in proceedings against a state citizen who actively violated criminal law while outside the country, and who then chose to return to his/her country of citizenship. This connection prevents the state from becoming a sanctuary for its citizens who are accused of committing offenses while abroad, since the state puts them on trial. This jurisdiction can also be used as an alternative to extradition of the offender to the state where the crime was committed.

It is in light of this understanding of the territorial jurisdiction principle and of the connection that allows deviation from it that one must see the special significance of the "Security of the Jews" clause that exists in the Israeli penal code. When the Knesset added the "Security of the Jews" clause in 1994, it established a new extraterritorial principle, an additional connection that makes possible the application of Israeli criminal norms outside the borders of the state. The significance of the clause is that the State of Israel sees the protection of all Jews as one of its supreme responsibilities and considers every Jew, wherever he or she may reside, to be covered by its legal protection.

The legislators' intent to create a new and special extraterritorial connection can be evaluated through the reading of the explanatory remarks offered on the bill, and the remarks made by then justice minister Dan Meridor in the Knesset plenum, when the bill was going through its first reading. The explanatory remarks said:

> Likewise it should be emphasized that special protection is granted in Section 13(b)(2) to the life, health, freedom or property of a Jew, because he is a Jew, and that this is without any other connection to the State of Israel. The point of this is that just as when such an injury is directed against an Israeli, or an Israeli public servant because he holds such a position, the real injured party—according to the motive and object of the crime—is the state and the physically injured party is apprehended as someone who represents it or who is part of it, so, too, a similar rationale lies behind the protective application regarding injuries to a Jew or to Jewish institutions because they are such. This is an expression of the State of Israel's existence as the State of the Jewish people.

In his remarks to the Knesset during the bill's first reading, Meridor said:

> We accept in the bill Professor Feller's proposal to take upon ourselves as a Jewish state the responsibility to protect the life of a Jew, if he is harmed because he is Jewish. One may ask, of course, if there is a convention like this in other countries, and perhaps there is not. But there is no state that has written in another Basic Law, as in our Basic Law: The Knesset, Section 7a, the definition of Israel as the "state of the Jewish people." When a Jew is persecuted anywhere because he is a Jew, not because he committed a criminal act, I think that it has to be made possible for us to apply the criminal laws of the State of Israel against the party who injures him, according to our judgment.

Significance and Application

The practical significance of the "Security of the Jews" clause is that Israeli courts have jurisdiction over acts committed by foreigners against Jews because of their Jewishness. This means that from the point of view of the State of Israel, there is no substantive difference whether anti-

Semitic offenses are committed inside or outside of Israel. In other words, in contrast to every other offense committed against Israeli citizens or Jews outside of Israel, and for which the court is not ordinarily empowered to judge, when an offense is motivated by anti-Semitism, the court has full jurisdiction. In addition, the conferment of judicial jurisdiction on an Israeli court, and the treatment of the offense as if it was committed within the borders of Israel, provides the State of Israel the authority to demand the extradition of the offender.

Presumably, an extradition request would, in this case, run up against the commonly known roadblock of "dual criminality," the requirement that necessitates that the offense prompting the extradition request exist in both the petitioning state and the state being petitioned. Since this clause in the Israeli penal code is unique and does not exist in the laws of other states, it appears that such an extradition request will not be heeded in practice. Nevertheless, much depends on the rules and laws of extradition, and situations may exist wherein the country where a crime was committed would be prepared to find a way to facilitate the extradition of a suspect to Israel.

To the best of my knowledge, the "Security of the Jews" clause has yet to be activated. This in no way diminishes the declarative and ideological importance of this law. It cannot be seen as beyond the realm of possibility that in the future, in certain circumstances, the law will cease to be merely words and will become a living and breathing reality.

Notes

1. I consider the case of the Jewish diaspora and its links to Israel to be an *arche-typical* rather than *idiosyncratic* one. This case provides a fully developed paradigm of relations between diaspora and homeland from preindependence, via attainment of statehood, to the period of postindependence state consolidation. Indeed, this case is often singled out by other diasporas as a model to be emulated and is frequently cited as such by both scholars and international actors alike. Other diasporic-homeland interactions may only partially match this paradigm. This, of course, does not indicate that they are qualitatively different but rather that they represent only part of the full range of the paradigmatic diaspora-homeland nexus.

2. Steven Grosby, "The Biblical 'Nation' as a Problem of Philosophy," *Hebraic Political Studies* 1, no. 1 (fall 2005): 11. Also see Steven Grosby, *Biblical Ideas of Nationality: Ancient and Modern* (Winona Lake, IN: Eisenbrauns, 2002), 58.

3. David Vital, *A People Apart: The Jews in Europe, 1789–1939* (Oxford: Oxford University Press, 1999), 368.

4. See Peter Hagel and Pauline Peretz, "States and Transnational Actors: Who's Influencing Whom? A Case Study in Jewish Diaspora Politics during the Cold War," *European Journal of International Relations* 11, no. 4 (December 2005): 467–93.

5. Robert Gilpin, "No One Loves a Political Realist," *Security Studies* 5, no. 3 (spring 1996): 26.

6. Alexander Hamilton, John Jay, and James Madison, *The Federalist Papers*, ed. George W. Carey and James McClellan (Indianapolis: Liberty Fund, 2001), 6.

7. See Amos Elon, *The Pity of It All: A Portrait of the German-Jewish Epoch, 1743–1933* (New York: Picador, 2002), 95.

CHAPTER ONE

An earlier version of this chapter was published with Martin Sherman in *Nations and Nationalism* (summer 1998). The first draft was presented at the Harvard-MIT MacArthur Seminar in March 1996. The authors wish to thank Juan J. Linz,

Myron Weiner, Zvi Gitelman, Aharon Klieman, and Michael Kochin for their helpful comments.

1. As I discussed in earlier work, the Czechoslovakian case proves extremely instructive. See Yossi Shain, "Ethnic Diasporas and U.S. Foreign Policy," *Political Science Quarterly* 109 (1994–95) and Yossi Shain, *Marketing the American Creed Abroad: Diasporas in the U.S. and Their Homelands* (Cambridge: Cambridge University Press, 1999).

2. Walker Conner, "The Impact of Homelands upon Diaspora," in Gabriel Sheffer, ed., *Modern Diasporas in International Politics* (London: Croom Helm, 1986), 20.

3. Such as present-day relations between Armenians in Nagorno-Karabakh and independent Armenia.

4. Elie Kedourie, *Nationalism* (London: Hutchinson, 1966), 58. See also Fredrick Hertz, *Nationality in History and Politics* (London: Routledge and Kegan Paul, 1966), 12; Hans Kohn, *The Idea of Nationalism: A Study in Its Origins and Background* (New York: Macmillan, 1946), 92.

5. Aviel Roshwald writes: "Because, in principle, civic nationalism is inclusive of all who choose to participate in the common political culture, regardless of their parentage or mother tongue, most authors associate it with liberal, tolerant values and respect for the rights of the individual." Roshwald, *Ethnic Nationalism and the Fall of Empires: Central Europe, Russia, and the Middle East, 1914–1923* (New York: Routledge, 2001), 5.

6. Yossi Shain, *The Frontier of Loyalty: Political Exiles in the Age of the Nation-State* (Middletown, CT: Wesleyan University Press, 1989; 2d ed., Ann Arbor: University of Michigan Press, 2005).

7. Donald L. Horowitz, *Ethnic Groups in Conflict* (Berkeley: University of California Press, 1985).

8. Whatever the details of such a model may turn out to be, it seems likely that the causal roots of a failure to create (impose) a national identity may be traced, albeit not exclusively, to inappropriate delineation of political boundaries in relation to political allegiances, while those of failures to maintain national identity may be attributed, at least partially, to the obsolescence or loss of relevance of some formerly unifying ideology.

9. Since Moldova declared its independence from the Soviet Union, the new country has faced secessionist claims by republics in southern and eastern Moldova, Gagauzia and Transnistria (which has a large Russian-speaking community). At the same time, some ethnic Moldovan elites pressed their case for a pan-Romanian nation and called for the reintegration of Moldova with Romania. The Gagauzi and Transnistrians feared that the pan-Romanianism would lead to a forced "romanianization" and a quick union of Moldova and Romania. See Charles King, "Moldovan Identity and the Politics of Pan-Romanianism," *Slavic Review* 53, no. 2 (1994): 358. The fighting between the Dniester Republic and the Moldovans claimed the lives of hundreds and led to the dispatch of Russian troops into action on the side of the Dniester Republic. Eventually, the Conference on Security and Cooperation in Europe (CSCE) sent a representative mission that formulated a comprehensive proposal for cantonizing the region. On February 1, 1994, after political and military pressure from the Russian state, the Moldovan government

officially approved autonomy for Transdniestria, granting it a high degree of self-government that fell short of federal status. See *Economist*, July 10, 1993; *Keesing's Report of World Events*, February 1994, 39876.

10. One observer has written that "if the Armenians do ultimately carve out an independent region in Azerbaijan for themselves . . . it will be largely a result of the efforts of zealous diaspora Armenians." *Financial Times*, September 16, 1994.

11. British foreign secretary Lord Curzon criticized the action as "a thoroughly bad and vicious solution for which the world will pay a heavy penalty for hundred years to come." Winston Churchill, however, argued that "the dis-entanglement of populations which took place between Greece and Turkey . . . was in many ways a success, and has produced friendly relations between Greece and Turkey ever since." At the Nuremberg trials, population transfers were defined as war crimes. Cited in Alan Dowty, *Closed Borders: The Contemporary Assault on Freedom of Movement* (New Haven: Yale University Press, 1987), 88, 97.

12. Cited in Philip Robins, "The Overlord State: Turkish Policy and the Kurdish Issue," *International Affairs* 69 (1993): 65.

13. Ofra Bengio, "The Challenges to the Territorial Integrity of Iraq," *Survival* 37, no. 2 (1995): 82.

14. In their common struggle to depose an existing tyrannical regime, nationalist exiles may collaborate with ethnic secessionists. See Shain, *Frontier of Loyalty*.

15. An important and very complex question is to what extent ideological divisions and large differences in regime type eventually may lead to ethnic divisions. In the case of Korea, there are many indications that the physical division at the 38th parallel gradually created deep ideational disparities so that any future push toward unification must contend with the divergence in values adopted by both societies.

16. Myron Weiner, "Labor Migrations as Incipient Diasporas," in Sheffer, ed., *Modern Diasporas; International Herald Tribune*, August 20, 1996. According to *Israel Television Evening News* (August 23, 1996), one out of every six residents in Tel Aviv is a migrant foreign worker.

17. Weiner, "Labor Migrations."

18. Michael Lind, *The Next American Nation* (New York: Free Press, 1995), 46–47.

19. Myron Weiner, *The Global Migration Crisis: Challenges to States and Human Rights* (New York: HarperCollins, 1995), 141.

20. Roshwald, *Ethnic Nationalism*.

21. The Soviet model intended in theory, though failed in practice, to unite all ethnonational groups in the Soviet empire under the banner of socialist comradeship. In many respects Soviet policy seems to have been confused and self-contradictory. Thus, on the one hand it prohibited any other vision of its constituent republics and systematically attempted to obliterate traditional cultures and to erase the recorded histories and memories of its titular nations. See Khachig Tololyan, "National Self-determination and the Limits of Sovereignty: Armenia, Azerbaijan, and the Secession of Nagorno-Karabagh," *Nationalism and Ethnic Politics* 1, no. 1 (1995): 98. At the same time, and in apparent contradiction to its own political ideology, the Soviet state fostered and cultivated the titular nationalities. Indeed, the Constitution of the Soviet Union also provided in the famous article 17

that "the right freely to secede from the USSR is reserved to every Union Republic." Cited in Lee C. Buchheit, *Secession: The Legitimacy of Self Determination* (New
Haven: Yale University Press, 1978), 100.

22. The large Eritrean refugee diaspora (that resulted from Ethiopian ethnofocal imposition) became a major force in the war for Eritrean independence. This
pre-state mobilization remained very important after independence especially
when the diaspora became the lifeline in supporting their homeland during the
Eritrean-Ethiopian war of 1998–2000. See Ethiopiawi, "The Eritrian-Ethiopian
Conflict," in Astri Suhrke and Lela Garner Noble, eds., *Ethnic Conflict in International Relations* (New York: Praeger, 1977), 36–37.

23. Kedourie's account of the Turkish experience illustrates the complexity
involved in the creation of an ideofocal identity.

> Legal and political equality—however formal and empty of substance—
> made it difficult, if not impossible, to justify the *millet* system, with its com-
> munal institutions which acted as a shield to protect its members from the
> demands, and the usually unwelcome attentions of the government. If
> equality was now the rule there was no need for special privileges and for
> institutions to secure these. Under the new dispensation *millets* became
> minorities since equality necessarily meant that one citizen, whatever his
> religion, was to count no more than another citizen. This is indeed the logic
> of democracy, but the logic becomes somewhat oppressive when majorities
> and minorities are immutable. The majority is thus perpetually dominant,
> and imposes its norms and views on the minority, while the minority has lit-
> tle or no interest in maintaining the body politic of which it is ostensibly a
> member. A minority in such circumstances remains as much outside the
> *pays politique* in a modern *Rechtsstaat* as the *millet* had been when the state
> followed the laws of Islam. The minority may have a few representatives in
> parliamentary assemblies. But such representatives cannot possibly sway, or
> prevail against, the overwhelming numbers who belong to the majority reli-
> gion. Again, should they attempt to act as the representatives of a minority,
> their position becomes false and awkward, precisely because the polity is
> deemed to be nationally homogeneous, and to proscribe divisions based on
> religion. The recognized status of the *millet* is replaced by the insecurity and
> tension which the discrepancy between democratic rhetoric and political
> reality must generate.

See Elie Kedourie, *Politics in the Middle East* (New York: Oxford University Press,
1992), 44–45.

24. In India, where secular nationalism (associated with the Congress Party)
served for decades as the official doctrine of national identity, many consider the
rise of the Bharatiya Janata Party (BJP) and its connection with the Hindu nationalist group, Rashtria Swayamsewak Sangh (RSS) as the greatest threat to the
supraethnic vision of the nation. Mita Menezes, "The Rise and Domination of
Hindu Nationalism: The Future of India's National Identity" (essay, Georgetown
University, December 2002).

25. *New Republic*, March 22, 1993.

26. Sherman, for example, has developed a theoretical model, showing how the
differences in the internal structures of regimes affect the harshness of their policy

choices. See Martin Sherman, *Despots, Democrats, and the Determinants of International Conflict* (London: Macmillan, 1998).

27. Indigenous peoples include aboriginal—i.e., "the residents of a place from earliest known times"—or colonialist settlers. See Myron Werther, "Labor Migrations as Incipient Diasporas," in Sheffer, ed., *Modern Diasporas*, 7.

28. Benny Morris, *The Birth of the Palestinian Refugee Problem, 1947–1949* (Cambridge: Cambridge University Press, 1989). Israel provides an interesting duality of both ethnofocal and ideofocal traits. If "Jewishness" is considered an ethnically homogenous feature, then in this regard Israel is indeed an ethnofocal state. If, however, the more commonly perceived ethnic traits, such as ancestral origin, social and cultural norms or mother tongue, or even physiological features are considered, then the Jewish population of Israel may be perceived as a highly diverse ethnic community, united by the ideofocal principle of Zionism. In fact, some have argued that the ethnofocal component of the Jews in modern times is more the result of global animosity and of persecution by external groups than of any inherent sense of a common national identity.

29. Mark E. Brandon, "No Exit? Secession and Constitutional Order" (paper presented at the 1992 annual meeting of the American Political Science Association).

30. Refugees forced out of their homeland frequently resist adaptation while awaiting their return. By contrast, economic migrants tend to try to adopt a new identity associated with the host country. However, with the passage of time, even the most dedicated exile communities begin to adopt immigrant-like characteristics such as in the case of the anti-Castro Cubans in the United States. Migrant communities are at times drawn into ethnonational existence abroad when they face difficulties in assimilating in their host societies or conversely when their full empowerment in the host country mobilizes them to intervene in the politics of the homeland. The reluctance to integrate may be also encouraged by religious obligations as in the case of certain orthodox followers of the Muslim faith. They cannot, in principle, integrate into a system that requires loyalty to a liberal democratic state.

31. Alexander DeConde, *Ethnicity, Race, and American Foreign Policy: A History* (Boston: Northeastern University Press, 1992), 88–91.

32. Dominique Aron Schnapper, "A Host Country of Immigrants that Does Not Know Itself," trans. L. Shirinian, *Diaspora* 1, no. 3 (1991); Rogers Brubaker, ed., *Immigration and the Politics of Citizenship in Europe and North America* (Langham, MD: University Press of America, 1992); Rogers Brubaker, *Citizenship and Nationality in France and Germany* (Cambridge, MA: Harvard University Press, 1992); Douglas Klusmeyer, "Aliens, Immigrants, and Citizens: The Politics of Inclusion in the Federal Republic of Germany," *Daedalus* 122, no. 3 (1993); Ekkart Zimmerman, "Xenophobic Movements in Contemporary Germany," in Yossi Shain and Aharon Klieman, eds., *Democracy: The Challenges Ahead* (London: Macmillan, 1995).

33. Will Kymlicka, *Multicultural Citizenship* (Oxford: Oxford University Press, 1995).

34. See www.auswaertiges-amt.de/www/en/willkommen/staatsangehoerigkeitsrecht/index_html (accessed February 15, 2007).

35. Weiner, "Labor Migrations," 55; Weiner, *Global Migration Crisis*, 207.

36. Kymlicka, *Multicultural Citizenship*, 182.

37. Guntram Werther, *Self-Determination in Western Democracies: Aboriginal Politics in a Comparative Perspective* (Westport: Greenwood, 1992), xvii.

38. "Minorities: That Other Europe," *Economist*, December 25, 1993.

39. Here I must distinguish between (1) an "irredentist" diaspora and (2) a "far-removed" diaspora. Though members of the first category reside outside the national state, they remain within the geographical confines of the homeland as defined by nationalists. In this sense they are not really a diaspora. Moreover, not all transborder communities consist of indigenous people, and, in fact, many are simply immigrants. Yet, even in the latter case, the sense of indigenousness may be developed and irredentist claims may ultimately form. For example, the Mexican-American population in the Southwest of the United States has been cited as a potential source of irredentist aspirations. See Morris Janowitz, *The Reconstruction of Patriotism: Education for Civic Consciousness* (Chicago: University of Chicago Press, 1983), 137.

40. In the early 1990s Latvia and Estonia disenfranchised many ethnic Russians by making fluency in their national languages and knowledge of Baltic history a requirement for citizenship. They also introduced residency requirements and made provisions barring former military and KGB officials from citizenship. See the *Chicago Tribune*, November 26, 1994. Also see Igor Zvelev, *Russia and Its New Diasporas* (Washington, DC: United States Institute of Peace, 2000), and Michael Mandelbaum, ed., *The New European Diasporas: National Minorities and Conflict in Eastern Europe* (New York: Council on Foreign Relations, 2000).

41. Alan Cowall, "War on Kurds Hurts Turks in U.S. Eyes," *New York Times*, November 17, 1994; Chris Hedges, "Turkey Offers Kurd Rebels Reform Plan," *New York Times*, March 16, 1995.

42. Arend Lijphart, *Democracy in Plural Societies: A Comparative Exploration* (New Haven: Yale University Press, 1977), 45.

43. Charles Taylor, "Politics of Recognition," in Amy Gutmann, ed., *Multiculturalism and "the Politics of Recognition"* (Princeton: Princeton University Press, 1992), 52.

44. Lord Acton, "Nationality," in *Freedom and Power* (Glencoe: Free Press, 1949), 185.

45. Michael Walzer, "Comment," in Gutmann, *Multiculturalism*, 101.

46. Ashutosh Varshney, "Contested Meanings: India's National Identity, Hindu Nationalism, and the Politics of Anxiety," *Daedalus* 122, no. 3 (1993): 236.

47. The fear of American disunity has received new theoretical backing in Samuel Huntington's recent thesis about the expanding dominance of "civilizations" in world affairs. Huntington has argued that the persistence of "kin-country" loyalties in the United States run much deeper than assimilationists are willing to admit, and has questioned whether the trend toward "the de-Westernization of the United States . . . means its de-Americanization in the democratic sense." Samuel Huntington, "If Not Civilizations, What? Paradigms of the Post–Cold War," *Foreign Affairs* 72 (1993), 189–90.

48. Shain, *Marketing the American Creed Abroad.*

49. Anatoly N. Yamskov, "Russian Diaspora: Political Implications," memo. However, if settler populations evolve demographically into a large minority (or even a majority) and become well-blended in cultural-linguistic terms with the

indigenous group—so that many of its members no longer even speak the language of their respective nationalities—regional identity, and not ethnicity, may emerge as the new basis for the seceding areas. Such newly established sovereign entities now constitute a community with a distinct version of culture whose members do not perceive themselves as part of a diaspora, even though the new state maintains strong connections with the state from which they secede.

50. Cited in Shain, *Frontiers of Loyalty*, 33.

51. Khachig Tololyan, "Exile Governments in the Armenian Polity," in Yossi Shain, ed., *Governments-in-Exile in Contemporary World Politics* (New York: Routledge, 1991).

52. Tololyan, "National Self-determination," 98.

53. Lind, *Next American Nation*, 355–57.

54. See, for example, Paula Franklin Lytle, "Electoral Transitions in Yugoslavia," in Yossi Shain and Juan Linz, eds., *Between States: Interim Governments and Democratic Transition* (New York: Cambridge University Press, 1995), 239.

55. Susan L. Woodward, "Diaspora, or the Dangers of Disunification? Putting the 'Serbian Model' into Perspective," in Mandelbaum, ed., *The New European Diasporas*, 161.

56. Daphne N. Winland, "'We Are Now an Actual Nation': The Impact of National Independence on the Croatian Diaspora in Canada," *Diaspora* 4, no. 1 (1995): 3–4.

57. Juan Linz, "State Building and Nation Building," *European Review* 1, no. 4 (1993): 2.

CHAPTER TWO

An earlier version of this chapter was published with Martin Sherman in *Nationalism and Ethnic Politics* (winter 2001).

1. Erich Gruen, *Diaspora: Jews amidst Greeks and Romans* (Cambridge, MA: Harvard University Press, 2002), 245.

2. Gruen, *Diaspora*, 246.

3. Moses Naim, "The New Diaspora," *Foreign Policy* (July–August 2002): 95–97.

4. Kalevi J. Holsti, *The State, War, and the State of War* (Cambridge: Cambridge University Press, 1996), 127.

5. Robert Jervis, "Realism in the Study of World Politics," *International Organization* 54, no. 2 (1998): 988.

6. Amy Dockers Marcus, "Burden of Peace: American Jews Grapple with an Identity Crisis as Peril to Israel Ebbs," *Wall Street Journal*, September 14, 1994; J. J. Goldberg, *Jewish Power: Inside the American Jewish Establishment* (Reading, MA: Addison Wesley, 1995), 359–62.

7. I adopt this term and the attendant abbreviation (IEIS) not only for reasons of notational brevity but also for reasons of substance. It conveys well the notion that I focus on: money flows *within* a given ethnic group but *between* segments thereof residing in different states.

8. Tom Gravin, *Nationalist Revolutionaries in Ireland, 1858–1928* (Oxford: Clarendon Press, 1987), 34.

9. Alexander Kitroeff, "Continuity and Change in Contemporary Greek His-

toriography," in M. Blinkhorn and T. Veremis, eds., *Modern Greece: Nationalism and Nationality* (Athens: Sage, 1990), 170–71. Nancy Foner, "What's New about Transnationalism? New York Immigrants Today and at the Turn of the Century," *Diaspora* 6, no. 3 (1997): 357.

10. Helena Z. Lopata, *Polish Americans: Status Composition in an Ethnic Community* (Englewood Cliffs, NJ: Prentice-Hall, 1976), 22–25.

11. Manuel Orozco, "Remittances and Markets: New Players and Practices" (Washington, DC: Inter-American Dialogue and the Tomas Rivera Policy Institute, 2000); Louis Desipio, "Sending Money Home . . . for Now: Remittances and Immigrant Adaptation in the United States" (Washington, DC: Inter-American Dialogue and the Tomas Rivera Policy Institute, 2000).

12. Peggy Levitt, "The Many Levels of Transnational Politics: Lessons from the Dominican Republic" (paper presented at the International Migration and Globalization of Domestic Politics workshop, Rutgers University, Newark, May 14–15, 1999).

13. Naim, "New Diaspora," 96.

14. See "The Longest Journey: A Survey of Migration," *Economist*, November 2, 2002, 11; Rama Lakshmi, "India Reaches Out to Emigrants," *Washington Post*, January 12, 2003, 21. Also see Amy Waldman, "India Harvests Fruits of Diaspora," *New York Times*, January 12, 2003, 1.

15. V. Lal, "The Politics of History on the Internet: Cyber-Diasporic Hinduism and the North American Hindu Diaspora," *Diaspora* 8, no. 2 (1999).

16. A. Chander, "Diaspora Bonds," *New York University Law Review* 76 (2001): 1064.

17. In the case of Eritrea, money is extracted from the diaspora community not only in a voluntary manner. About 95 percent of diasporic Eritreans took part in the 1993 Referendum for Independence. The diaspora was also closely involved with drafting and the ratification of the country's constitution and had formal representation in the Assembly of the Constitutional Committee, amounting to six members of a fifty-member assembly. See Nadie Al-Ali, Nadje, Richard Black, and Khalid Koser, "The Limits to 'Transnationalism': The Experience of Bosnian and Eritrean Refugees in Europe as Emerging Transnational Communities," *Ethnic and Racial Studies* 24, no. 4 (2001): 590 and *Economist*, "Diasporas: A World of Exiles," January 2, 2003.

18. Hong Liu, "Old Linkages, New Networks: The Globalization of Overseas Chinese Voluntary Associations and Its Implications," *China Quarterly* 155 (1998): 594; Gary G. Hamilton, "Overseas Chinese Capitalism," in Tu Wei-Meng, ed., *Confucian Traditions in East Asian Modernity: Moral Education and Economic Culture in Japan and the Four Mini Dragons* (Cambridge: Harvard University Press, 1996).

19. Rey Koslowski, ed., *International Migration and the Globalization of Domestic Politics* (New York: Routledge, 2005).

20. W. Stanley, "Blessing or Menace? The Security Implications of Central American Migration," in Myron Weiner, ed., *International Migration and Security* (Boulder: Westview, 1993), 231.

21. Robert W. Franco, "Review Essay," *Contemporary Pacific* 6, no. 1 (1994). Bernard Poirine, "Should We Hate or Love MIRAB," *Contemporary Pacific* 10, no. 1 (1998): 65–105, at 66–67.

22. This attention to detail in articulating the logical link between the specification of the concept of nation is not mere semantic gymnastics but an essential methodological clarification in a field where surrender to methodological sloth

has become almost a sanctified principle. Indeed because of the alleged "complexity" of the subject matter, scholars contend that matters relating to nationalism "def[y] exact definition . . . [and] have many facets which stand in the way of rigorous and complete analysis," and argue that "the scientific form of inquiry may be inappropriate." A. Philips, "European Nationalism in the Nineteenth and Twentieth Centuries," in R. Mitchison, ed., *Roots of Nationalism* (Edinburgh: John Donald, 1980), 1–4. Apart from the fact that this "unscientific" approach appears to have the ring of intellectual surrender, it leaves open the question of precisely what form of *unscientific* inquiry would in fact be appropriate. It is thus little wonder that Israel Zangwill deemed issues related to nationalism to be "one of those tropical jungles of thought in which [the dangerous and imprecise colloquialisms] of politics and journalism flourish." Quoted in L. L. Snyder, *The Meaning of Nationalism* (New Brunswick: Rutgers University Press, 1954), 5.

23. John Stuart Mill, "Considerations on Representative Government" (1861), in R. B. McCallum, ed., *On Liberty and Considerations on Representative Government* (Oxford: Basil Blackwell, 1946), 291.

24. The former embodies the idea of a nation characterized by monolithic (sociocultural) uniformity; the latter, the idea of a nation characterized by harmonious (sociocultural) diversity, bonded by a common *political* allegiance. See Lord Acton, "Nationality," in *Essays in Freedom and Power* (Boston: Beacon, 1949), 183–85.

25. According to the former, the nation is seen as an organic division of humanity, decreed by some divine or natural edict, and the ties that bind the nation and determine the political allegiance of its members are objectively discernible attributes such as ethnoracial, cultural, or linguistic traits. According to the latter perception, the idea of nation denotes "a number of individuals who have signified their will as to the manner of their government." This view, which emphasizes the exercise of human volition as a generating force of nations, is underscored in the works of Mazzini where the binding force of a nation "does not depend upon race or descent, but upon common thought and a common goal." See Hans Kohn, *Prophets and Peoples: Studies in Nineteenth Century Nationalism* (New York: Colliers, 1961), 89.

26. Clifford Geertz, *Islam Observed: Religious Development in Morocco and Indonesia* (New Haven: Yale University Press, 1968); Yael Tamir, *Liberal Nationalism* (Princeton: Princeton University Press, 1993); Rogers Brubaker, *Citizenship and Nationhood in France and Germany* (Cambridge: Harvard University Press, 1992); John Hutchinson and Anthony D. Smith, eds., *Nationalism* (New York: Oxford University Press, 1994).

27. Although it is true that in many respects this division parallels that of the more familiar distinction between ethnic and civic nations, it does however deviate from it in two substantively important aspects. First, the *ideofocal* term is more inclusive than the *civic* one. For while the latter is almost universally associated with multiethnic-libertarian connotations, the former is intended to incorporate multiethnic-authoritarian contexts as well, in which the use of the term *civic* would be at best misleading if not entirely misplaced. By contrast, the term *ideofocal* focuses on the allegedly unifying ideal (such as Soviet communism) rather than the rights exercised by those allegedly unified by it. Second, and more important for the purposes of this study, while the ethnic/civic distinction focuses more on the *end results*

of political process (the kind of states and/or nations that reflect the *culmination* of a process of nation building), our terminology places greater emphasis on the *causal origins* of political process (the nature of the nuclei around which national collectivities coalesce and that seed the nation-building process). It is thus better suited for an analysis of effects on the causal determinants of national identities, induced by factors such as financial flows to and from home and host countries, which make up the central focus of this investigation.

28. Weiner, *International Migration and Security*, 126; Arthur W. Helweg, "India's Sikhs: Problems and Prospects," *Journal of Contemporary Asia* 17, no. 2 (1987), 140–59; Heather Horst, "Indians Imagine the Indian Diaspora: The Dialectic between National and Transnational," manuscript, UCSB Anthropology Lecture Series, October 15, 1997.

29. Robert Dahl, *Democracy and Its Critics* (New Haven: Yale University Press, 1989).

30. David Rieff, "From Exiles to Immigrants: The Miami Cubans Come Home," *Foreign Affairs* 74, no. 4 (1995); Lucia Newman, "The Posturing and Potential of the Latest U.S. Changes in Cuba," January 15, 1999, http://cnn.com/SPE CIALS/views/y/1999/01/newman.cuba.jan15 (accessed February 15, 2007).

31. Steven Krasner, *Sovereignty: Organized Hypocrisy* (Princeton: Princeton University Press, 1999), 5.

32. Gil Merom, "Israel National Security and the Myth of Exceptionalism," *Political Science Quarterly* 114 (1999): 411–12.

33. Martin Buber, *On Judaism* (New York: Schocken, 1967), 249–52.

34. Yossi Shain, *Marketing the American Creed Abroad: Diasporas in the U.S. and Their Homelands* (Cambridge: Cambridge University Press, 1999), 113. According to some sources, up to half of the Hamas Islamic organization's budget of about $40 million was financed by Palestinian diasporic sources in Europe and the United States. The money was collected via charitable organizations and religious institutions and was recognized in the United States as qualifying for tax exemptions. See Shaul Mishal and Avraham Sela, *The Hamas Wind: Violence and Coexistence* (Tel Aviv: Yedioth Ahronoth, 1999), 127 (in Hebrew).

35. Susan Woodward, "Diaspora, or the Dangers of Disunification? Putting the 'Serbian Model' into Perspective," in Michael Mandelbaum, ed., *The New European Diasporas: National Minorities and Conflict in Eastern Europe* (New York: Council of Foreign Relations, 2000), 162–63.

36. For example, when in March 1998 the Kosovo Liberation Army (KLA) began its armed campaign against Milošević, the rebels appealed to their kin diasporas in the United States for financial support. As NATO bombing commenced and the misery of the Albanian population in the region intensified, Albanian-Americans united in a show of force and donated considerable sums of money to the guerrilla forces. Subsequently, hundreds of young Albanian-Americans, driven by sentiments of kindred allegiance, left the United States and enlisted to fight alongside their ethnic brethren in the ranks of the KLA (*International Herald Tribune*, April 13, 1999).

37. Melvin Urofsky, *We Are One: American Jewry and Israel* (New York: Anchor Press, 1978), 150–78.

38. Mishal and Sela, *Hamas Wind*.

39. Golda Meir, *My Life* (Jerusalem: Steimatzky, 1975), 206.

40. Razmik Panossian, "Between Ambivalence and Intrusion: Politics and Identity in Armenia-Diaspora Relations," *Diaspora* 7, no. 2 (1998): 175.

41. R. Hrair Dekmejian and Angelos Themelis, "Ethnic Lobbies in U.S. Foreign Policy," Occasional Research Paper 13 (Athens: Institute of International Relations, 1997), 31; Levon A. Abrahamian, "Armenian Homeland and Diaspora: Divergence and Encounter" (paper presented at the conference Diasporas: Transnational Identity and the Politics of Homeland, University of California, Berkeley, November 11–14, 1999).

42. Khachig Tololyan writes, "No overview of the Diaspora's influence on the NKR [Nagorno-Karabakh] conflict, whether directed or mediated through Armenia, can neglect the economic dimension. First, the two Armenian lobbies in Washington have been crucial in securing for Armenia over $1 billion since 1991 in U.S. aid. A small part of that would have gone to Armenia without such lobbying, but not most of it. That averages to about $86.5 million a year for a government whose budget sank to less than $200 million at its nadir (the 2003 budget was $574 million in expenditures and $493 million in revenues). In 2003, Armenia's GDP was $2.7 billion. NKR's was $62 million and growing at close to 20% a year. Estimates for remittances to Armenia from Armenians working abroad, primarily in Russia, are between $200 and $300 million in 2003. Analogous figures are not available for NKR, but likely to be in comparable proportions. Tourism by some 200,000 tourists (most Armenians, either post-1988 emigrants returning for a visit, many others members of the older diaspora) contributed an estimated $120 million to GDP. Philanthropic organizations like the Hayastan Fund, the AGBU, the United Armenian Fund and the Armenian Relief Society have also contributed millions, though here the figures are less reliable because much of the assistance came in the form of goods, from aging kidney dialysis machines to computers to clothes and medications. In these various ways, the old and new diasporas together contribute a significant percentage of Armenia's and NKR's GDP. These sums are of material significance. They raise morale and the will to resist a settlement of the Karabakh issue regarded as unfavorable. And that difference in morale has been a major factor throughout the conflict. Not surprisingly, Azerbaijan's leadership has taken steps to promote the organization of its own dispersed emigrant populations into diasporas." See "The Armenian Diaspora and the Karabagh Conflict, from 1988 to the Future," in Hazel Smith and Paul Stares, eds., *Diasporas in Conflict: Peacemakers or Peace Wreckers?* (United Nations University Press, 2007), 122.

43. Alfred C. Stepan, *Rethinking Military Politics: Brazil and the Southern Cone* (Princeton: Princeton University Press, 1988), 4.

44. Madeleine Nash, "From Polonia with Love," *Time*, November 27, 1989, 22–23. The transfer of $150 million by Polish Americans to Polish nonstate organizations in the 1980s is a good case in point.

45. In 1989, Israel transferred $3.2 million to Romania in return for exit permits for Jews, in addition to the hundreds of millions paid out in previous decades. *Ha'aretz* (English), May 29, 1998.

46. Seymor M. Lipset and Earl Raab, *Jews and the New American Scene* (Cambridge, MA: Harvard University Press, 1995), 113.

47. Baruch Kimmerling, "Between Hegemony and Dormant Kulturkampf in Israel," in Dan Urian and Efraim Karsh, eds., *In Search of Identity: Jewish Aspects of Israeli Identity* (London and Portland, OR: Frank Cass, 1999).

48. David Schoenbaum, *The United States and the State of Israel* (Oxford: Oxford University Press, 1993), 63.

49. Arthur Hertzberg, "Israel and the Diaspora: A Relationship Reexamined," *Israel Affairs* 2, no. 3–4 (1996): 172.

50. Schoenbaum, *United States.*

51. See the remarks of Rabbi Morris Kertzer, cited in Samuel Heilman, *Portrait of American Jews: The Last Half of the Twentieth Century* (Seattle: University of Washington Press, 1998), 17.

52. Menahem Kaufman, "Envisaging Israel: The Case of the United Jewish Appeal," in Allon Gal, ed., *Envisioning Israel: The Changing Ideals and Images of North American Jews* (Jerusalem: Magnes Press, 1996), 224.

53. http://www.israelbonds.com/aboutus.html (accessed February 15, 2007).

54. Schoenbaum, *United States*, 65.

55. Marshall Sklare, *America's Jews* (New York: Random House, 1971), 216.

56. Max Beloff, "The Diaspora and the Peace Process," *Israel Affairs* 1, no. 1 (1994): 33.

57. Kaufman, "Envisaging Israel," 222; Goldberg, *Jewish Power*, 359.

58. Andrew Furman, *Israel through the Jewish-American Imagination: A Survey of Jewish-American Literature on Israel, 1928–1995* (Albany: State University of New York, 1997); Jonathan Broder, "Netanyahu and the American Jews," *World Policy Journal* 15, no. 1 (1998).

59. *The New Israel: Mosaic of Identities*, New Israel Fund, Annual Report, 1998.

60. Broder, "Netanyahu and the American Jews," 95; Avraham Ben Zvi, *Partnership Under Stress: The American Jewish Community and Israel* (Tel Aviv: Jaffe Center for Strategic Studies, 1998), 36–37; Reed Abelson, "Seeking Unity in Jewish Giving," *New York Times*, August 9, 1998, section 3, 1, 10.

61. *International Herald Tribune*, October 10, 1997.

62. Jack Wertheimer, "Politics and Jewish Giving," *Commentary* (December 1997): 35.

63. *The Forward*, September 17, 1999; *Jerusalem Post*, November 21, 1999.

64. *Ha'aretz*, November 17, 1999.

65. http://www.best.com/~ray673/search/database/is39.9.html; http://www.detnews.com/1997/nation/9709/18/09180110.htm.

66. Shain, *Marketing the American Creed Abroad*, 171.

67. *Ha'aretz*, January 28, 2000; *Washington Post*, January 31, 2000.

68. Nir Boms, "Redefining Israel: The Changing American Jewish Community Perception of Israel as Indicated by Changes in Jewish American Philanthropy" (master's thesis, Baltimore Hebrew University, May 2001).

69. See "The Role and Contributions of NGO's that Educate for Judaism as Culture in the General School System of Israel and the Secular Arena" (draft paper by PANIM for Jewish Renaissance in Israel written by Uzi Arad and Meir Yoffe, January 2003).

70. See the survey conducted by Steven Cohen in "The More Jewish the More Vulnerable," *Ha'aretz*, February 2, 2003.

71. *Jerusalem Post*, June 27, 2002; *Ha'aretz*, August 27, 2002.

72. Ronald L. Jepperson, Alexander Wendt, and Peter Katzenstein, "Norms, Identity, and Culture in National Security," in Katzenstein, ed., *The Culture of National Security: Norms and Identity in World Politics* (New York: Columbia University Press, 1966), 60.

73. Jeffrey T. Checkel, "The Constructivist Turn in International Relations Theory," *World Politics* 50, no. 2 (1998): 325.

CHAPTER THREE

1. Robin Cohen, *Global Diasporas: An Introduction* (London: UCL Press, 1997); Gabriel Sheffer, ed., *Modern Diasporas in International Politics* (London: Croom Helm, 1986); Thomas Sowell, *Migrations and Cultures: A World View* (New York: Basic Books, 1996); Charles King and Neil Melvin, *Nations Abroad: Diaspora Politics and International Relations in the Former Soviet Union* (Boulder: Westview, 1998).

2. Cited in Aryeh Gershoni, "The United States Jews and the Disengagement from Gaza" (paper, Tel Aviv University, October 1, 2005).

3. See Prema Kurien, "Opposing Construction and Agendas: The Politics of Hindu and Muslim Indian-American Organizations," in Rey Koslowski, ed., *International Migration and the Globalization of Domestic Politics* (New York: Routledge, 2005), 161.

4. Naftali Rothenberg, "Jews in Israel and the United States: Diverging Identities," in Ernest Krausz and Gitta Tulea, eds., *Jewish Survival: The Identity Problem at the Close of the Twentieth Century* (New Brunswick, NJ: Transaction, 1999), 166–67. See also Steven T. Rosenthal, *Irreconcilable Differences? The Waning of the American Jewish Love Affair with Israel* (Hanover, NH: Brandeis University Press, 2001). On August 17, 2004, Moshe Katzav, Israel's president, wrote in the *Jerusalem Post*, "I cannot feel complacent when the majority of the Jewish people still does not reside here, and when the majority of the Jewish people abroad do not provide their children with Jewish education and are becoming detached from their Jewish roots. In Israel too there is a similar phenomenon: It is a fact that students who grow up here and have graduated from the public school system are not sufficiently knowledgeable about the basics of Judaism."

5. Jerome A. Chanes, "Who Does What? Jewish Advocacy and Jewish 'Interest,'" in L. Sandy Maisel and Ira N. Forman, eds., *Jews in American Politics* (New York: Rowman and Littlefield, 2001), 101.

6. Studies by Yochanan Peres and Epharim Yuchtman-Yaar present the following categories of Israeli Jews according to their self-definition: 10 percent *haredim* (ultra-Orthodox), 10 percent religious, 29 percent traditional, and 51 percent secular. These studies also reveal that 23 percent of the Jewish-Israeli public worship in synagogues on a daily basis, and 26 percent do not drive a car on the Jewish Sabbath. See *Between Consent and Dissent: Democracy and Peace in the Israeli Mind* (Jerusalem: The Israel Democracy Institute, 1998), 162–63. According to Asher Arian, "About a quarter of Israeli Jews are observant in an Orthodox sense or even beyond that, including 6 to 10 percent haredi, or ultra-Orthodox, [while] about 40 percent are determinedly secular." See *The Second Republic: Politics in Israel* (Chatham, NJ: Chatham House, 1998), 10.

7. For an excellent analysis of the dynamics of the ultra-Orthodox economy, see Eli Berman, "Sect, Subsidy, and Sacrifice: An Economist's View of Ultra-Orthodox Jews" (paper, Boston University, National Bureau of Economic Research, March 1999).

8. See Ari Shavit, "A Jewish Soul," *Haaretz Magazine*, February 13, 2004.

9. Arian, *Second Republic*, 3.

10. Rabin was assassinated in November 1995 by Yigal Amir, a young Israeli religious nationalist student who was influenced by Rabinic authorities of his camp (in Israel and the United States) that articulated the view that by agreeing to relinquish segments of the Holy Land to Gentiles Rabin was deemed "rodef" and "moser;" two obscure Halachic precepts that made the prime minister liable to be killed. See Milton Viorst, *What Shall I Do with This People: Jews and the Fractious Politics of Judaism* (New York: Free Press, 2002), 239–42, and Martin Kramer, "The Middle East, Old and New," *Daedalus* (spring 1997): 94.

11. *Ha'aretz*, June 26, 2000.

12. *Ha'aretz*, October 5, 2000.

13. For a discussion of these early efforts see Zalman Abramov, *Perpetual Dilemma: Jewish Religion in the Jewish State* (Cranbury, NJ: Associated University Press, 1976), 375–76.

14. Abramov, *Perpetual Dilemma*, 206.

15. This view is echoed in the work of Yair Sheleg, an Israel journalist on religious affairs who recently observed that "while the demographic, financial, and spiritual center of gravity of non-Orthodox movements is in the United States, Israel is the world center for almost every Orthodox group. See "The North American Impact on Israel Orthodoxy," American Jewish Committee, New York, 1999, 6.

16. Alan Dershowitz put forward the "Jewish Question" for the twenty-first century as "Can we survive our success?" He writes, "The good news is the American Jews—as *individuals*—have never been more secure, more affluent, and less victimized by discrimination or anti-Semitism. The bad news is that American Jews—as a *people*—have never been in greater danger of disappearing through assimilation, intermarriage, and low birth rates." See Alan M. Dershowitz, *The Vanishing American Jew: In Search of Jewish Identity for the Next Century* (Boston: Little, Brown, 1997), 1.

17. For the debate over the study of Jewish-American demography and the different interpretations of population surveys, see Bernard Wasserstein, "Post-Diaspora Jewry and Post-Zionist Israel" (paper presented at the International Conference on Diasporas: Transnational Identities and the Politics of the Homeland, University of California, Berkeley, November 12–13, 1999).

18. Egon Mayer, Barry Kosmin, and Ariela Keysar, "American Jewish Identity Survey 2001," published by the Graduate Center of the City University of New York, February 2002.

19. Sidney Goldstein, "Profile of American Jewry: Insights from the 1990 National Jewish Population Survey," in David Singer and Ruth R. Seldin, eds., *American Jewish Year Book 1992*, vol. 92 (New York: American Jewish Committee, 1992), 12–132.

20. Interview with Rabbi Ammiel Hirsh, December 29, 1999.

21. David Abel, "Jews Find New Meaning in Ritual," *Boston Globe*, December 5, 2001, B1.

22. Cited in Jonathan D. Sarna, *American Judaism: A History* (New Haven: Yale University Press, 2004), 326.

23. See Ori Z. Soltes, "Memory, Tradition, and Revival: Mapping and Identi-

fying the Political Structure of the Jewish Community Worldwide," in "Occasional Papers on Jewish Civilization Israel and the Diaspora" (Program for Jewish Civilization, Georgetown University, summer 2005), 14.

24. The term is borrowed from Robert Wuthnow.

25. See Avi Beker, "A Different Model of a Jew," *Ha'aretz* (Hebrew), August 14, 2000, B2.

26. Conor Cruise O'Brien, *God Land: Reflections on Religion and Nationalism* (Cambridge, MA: Harvard University Press, 1987), 3.

27. "Jewish Sovereignty as a Theological Problem," *Azure* 16 (winter 2004), 123–24.

28. See Bernard Wasserstein, "The Politics of Holiness in Jerusalem," *Chronicle Review*, September 21, 2001 (section 2 of *The Chronicle of Higher Education*).

29. Rabbi Joseph B. Soloveitchik, *Fate and Destiny: From the Holocaust to the State of Israel* (Hoboken, NJ: Ktav Publishing House, 2000).

30. Two political scientists at Bar Ilan University argued recently that the notion of Israel being "the first flowering of our redemption"—a term used in the in the Prayer for the State and recited on Shabbat as part of the regular service—"is essentially a symbolic ritual messianism that does not impact on quotidian life and on general and political behavior patterns" of the "silent majority" of religious Zionists. And yet, this messianic approach is the most vocal among religious Zionist leaders and their radicalized followers. See Asher Cohen and Stuart Cohen, "Tarred with the Brush of Extremism: In the Public and Academic Discourse, All Religious Zionists Are Branded as Deviants—Despite the Facts," *Haaretz*, November 30, 2005, 8.

31. While fewer than 10 percent of American Jews are Orthodox they comprise over 80 percent of American immigrants. Yair Sheleg, "The North American Impact on Israel Orthodoxy," *The Forward* (October 1999).

32. See "American Jewish Attitudes towards Israel and the Peace Process," a public opinion survey conducted for the American Jewish Committee by Market Facts, Inc., August 7–15, 1995, 63.

33. As early as 1885, the blueprint of American Reform Judaism declared, "We consider ourselves no longer a nation, but a religious community, and, therefore, expect neither a return to Palestine . . . nor the restoration of the laws concerning the Jewish state." See "Reform Judaism and Zionism: A Centenary Platform," *CCAR Journal* (spring 1998): 10.

34. See statement by the Central Conference of American Rabbis, May 1999. For the opinions of the two leading shapers of the political ideology of the Reform movement on this issue, see Albert Vorspan and David Saperstein, *Jewish Dimensions of Social Justice: Tough Moral Choices of Our Time* (New York: UAHC Press, 1998), 137.

35. *Electronic Newsletter of the World Union for Progressive Judaism* (*WUPJ News*) 9, no. 11 (March 1999).

36. See Harvey Meirovich, "The Shaping of the Masorti Movement in Israel," American Jewish Committee, New York, January 1999, 6.

37. Asher Arian, *Politics in Israel: The Second Generation* (Chatham, NJ: Chatham House, 1985), 5.

38. For the best book on the subject, see Charles S. Liebman and Eliezer Don-Yehiya, *Civil Religion in Israel* (Berkeley: University of California Press), 1983. For

an analysis of how the civil religion helped in creating Israel's perceived sense of "exceptionalism," and the implications of this collective identity for the foundation of Israel's national security, see Gil Merom, "Israel's National Security and the Myth of Exceptionalism," *Political Science Quarterly* 114, no. 3 (fall 1999): 409–93.

39. Baruch Kimmerling, "Between Hegemony and Dormant *Kulturkampf* in Israel," in Dan Urian and Efraim Karsh, eds., *In Search of Identity: Jewish Aspects of Israeli Culture* (London: Frank Cass, 1999), 49–72.

40. Peter Berkowitz, "A Dramatic Struggle over Self-Definition," *Wall Street Journal*, June 1, 2000, A20.

41. See Yoav Peled, "Towards a Redefinition of Jewish Nationalism in Israel? The Enigma of Shas," *Ethnic and Racial Studies* 21, no. 4 (July 1998): 703.

42. Studies by Arye Ratner show that the main cleavage among Jews in Israel today is between the secular and the religious camps. These studies also indicate a growing affinity between religious Zionists and the haredi community. While religious Zionists are gradually adopting more conservative religious practices, the haredi camp is taking hard-line and ultranationalist positions on matters of peace and war with the Palestinians, and adopt the posture of religious Zionists in the settler community regarding the sanctity of the occupied territories. Altogether, Ratner points out, there is a growing tendency within the Israeli religious community to delegitimate Israel's legal system in favor of religious dogmas in a process that endangers the Israeli *Rechtsstaat*. See Arye Dayan, "Goodbye Old Cleavage, Hello New One," *Ha'aretz* (Hebrew), July 30, 2000, B 3.

43. Bernard Susser and Charles S. Liebman, *Choosing Survival: Strategies for a Jewish Future* (Oxford: Oxford University Press, 1999), 94.

44. Cited in Avi Beker, "Introduction: The Jewish Identity," http://www.wzo.org.il/encounter/ identity/htm.

45. Yoram Hazony, *The Jewish State: The Struggle for Israel's Soul* (New York: Basic Books, 2000).

46. See Jeffrey Smith, "'A War Over Culture': Israel's Shas Party Treads Traditional, Politically Powerful Path," *Washington Post*, May 3, 2000.

47. Am Ve'olam: "Nation and World: Jewish Culture in a Changing World," Recommendations of the Committee for Investigation into Judaic Studies in State Education. Israeli Ministry of Education 1994. Yosef Dan, a leading Israeli scholar of Judaic studies, has argued that the hostility of many Israelis toward religious politics has led them to abandon Judaism altogether, thereby downgrading the validity of Jewish pluralism and Jewish cultural aspects, and unintentionally legitimating the ultraorthodox religious hegemony. This process has contributed to the decline of Judaic scholarship inside Israel, while in the West, Judaic studies have flourished under the new creed of diversity and multiculturalism. Yosef Dan, "Empty Hands," *Free Judaism* (Hebrew) 11–12 (October 1997): 9.

48. The platform stated, "Extortion and exploitation of the public treasury for religious purposes have to end. The ultra-Orthodox establishment is a threat to the orderly administration of a free society and to the individual freedom that characterizes a democratic state. Attempts to turn Israel into a state based on Halacha (Jewish religious law) endanger our future. We seek to separate state and religion, while preserving the country's Zionist character."

49. See David Arnow, "Barak's Mandate," *Forward* (New York), July 2, 1999.

50. A 1993 study by the Louis Guttman Israel Institute of Applied Social

Research maintains that "Israeli society has a strong traditional bent, and, as far as religious practices are concerned there is a continuum from the 'strictly observant' to the 'nonobservant.'" Shlomit Levy, Hanna Levinson, and Elihu Katz, "Beliefs, Observances, and Social Interactions among Israeli Jews," the Louis Guttman Israel Institute of Applied Social Research, Jerusalem, December 1993, 2. Arian writes that "in 1996, the overwhelming majority of Jews identified themselves as 'Jewish' and 'Israeli.' Respondents were given four identities to rank: Jewish, Israeli, their ethnic classification (Ashkenazi or Sepharadi), or religion (observant or secular). . . . More than 40 percent of the respondents chose each of 'Jewish' and 'Israeli' as both first and second choice. Ethnic and religious observance identities were left far behind." Asher Arian, *The Second Republic: Politics in Israel*, 7.

51. Charles Liebman, "Comment" on Yossi Klein Halevi's essay, in "Jewish Identities in Post-Rabin Israel." Publication of Institute on American Jewish Israeli Relations, July 1998, 23.

52. Daniel J. Elazar and Shmuel Sandler, "Introduction: The Battle over Jewishness and Zionism in the Post-Modern Era," *Israel Affairs* 4, no. 1 (autumn 1997): 17.

53. Moshe Shokeid has found a great degree of similarity between the synagogue practices of Mizrahim in Israel and the religious practices of Conservative American Jews. "Like the Mizrahim in Israel, Jewish-Americans developed a social infrastructure of a communal-family migratory base that unified and preserved the Jewish-American synagogue communities for many decades." Moshe Shokeid and Shlomo Deshen, *The Generation of Transition: Community and Change among North African Immigrants in Israel* (Jerusalem: Yad Izhak Ben-Zvi, 1999), 243–44 (translated by the author from Hebrew).

54. See Yair Sheleg, "Russian Jews Choosing Reform Judaism," *Ha'aretz*, December 21, 1999; Haim Shapiro, "Melchior Unveils Plan to Convert Immigrant Children," *Jerusalem Post*, December 21, 1999.

55. For an analysis of the media campaigns of the movements, see Michal Schwartzman, "The Media Campaign of the Reform and Conservative Movements in Israel" (paper, Tel Aviv University, 1997).

56. See Elan Ezrachi, "Jewish Renaissance and Renewal in Israel: A Report of the Dorot and Nathan Cummings Foundation," January 2001, 18.

57. See the statement by Samuel H. Sislen, executive director of the Masorti Foundation for Conservative Judaism in Israel, in "Strengthening Israel, Strengthening Conservative Judaism," *Women's League Outlook* (fall 1999).

58. See Ellen Schnitser, "The Impact of American Liberal Jewish Identity in Israel: The Case Study of Russian Speaking Immigrants" (paper, Tel Aviv University, April 2003).

59. In November 1999, activists of the General Assembly of America's Jewry met in Atlanta and moved to establish a single umbrella organization, the United Jewish Communities (UJC). In what was described by one Israeli journalist as "more than a bureaucratic upheaval," the new body took aim at redirecting funds to bolster Jewish identity in a process that empowers U.S.-based local federations and gives them greater say over spending in Israel. The new body unified all Jewish communities across America—through a merger of the UJA, the United Israel Appeal (UIA), and the Council of Jewish Federations (CJF). See Nitzan Horowitz, "Historic Assembly to Be a Melting Pot, as U.S. Jewish Organizations Merge,"

Ha'aretz, November 17, 1999; Marilyn Henry, "GA Ends with United Body, Divisive Issues," *Jerusalem Post*, November 21, 1999.

60. See Nir Boms, "Redefining Israel: The Changing American-Jewish Community of Israel as Indicated by Changes in Jewish-American Philanthropy" (master's thesis, University of Maryland, Baltimore Hebrew University, 2000), 98.

61. Yossi Shalom and Shahar Ilan, "Chief Rabbi: Holocaust Pales Next to Reform," *Ha'aretz*, January 26, 1999, 1.

62. Jack Wertheimer, "Judaism Without Limits," *Commentary* (July 1997): 24.

63. With the rise of intermarriages among Jews in the United States, American Reform rabbis have eased the difficult process of Jewish conversion in order to enable tens of thousands of American gentiles to become Jewish. The Orthodox do not recognize these conversions and regard Reform and Conservative converts as non-Jews. J. J. Goldberg, *Jewish Power: Inside the American Jewish Establishment* (Reading, MA: Addison-Wesley, 1996), 338.

64. According to J. J. Goldberg, the Lubavitcher Rebbe "had built a powerful trans-Atlantic political machine to press his view on a reluctant Israeli Orthodox political establishment. They in turn, had pressured [Prime Minister] Shamir." *Jewish Power*, 338.

65. David Landau, "Who Is a Jew? A Case Study of American Jewish Influence on Israeli Policy," American Jewish Committee, 1996, 10–11.

66. While the vast majority of Israeli Orthodox and ultra-Orthodox (about 80 percent) reject the idea of a Palestinian state in the occupied territories, a large majority of "non-observant" (75 percent) or "somewhat-observant" (62 percent) Israeli Jews support such an outcome as part of a permanent agreement. These divisions resemble those within the diaspora. See Asher Arian, "Israeli Public Opinion on National Security," Jaffe Center for Strategic Studies (JCSS) Memorandum no. 53, August 1999, 46.

67. Abraham Ben Zvi, "Partnership under Stress: The American Jewish Community and Israel," Jaffe Center for Strategic Studies, August 1998, 35.

68. For the statement see Shahar Ilan, "Progressive Jews: 'What Synagogue Are We Not Going To?" *Ha'aretz* (English), February 21, 1999, 6.

69. Cited in Rabbi G. Hirsch's keynote address, published in the Electronic Newsletter of the World Union for Progressive Judaism, Special Convention Issue, March 11, 1999, 5. The writers were attacked vehemently by secular Israelis who argued that by endorsing Reform and Conservative Judaism and by calling on Israelis to join these movements, they were undermining the vision of a secular-humanistic Jewish-Israeli movement. For A. B. Yehoshua's response to these charges, see *Free Judaism* (Hebrew) 14 (April 1999): 38.

70. "What Do American Jews Believe?" *Commentary*, August 1996, 30.

71. Yossi Klein Halevi has articulated a vision of how Israel should develop a new, indigenous Judaism that builds on American diasporic innovation. See his essay "Jewish Identities in Post-Rabin Israel" (Institute on American Jewish Israeli Relations, Jerusalem, July 1998).

72. Cited in the periodical report of the Minister of Diaspora and Social Affairs, Jerusalem, February 20, 2000.

73. Cited in "Making Meaning: Participants' Experience of Birthright Israel," a publication of the Maurice and Marilyn Cohen Center for Modern Jewish Studies, Brandeis University, November 2000, 1.

74. Ezra Mendelsohn, *On Modern Jewish Politics* (New York: Oxford University Press, 1993), 79, 133.

75. Jewish-Americans organized large rallies on behalf of the new state, pleaded with the Truman government to recognize and stand behind it, and raised tens of million of dollars for arms procurement in support of its 1948 war efforts. See David Schoenbaum, *The United States and the State of Israel* (Oxford: Oxford University Press, 1993), 58–62. For a discussion of the Jewish-American role in President Truman's decision to accord recognition to the State of Israel, see Alexander DeConde, *Ethnicity, Race, and American Foreign Policy: A History* (Boston: Northeastern University Press, 1992), 131–36.

76. Schoenbaum, *United States*, 64.

77. Arthur Hertzberg, "Israel and the Diaspora: A Relationship Reexamined," *Israel Affairs* 2, no. 3–4 (spring–summer 1996): 172.

78. Abraham Ben Zvi, *Decade of Transition: Eisenhower, Kennedy, and the Origins of the American-Israeli Alliance* (New York: Columbia University Press, 1998), 56–57, 96.

79. See "Jewish-Americans Beyond the Pale," *Economist*, November 2, 1991, 29.

80. Jonathan D. Sarna and David G. Dalin, *Religion and State in the American Jewish Experience* (Notre Dame: University of Notre Dame Press, 1997), 246.

81. Heilman, *Portrait of American Jews: The Last Half of the Twentieth Century* (Seattle: University of Washington Press, 1995), 146.

82. Sarna and Dalin, *Religion and State*, 262.

83. Paul Breines, "Deliver Us from Evil," *Washington Post Book World*, February 4, 2001, 13. For a critical treatment of such Holocaust-related dynamics, see Peter Novick, *The Holocaust in American Life* (New York: Houghton Mifflin, 1999).

84. Menahem Kaufman, "Envisaging Israel: The Case of the United Jewish Appeal," in Allon Gal, ed., *Envisioning Israel: The Changing Ideals and Images of North American Jews* (Jerusalem: Magnes Press, 1996), 222.

85. Paul Berman has written that "it was sometimes believed that Palestinian skin tone was darker than that of the Israeli Jews, as if in pigmental confirmation of the proposed new link between Palestinians and African-Americans." Paul Berman, "The Other and Almost the Same," *New Yorker*, February 28, 1994, 68.

86. The Reform leader Albert Vorspan wrote that the UN's decision "made all Jews consider themselves Zionists." See Albert Vorspan, *Great Jewish Debates and Dilemmas: Jewish Perspectives on Moral Issues in Conflict in the Eighties* (New York: Union of American Hebrew Congregations, 1980), 19.

87. Charles S. Liebman, "Israel in the Mind of American Jews," in Eliezer Don-Yehiya, ed., *Israel and Diaspora Jewry: Ideological and Political Perspectives* (Jerusalem: Bar-Ilan University Press, 1991), 34.

88. According to one source, by the late 1980s, Israeli ties with South Africa had become the "most divisive issue in Black-Jewish relations" in the United States. See Yvonne D. Newsome, "International Issues and Domestic Ethnic Relations: African Americans, American Jews, and the Israel—South Africa Debate," *International Journal of Politics, Culture, and Society* 5, no. 1 (1991): 39.

89. For an extensive treatment of the widening gulf between Israeli and American Jews since the 1980s, see Steve T. Rosenthal, *Irreconcilable Differences? The Waning of the American Jewish Love Affair with Israel* (Hanover, NH: Brandeis University Press, 2001).

90. By that time a web of over seventy pro-Israel political action committees had been established that channeled $4.7million to pro-Israel candidates during the 1987–88 election cycle. See Eisenstat, "Loving Israel," 93.

91. Aaron S. Klieman, *Israel and the World after Forty Years* (Washington, DC: Pergamon-Brassey's, 1990), 178.

92. David Vital, *The Future of the Jews: A People at the Crossroads* (Cambridge, MA: Harvard University Press, 1990), 136.

93. See "American Jewish Attitudes," survey by Market Facts, 45, 55.

94. Goldberg, *Jewish Power*, 359.

95. Arthur Hertzberg, "Less Religious on Israeli Matters," *Ha'aretz* (Hebrew), October 10, 1993, B2.

96. During negotiations between Israel and Syria, haredi and religious Zionists protested against Prime Minister Ehud Barak's intention to trade land for peace and chanted "traitor, go home!" while leaders of the Reform movement visited the Israeli Embassy and other consulates across America to show their support for the Israeli prime minister. See Caryle Murphy, "Reform Jewish Leaders Urge Support," *Washington Post*, January 11, 2000; Shlomo Shamir, "Reform Jews Try Rallying for Peace," *Ha'aretz*, January 10, 2000.

97. See "American Jewish Attitudes," survey by Market Facts.

98. Thomas L. Friedman, "Mischief Makers," *New York Times*, April 5, 1995.

99. See David Landau, "The Voice of Post-Tolerance" (Kol Ha' Post-Metinut), *Ha'aretz* (Hebrew), October 17, 1996.

100. See Janine Zacharia, "The Unofficial Ambassadors of the Jewish State," *Jerusalem Post*, April 2, 2000, 1.

101. Dimitri Slivanik, "Emigration According to Herzel," *Eretz Acheret* (Hebrew) 19 (November–December 2003): 18–21.

102. They advocate a balance between civil and religious life in Israel based on the idea that the "ways of the Torah are ways of pleasantness and all its pathways are peace." See David Berger, "Reflections on the State of Religious Zionism," *Jewish Action* 60, no. 1 (fall 1999): 12–15.

103. For a detailed discussion of this phenomenon, see Jonathan Broder, "Netanyahu and American Jews," *World Policy Journal* 15, no. 1 (spring 1998): 89–98.

104. "The Many Faces of Judaism in Israel: Mapping Jewish Unity Organizations," Jewish Agency for Israel, December 2000, 3.

105. Tamar Hausman, "Sacrifice of Temple Mt. 'Risks Ties to U.S. Jews,'" *Ha'aretz*, January 5, 2001.

106. Cited in *Jerusalem Report*, August 28, 2000, 56.

107. See Gail Lichtman, "Mounting Temple Controversy," *Jerusalem Post Magazine*, January 26, 2001, 10–13.

108. Hank Scheinkopf, quoted in Rachel Donadio, "GOP Woos Arabs and Hawks; Dems on Mideast Defensive," *Ha'aretz*, October 26, 2000.

109. Sharon's speech to AIPAC, delivered on March 19, 2001, may be found at http://www.mfa.gov.il/MFA/Government/Speeches+by+Israeli+leaders/2001/Address+by+Prime+Minister+Ariel+Sharon+to+AIPAC+Po.htm (accessed February 15, 2007).

110. "A survey conducted by *The Forward* found that 75 per cent of American Jews felt more threatened than they did prior to September 11 and half of these

Jews cited their Jewishness as the reason for their increased fear." Cited in Eliahu Salpeter, "World Jewry and the War against Global Terrorism," *Ha'aretz*, November 7, 2001.

111. Jonathan Rosen, "The Uncomfortable Question of Anti-Semitism," *New York Times Magazine*, November 4, 2001, 48.

112. Eliahu Salpeter, "Unfortunate Utterances on the Diaspora," *Ha'aretz Daily—English Internet Edition* (op-ed), September 20, 2000. Also see Gil Hoffman, "Katzav: More Cash Needed for Western Aliya," *Jerusalem Post*, September 15, 2000.

113. See Yossi Shain and Barry Bristman, "The Jewish Security Dilemma," *Orbis* (winter 2002): 1–25.

114. These comments were made at "The Herzliya Conference on the Balance of National Strength and Security: 2000 Conference Protocol," Institute of Policy and Strategy, Interdisciplinary Center, Herzliya, December 19–21, 2000.

115. Nahum Barnea, *Yediot Ahronot* (Hebrew), March 3, 2002, 1.

116. Alan Cooperman, "Orthodox Jews in the U.S. Quiet on Israeli Conversion Ruling," *Washington Post*, February 24, 2004, A6.

117. See *Ha'aretz*, March 12, 2002.

118. Mendelsohn, *On Modern Jewish Politics*, 144–45.

119. "The spiritual leader of the Religious-Zionist camp, former Askenazi Chief Rabbi Avraham Shapira, called on soldiers to disobey orders to evacuate Gaza, even at risk of death or imprisonment. However, Rabbi Shlomo Aviner, head of the large yeshiva in the Beit El settlement, argued that civil disobedience was legitimate, but that soldiers had to follow commanders' orders, otherwise the Israeli army would collapse. Yet the rabbi of Beit El, Rabbi Zalman Melamed, joined with Shapira in objecting to the order for withdrawal, claiming that if Rabbi Kook was alive today he, too, would have called on the soldiers to object." These quotes are part of an excellent analysis of Israeli debates about the Gaza withdrawal; see Meyrav Wurmser, "Color War: Two Flags and an Israeli Schism." *National Review Online*, August 24, 2005, available at http://www .nationalreview.com/comment/wurmser200508240819.asp (accessed February 15, 2007).

120. See letter to Ambassador Ayalon, July 21, 2005, at http://www.ou.org/ pdf/5765/AmbAyalonLtr.pdf (accessed March 20, 2007).

121. See Yossi Shain, *Marketing the American Creed Abroad: Diasporas in the U.S. and Their Homelands* (New York: Cambridge University Press, 1999).

122. See Kurien, "Opposing Constructions and Agendas," 148–72.

123. Israel's victory in 1967 was taken by many evangelists as a confirmation of the accuracy of biblical prophecies and the nearness of Christ's own reign. In the words of religious right leader Jerry Falwell, "The most dramatic evidence for His imminent return is the rebirth of the nation of Israel." Christian Right leaders, similar to many Orthodox Jews inside and outside Israel, find modern political meaning in Israel's conflict with Palestinians over the control of God's territorial gift to Abraham, not only as a matter of contemporary political battle but in fact, in the words of Oklahoma senator James Inhofe, a born-again fundamentalist, as "a contest over whether the word of God is true." For this analysis see Jeremy Mayer, "Christian Fundamentalists and Public Opinion toward the Middle East: Israel's New Best Friends," *Social Science Quarterly* 85, no. 3 (2004): 695–712.

124. Alan Cooperman, "Israel Divestiture Spurs Clash," *Washington Post*, September 29, 2004, A 8.

125. Cited in Robert A. Burt, "On the Bench: The Jewish Justices," in Maisel and Forman, eds., *Jews in American Politics*, 69.

CHAPTER FOUR

1. There are generally four types of conflict-resolution situations and related peace processes in which far-removed diasporas may play an important role: (1) State-to-state conflicts that deal primarily with resources or boundaries, where neither side is seeking to eliminate the other (Eritrea-Ethiopia or India-Pakistan); (2) State-to-state conflicts that have a distinct minority dimension (Armenia-Azerbaijan on Nagorno-Karabakh); (3) Intrastate conflicts, where a minority is seeking secession/irredentism (Sri Lanka–Tamils; United Kingdom–Northern Irish Catholics, India–Kashmiris/Sikhs); (4) Intrastate conflicts in which diasporas have the limited objective of regime change, without questioning the legitimacy of the state or its boundaries. Such conflicts involve political exiles, who by definition would expect to return home once the conflict ceases (exiles from Iraq prior to the downfall of Saddam Hussein, Iranian exiles, or anti-Castro Cubans in Miami). In all of these conflicts when sizable and organized diasporas are present, they are likely to exert influence on outcome and processes.

2. With the Armenian-American diaspora consisting of nearly one million people, and the Jewish-American diaspora numbering roughly six million, these two minority groups are acknowledged to be (alongside Cuban-Americans) the most effective at advocating their priorities in the U.S. political system. Armenia and Israel are the largest per capita recipients of U.S. foreign aid. The ways in which diaspora involvement in these cases influences the prospects for conflict perpetuation or conflict resolution are therefore of direct concern to the United States and other states that invest time and money in peacekeeping, diplomatic initiatives, and economic development in these regions. See Michal Dobbs, "Foreign Aid Shrinks but Not for All," *Washington Post*, January 24, 2001, 1.

3. The role of diasporas most frequently cited in the news media is their financial role in sustaining a conflict by funding armed insurrectionist groups, terrorists, or government efforts to eradicate the latter. See Paul Collier and Anke Hoeffler, "Greed and Grievance in Civil War," Policy Research Working Papers (World Bank, Washington, DC, May 2000).

4. Michael Mandelbaum, ed., *The New European Diasporas: National Minorities and Conflict in Eastern Europe* (New York: Council on Foreign Relations, 2000).

5. We are not addressing the eventual outcome of peace diplomacy but rather the evolution of support and opposition within the process itself.

6. On this subject see Yossi Shain, ed., *Governments-in-Exile in Contemporary World Politics* (New York: Routledge, 1991).

7. See, inter alia, Benedict Anderson, *Imagined Communities: Reflections on the Origin and Spread of Nationalism* (London: Verso, 1983); Anthony Smith, *National Identity* (Reno: University of Nevada Press, 1991).

8. Peter Katzenstein, "Introduction: Alternative Perspectives on National Security," in *The Culture of National Security: Norms and Identity in World Politics*, ed. Katzenstein (New York: Columbia University Press, 1996), 19. For an important dis-

cussion on this topic, see also David Campbell, *Writing Security: United States Foreign Policy and the Politics of Identity* (Manchester: Manchester University Press, 1992).

9. Ronald Suny, "Provisional Stabilities: The Politics of Identity in Post-Soviet Eurasia," *International Security* 24, no. 3 (winter 1999–2000): 147.

10. Gil Merom, "Israel's National Security and the Myth of Exceptionalism," *Political Science Quarterly* 114, no. 3 (fall 1999): 412–13.

11. In the last decade we have witnessed a basic rethinking of the relationship between Israel and Jewish-Americans in terms of legitimacy, status, power, and identity—away from the context of Zionist vision of the gathering of the exiles toward partnership and normalization with the diaspora. See Yossi Beilin, *His Brother's Keeper: Israel and Diaspora Jewry in the Twenty-first Century* (New York: Schocken Books, 2000).

12. See Yossi Shain and Barry Bristman, "The Jewish Security Dilemma," *Orbis* 46, no. 1 (winter 2002): 47–71.

13. Khachig Tololyan and Krikor Beledian, interview by Arpi Totoyan in *Haratch* (Paris), July 2–3, 1998, reprinted in Vincent Lima, "Fresh Perspectives on Armenia-Diaspora Relations," *Armenian Forum* 2, no. 2 (December 20, 2000), www.gomidas.org/forum/af3c.htm (accessed June 14, 2002).

14. Robert D. Putnam, "Diplomacy and Domestic Politics: The Logic of Two-Level Games," *International Organization* 42 (summer 1988): 427–60.

15. Jeffrey W. Knopf, "Beyond Two-Level Games: Domestic-International Interaction in the Intermediate-Range Nuclear Forces Negotiations," *International Organization* 47 (autumn 1993): 599–628. Lee Ann Patterson expanded Putnam's model into a "three-level analysis" when she studied agricultural policy reform in the European Union. See Lee Ann Patterson, "Agricultural Policy Reform in the European Community: A Three-Level Game Analysis," *International Organization* 51 (winter 1997): 135–65.

16. Some stateless diasporas may play a critical role in the struggle for the creation of a new ethnocentric state in the traditional homeland. This has been the case with diasporic Sikhs who have led the struggle for an independent Khalistan in India, or the diasporic Tamils who are the core supporters of the separatist Liberation Tigers of Tamil Eelam. Gabriel Sheffer has argued that, with the establishment of independent states in their claimed homelands, stateless diasporas are likely to shift their methods of activism from an aggressive posture, which often includes being a source for military recruits or terrorists, to more "innocuous exchanges" involving cash transfers, tourism, and other nonlethal activities that help consolidate their kin states. Gabriel Sheffer, "Ethno-National Diasporas and Security," *Survival* 36, no. 1 (spring 1994): 64.

17. Tamar Hausman, "Sacrifice of Temple Mt. 'Risks Ties to U.S. Jews,'" *Ha'aretz Daily* (English Internet edition), January 5, 2001, www.haaretz.co.il/eng (accessed January 5, 2001).

18. Yair Sheleg, "World Jewry Thinks Jerusalem and Temple Mount Is an Issue for All Jews—Not Just Barak—to Decide," *Ha'aretz Daily* (English Internet edition), January 1, 2001, www.haaretz.co.il/eng (accessed January 1, 2001).

19. The address of Prime Minister Sharon to the Conference of Presidents was given February 20, 2003, in the Inbal Hotel in Jerusalem and is available at http://www.pm.gov.il/PMOEng/Archive/Speeches/2003/02/Speeches7098.htm (accessed February 15, 2007).

20. One Israeli activist responded to such sentiments by saying, "Israel is a make-believe land for American Jews. It's a symbol. They don't live here, they don't drive on the roads, or send their sons to the army . . . I don't make light of Jerusalem and the Temple Mount. But it's nice to live in New York, Philadelphia, and L.A. and to know that the Temple Mount is in our hands. But what is really to see up there? Mosques. And for what price?" Rabbi David Clyman, quoted in Hausman, "Sacrifice of Temple Mt. 'Risks Ties to U.S. Jews.'" See also Neil Mac-Farquhar, "300 Rabbis in U.S. Group Say Jerusalem Is Shareable," *New York Times*, January 20, 2000.

21. A leading scholar of the Armenian diaspora, H. Stephen Astourian, argues that on issues of national mythology, neither the homeland nor the diaspora communities are monolithic. "It is difficult to talk of the Armenian diaspora as a united entity . . . The ARF was rabidly opposed to any and all of the tentative peace deals. The Ramgavar Party had split into at least two groups. Those in Armenia opposed the final peace deal. Those in the United States were more ambiguous . . . The Hunchakian Party was also divided into three groups . . . Those in Armenia were in fact a dummy organization totally controlled by Ter-Petrossian. They supported the peace deals. The attitude of the other ones, who are in general of very little influence in Armenian life, is unclear . . . The Armenian Assembly . . . did not take a stance on that issue. Beyond these organizations, there was a group of diaspora Armenians under the influence of, or in agreement with, the views propounded in the columns of the *Armenian International Magazine* published in Glendale. They tended to support the peace deal in the name of realism, pragmatism, moderation, etc . . . These individuals [generally] consist of Armenians disaffected with the established organizations, some professionals, some half-assimilated Armenians, and some anti-ARF people." Astourian, telephone interview by author, January 25, 2001.

22. See "US Reform Leader Slams Ron Lauder for Addressing Jerusalem Rally," *Ha'aretz Breaking News*, January 9, 2001, www.haaretz.co.il/breaking news/jewishnews/346612.stm (accessed January 9, 2001).

23. For an analysis of this dynamic, see Yossi Shain and Barry Bristman, "Diaspora Kinship and Loyalty: The Renewal of Jewish National Security," *International Affairs* 78, no. 1 (January 2002): 69–96, and chapters 1 and 3 in this volume.

24. Eliahu Salpeter, "Israel Has a Right to Know on Whose Behalf Ron Lauder Will Speak from Now On," *Ha'aretz Daily* (English Internet Edition), January 17, 2001, www.haaretz.co.il/eng (accessed January 17, 2001).

25. See Matthew Frankel, "The $10 Billion Question: AIPAC and Loan Guarantees to Israel," *Fletcher Forum* (winter–spring 1995): 169.

26. Ross Vartian, executive director of the Armenian Assembly of America, interview by author, Washington, DC, March 8, 2000.

27. In the latest war between Eritrea and Ethiopia, for instance, the Eritrean and Ethiopian diasporas in the United States together contributed hundreds of millions of dollars toward weapons purchases by their homeland countries. For more on this topic, see Jesse Driscoll, "The Economics of Insanity: Funding the Ethiopia-Eritrea War" (paper, Georgetown University, fall 2000), 6–7.

28. Independent International Commission on Kosovo, *The Kosovo Report: Conflict, International Response, Lessons Learned* (Oxford: Oxford University Press, 2000).

29. Daniel Byman, Peter Chalk, Bruce Hoffman, William Rosenau, and David

Brannan, *Trends in Outside Support for Insurgent Movements* (Santa Monica, CA: RAND, 2001), 43–49.

30. Pradeep Jeganathan, "eelam.com: Place, Nation, and Imagi-Nation in Cyberspace," *Public Culture* 10, no. 3 (spring 1998): 515–28.

31. The survey data provided by Machon Dachaf at a recent meeting at the Jewish Agency for Israel in Tel Aviv shows a deep sense of kinship and commitment expressed by Israeli Jews toward their diasporic kin. See Machon Dachaf, *Survey Data*, May 12, 2002 (survey presented at a special meeting, Jewish Agency for Israel, Tel Aviv, Israel, May 22, 2002).

32. See Shlomo Shamir, "Jewish Leaders Lobbied Rice on Gaza Border Deal," *Ha'aretz*, November 18, 2005.

33. Benedict Anderson, "The New World Disorder," *New Left Review* 193 (1992): 3–13.

34. For an elaborate discussion of the anti-Oslo campaign by American Jews, see Steve T. Rosenthal, *Irreconcilable Differences? The Waning of the American Jewish Love Affair with Israel* (Hanover, NH: Brandeis University Press, 2001), 129–33. After the Oslo Accords were signed, those American Jews who opposed the peace process joined with conservative Israeli Likud members to obstruct improved U.S. relations with the Palestine Liberation Organization (PLO). Over the objections of the Clinton administration and despite lobbying by Israeli diplomats, anti-Oslo Jewish groups were able to convince the U.S. Congress to enact the Middle East Peace Facilitation Act in such a way as to limit U.S. participation in the donor efforts. Diaspora activists exacerbated the sharp divide within Israel over the peace process, even to the point that U.S.-based ultra-Orthodox rabbis issued rulings that sanctioned Israeli soldiers' insubordination and the defamation of Rabin as a traitor. One Brooklyn rabbi even announced that it would be "religiously permissible to kill Rabin."

35. Cited in Sarah Bronson, "Orthodox Leader: U.S. Jews Have No Right to Criticize Israel," *Ha'aretz*, August 2, 2004.

36. See *Maariv International*, June 24, 2004.

37. Shain and Bristman, "Jewish Security Dilemma," 52.

38. See Alan Cooperman, "Jewish Organizations Worried about Backlash for Iraq War," March 15, 2003.

39. Stephen John Stedman, "Spoiler Problems in Peace Processes," *International Security* 22, no. 2 (autumn 1997): 10–11.

40. John Dahlberg-Acton, *Essay in the Liberal Interpretation of History* (Chicago and London: University of Chicago Press, 1967), chap. 5, 134. Quoted in Benedict Anderson, *The Spectre of Comparisons: Nationalism, Southeast Asia, and the World* (London: Verso, 1998), 58.

41. Dahlberg-Acton, *Essay*, 9.

42. Paul Collier, *Breaking the Conflict Trap: Civil War and Development Policy*, World Bank Policy Research Report (World Bank: Oxford University Press, 2003), 22–44.

43. Paul Collier, "Policy for Post-conflict Societies: Reducing the Risk of Renewed Conflict" (paper at the Economics of Political Violence Conference, March 18–19, 2000, Princeton University).

44. Daniel L. Byman, *Deadly Connections: States That Sponsor Terror* (New York: Cambridge University Press, 2005), 253.

45. See Janine Zacharia, "The Unofficial Ambassadors of the Jewish State," *Jerusalem Post*, April 2, 2000, 1.

46. Indeed, war and peace are deeply influenced by historical images of hostility and friendliness among nations. As Kenneth Boulding observed, in conflict resolution the most critical images "are those which the nation has of itself and of those other bodies in the system which constitute its international environment . . . Whether transmitted orally and informally through the family or more formally through schooling and the written word, the national image is essentially a historical image—that is, an image which extends through time." Kenneth Boulding, "National Images and International Systems," in *Approaches to Peace: A Reader in Peace Studies*, ed. David P. Barash (Oxford: Oxford University Press, 2000), 46–47.

47. On the concept of an ethnonational group's "chosen trauma" and its effects on conflict resolution, see Vamik Volkan, *Bloodlines: From Ethnic Pride to Ethnic Terrorism* (New York: Farrar, Straus and Giroux, 1997).

48. Richard G. Hovannisian, "On Historical Memory and Armenian Foreign Policy," lecture, Haigazian University, Beirut, Lebanon, July 31, 2000, www.haigazian.edu.lb/announce/pressrelease.htm (accessed June 14, 2002).

49. In January 2001, President Jacques Chirac hosted President Robert Kocharian of Armenia and President Heydar Aliyev of Azerbaijan in Paris in an attempt to settle the conflict over Nagorno-Karabakh. The *New York Times* reported that "with municipal elections approaching in France, Mr. Chirac would like to have a settlement to offer the 400,000 ethnic Armenians in France." See Douglas Frantz, "Armenia and Azerbaijan Signal Progress in Talks on Enclave," *New York Times*, February 20, 2001.

50. Amit Gupta, "The Indian Diaspora's Political Efforts in the United States" (Observer Research Foundation, occasional paper, September 2004), 1.

51. Dr. Hafiz M. Pashayev, Azeri ambassador to the United States, interview by author, Washington, DC, October 21, 1999.

52. Inan Ozyildiz, Counselor, Turkish Embassy, interview by author, Washington, DC, November 4, 1999.

53. Zvi Gitelman, "The Decline of the Diaspora Jewish Nation: Boundaries, Content, and Jewish Identity," *Jewish Social Studies* 4 (winter 1998): 128.

54. Arthur Hertzberg, "Less Religious on Israeli Matters," *Ha'aretz* (Hebrew), October 10, 1993, B2.

55. Amy Dockers Marcus, "Burden of Peace: American Jews Grapple with an Identity Crisis as Peril to Israel Ebbs," *Wall Street Journal*, September 14, 1994, 1, 6.

56. J. J. Goldberg, *Jewish Power: Inside the American Jewish Establishment* (Reading, MA: Addison-Wesley, 1996), 359.

57. Quoted in Melissa Radler, "Presidents Conference Chairman: Arafat Has Unified the Jews," *Jerusalem Post*, July 13, 2001.

58. Tololyan and Beledian, interview.

59. Razmik Panossian, "Between Ambivalence and Intrusion: Armenia-Diaspora Relations," *Diaspora* 7, no. 2 (1998): 171.

60. Khachig Tololyan, "Exile Governments in the Armenian Polity," in *Governments-in-Exile in Contemporary World Politics*, ed. Yossi Shain (New York: Routledge, 1991), 166–87.

61. Samuel P. Huntington, *The Clash of Civilizations and the Remaking of World Order* (New York: Simon and Schuster, 1996), 280.

62. Panossian, "Between Ambivalence and Intrusion," 175.

63. R. H. Dekmejian and Angelos Themelis, "Ethnic Lobbies in US Foreign Policy," Occasional Research Paper 13 (Institution of International Relations, Athens, 1997), 31.

64. Armenian Assembly of America, "Armenia This Week," January 12, 2001.

65. The House leadership pulled the resolution only after then-president Clinton intervened with a letter to members of Congress.

66. Hafiz M. Pashayev, Azeri ambassador to the United States, interview by author, Washington, DC, October 21, 1999.

67. David B. Ottaway and Dan Morgan, "Jewish-Armenian Split Spreads on the Hill; Strategic Issues Put Onetime Lobbying Allies at Odds," *Washington Post*, February 9, 1999, A15.

68. See Connie L. Mcneely and Susan J. Tolchin, "On the Hill: Jews in the United States Congress," in *Jews in American Politics*, ed. L. Sandy Maisel and Ira N. Forman (New York: Rowman and Littlefield, 2001), 60.

69. Michael Dobbs, "Armenia Pins Economic Hopes on Peace," *Washington Post*, September 6, 2000, A13.

70. Michael Goldman, "Diplomacy Outside the Box: Behind the Good Friday Agreement," *Swords and Ploughshares* 11, no. 1 (spring 2002).

CHAPTER FIVE

1. Paul Collier and Anke Hoeffler, *Greed and Grievances in Civil War* (Washington, DC: World Bank, 2000), available at http://www.worldbank.org/research/conflict/papers/greed.htm (accessed February 15, 2007).

2. Eva Ostergaard-Nielsen, "From Remittance Machines to Euro-Turks: Ankara's Changing Perception of Citizens Abroad," London School of Economics Working Group on Perceptions and Policies of Sending Countries; Rey Koslowski, "International Migration and the Globalization of Domestic Politics: A Conceptual Framework" (manuscript).

3. Khachig Tololyan, "Exile Governments in Armenian Polity," in Yossi Shain, ed., *Governments-in-Exile in Contemporary Politics* (New York: Routledge, 1991); Robin Cohen, *Global Diasporas: An Introduction* (London: UCL Press, 1997); James Clifford, "Traveling Cultures," in Lawrence Grossberg, Cary Nelson, and Paula A. Treichler, eds., *Cultural Studies* (New York: Routledge, 1992); Tony Smith, "In Defense of Intervention," *Foreign Affairs* 73 (1993).

4. Tony Smith, *Foreign Attachments: The Power of Ethnic Groups in the Making of American Foreign Policy* (Cambridge: Harvard University Press, 2000); M. S. Saideman, *The Ties that Divide: Ethnic Politics, Foreign Policy, and International Politics* (New York: Columbia University Press, 2001).

5. Myron Weiner, ed., *International Migration and Security* (Boulder: Westview, 1993).

6. Louis Desipio, *Sending Money Home . . . For Now: Remittances and Immigrant Adaptation in the United States* (Austin: Tomas Rivera Policy Institute, 2000); Kate Gillespie, Edward Sayre, and Liesel Riddle, "Palestinian Interest in Homeland Investment," *Middle East Journal* 55 (2001).

7. Moses Naim, "The New Diaspora," *Foreign Policy* (July–August 2002): 95.

8. Samuel Huntington, *The Clash of Civilizations and the Remaking of World Order* (New York: Simon and Schuster, 1996); Gabriel Sheffer, "Ethno-National Diasporas and Security," *Survival* 36 (1994); Myron Weiner, *The Global Migration Crisis: Challenges to States and to Human Rights* (New York: HarperCollins, 1995).

9. Walker Connor, "The Impact of Homelands upon Diasporas," in Gabriel Sheffer, ed., *Modern Diasporas in International Politics* (London: Croom Helm, 1986).

10. William Safran is correct in his observation that recent scholarship on (and the use of the appellation) diasporas, especially in the field of anthropology and cultural studies, often has produced a maze of vagueness and open definitions that emphasize difference and "otherness" and that stretch the concept to include "a varied assortment of social phenomena that have little to do with dispersions and homelands." French scholar Stephane Dufoix characterizes this misuse as "oxymoronic" diaspora studies. See William Safran, "Recent French Conceptualizations of Diaspora," *Diaspora* 12, no. 3 (winter 2003).

11. Yossi Shain, *The Frontier of Loyalty: Political Exiles in the Age of the Nation-State* (Middletown, CT: Wesleyan University Press, 1989; 2d ed., Ann Arbor: University of Michigan Press, 2005).

12. Alicja Iwańska, *Exiled Governments: Spanish and Polish* (Cambridge: Schenkman, 1981).

13. Milton J. Esman, "Diasporas and International Relations," in Sheffer, ed., *Modern Diasporas*, 3403.

14. In the early 1990s the rallying call of protecting ethnic Russians in the "near abroad" had strong irredentist tones. Initially these voices were dominated by Russian right-wing nationalists and hard-core communist reactionaries. Yet public pronouncements regarding the centrality of the Russian diaspora are now part of the Russian mainstream and continue to alarm many policymakers in the West and in the former Soviet republic who consider "the seemingly virulent obsession with the fate of the Russians in adjoining states as a potentially destabilizing force." See Robert A. Saunders, "A Marooned Diaspora: Ethnic Russians in the Near Abroad and Their Impact on Russia's Foreign Policy and Domestic Politics," in Koslowski, ed., *International Migration and the Globalization of Domestic Politics*, 183.

15. See Yossi Shain and Tanja Flanagan, "The New Jewish and German Questions and the Transatlantic Alliance," *Israel Studies* 10, no. 1 (spring 2005): 188–209.

16. Michael Clough, "Grass-Roots Policymaking: Say Good-bye to the 'Wise Men,'" *Foreign Affairs* 73 (1994).

17. Smith, *Foreign Attachments.*

18. Samuel P. Huntingon, *Who Are We? The Challenge of America's National Identity* (New York: Simon and Schuster, 2004).

19. Yossi Shain, *Marketing the American Creed Abroad: Diasporas in the U.S. and Their Homeland* (New York: Cambridge, 1999); Myron Weiner and Michael S. Teitelbaum, *Political Demography, Demographic Engineering* (New York: Berghahn, 2001), 78.

20. Although other countries of immigrants, like Germany and France, are becoming more susceptible to diasporic influences, the American case (and perhaps the Canadian) remains quite unique in its accessibility and incorporation of diasporic

voices. Even Germany, with its deeply rooted ethnonational conception of citizenship and a semicorporatist social contracting between the state and leading institutions that dominates domestic politics, has started to see the seeds of such involvement. Yet because of its institutional and ideological design, Germany restrains diasporic lobbying of its government. Thus, diasporas have little influence over German foreign policy even when they are cohesive in their demands and well organized. See Nedim Ogelman, Jeannette Money, and Philip Martin, "Immigrant Cohesion and Political Access in Influencing Host Country Foreign Policy: A Comparison of Turks in Germany and Cubans in the United States," *SAIS Review* (2002).

21. Yossi Beilin, *His Brother's Keeper: Israel and Diaspora Jews in the Twenty-first Century* (New York: Schocken, 2000), 74.

22. Ronald Jepperson, Alexander Wendt, and Peter Katzenstein, "Norms, Identity, and Culture in National Security," in Katzenstein, ed., *The Culture of National Security: Norms and Identity in World Politics* (New York: Columbia University Press, 1996), 40.

23. "Rabbi's Anger at Israel Will Fuel Terror, Say Critics," *Times* (London), August 28, 2002.

24. *Jerusalem Post*, August 28, 2002, editorial.

25. Saideman, *Ties that Divide*, 138–41.

26. Weiner and Teitelbaum, *Political Demography*, 77–78.

27. Such a position was articulated by Israel's prime minister Ariel Sharon in his address to a large gathering at the American-Israel Public Affairs Committee's (AIPAC) 2001 annual meeting. Sharon announced that he considers himself "first and foremost as a Jew," and that he sees himself as having been given a mandate to unify not only Israel but also "Jews worldwide." He further declared that "the future of Israel is not just a matter for Israelis who live there. Israel belongs to the entire Jewish People." Cited in Yossi Shain and Barry Bristman, "Diaspora, Kinship, and Loyalty: The Renewal of Jewish National Security," *International Affairs* 78 (2002).

28. As one senior diaspora activist explained to the authors, "we are an organization that receives [many] million of dollars a year. We must continue to create issues to satisfy our donors and convince them of our importance."

29. Andrew Moravcsik, "Taking Preferences Seriously: A Liberal Theory of International Politics," *International Organization* 51 (1997): 525.

30. Peter Katzenstein, "Introduction: Alternative Perspective on National Security," in Katzenstein, *Culture of National Security*, 4.

31. Martha Finnemore, *National Interests in International Society* (Ithaca: Cornell University Press, 1996), 144–46.

32. Jeffrey Checkel, "The Constructivist Turn in International Relations Theory," *World Politics* 50 (1998): 326–27.

33. Emanuel Adler, "Seizing the Middle Ground: Constructivism in World Politics," *European Journal of International Relations* 3, no. 3 (1997); Ted Hopf, "The Promise of Constructivism in International Relations Theory," *International Security* 23 (1998): 176; Alexander Wendt, "Anarchy Is What States Make of It: The Social Construction of Power Politics," in F. Kratochwil and E. Mansfield, eds., *International Organization: A Reader* (New York: HarperCollins, 1994), 83–85.

34. Alexander Wendt, *Social Theory of International Politics* (New York: Cambridge University Press, 1999), 224–27.

35. Roxanne Doty, "Sovereignty and the Nation: Constructing the Boundaries of National Identity," in Thomas Bierstecker and Cynthia Weber, eds., *State Sovereignty as Social Construct* (New York: Cambridge University Press, 1996), 125–27.

36. Doty, "Sovereignty and the Nation," 125–27.

37. Paul Kowert and Jeffrey Legro, "Norms, Identity, and Their Limits: A Theoretical Reprise," in Katzenstein, *Culture of National Security*, 470–75.

38. Doty, "Sovereignty and the Nation."

39. Katzenstein, "Introduction," 5–6.

40. Adler, "Seizing the Middle Ground," 336.

41. William Bloom, *Personal Identity, National Identity, and International Relations* (New York: Cambridge University Press, 1990), 79–81.

42. While Doty apparently focuses on outside elements, her insight is applicable also to inside groups, i.e., diasporic communities. Furthermore, it should be noted that inside claims by diasporic elements are based only on an ethnic notion of membership; a civic notion, by definition, negates any claim of membership on the basis of kinship. Doty, "Sovereignty and the Nation."

43. Yossi Shain and Barry Bristman, "The Jewish Security Dilemma," *Orbis* 46, no. 1 (2002).

44. Emphasis in the original. Bloom, *Personal Identity*, 79–81.

45. Yosef Lapid, "Culture's Ship: Returns and Departures in International Relations Theory," in Yousef Lapid and Friedrich Kratochwil, *The Return of Culture and Identity to International Relations Theory* (Boulder: Lynne Rienner, 1996), 10.

46. Katzenstein, "Introduction," 23–25.

47. Moravcsik, "Taking Preferences Seriously," 516–17.

48. Matthew Evangelista, "Domestic Structure and International Change," in Michael Doyle and John Ikenberry, eds., *New Thinking in International Relations Theory* (Boulder: Westview, 1997), 223.

49. In this sense, diasporas function on both levels of Putnam's "two-level game" model. See Robert Putnam, "Diplomacy and Domestic Politics: The Logic of Two-level Games," *International Organization* 42 (1988).

50. Helen Milner, *Interests, Institutions, and Information: Domestic Politics and International Relations* (Princeton: Princeton University Press, 1997).

51. Jewish activists provided Israel's foreign office with warnings, gradually increasing in volume and urgency, that Israel's ties with the apartheid regime were fueling growing opposition to its interests, in the administration and Congress, and undermining Jewish relations with the African-American community. See Shain, *Marketing the American Creed Abroad*, 149–51.

52. Other than that, we are unaware of instances of diasporas in nondemocracies that are or were able to organize and exert influence on homelands' policies. To the extent that they exist, they are not independent.

53. These, then, are the two reasons why most of the literature dealing with ethnic foreign policy lobbies is focused on the United States. This country is both the most influential nation in international relations, and its foreign policy decision making is highly permeable to societal pressures.

54. True, failed states are beyond the pale; there is no policy-making and therefore no opening for exerting influence. A failing state, on the other hand, is another matter.

55. During the Oslo Peace Process, when Israel's economy was thriving, some

Israeli leaders rejected the need for diasporic assistance. Israel's deputy foreign minister Yossi Beilin told diaspora Jewry to spend their money on Jewish education abroad since Israel would no longer want to be treated as a charity case. See Steven Rosenthal, *Irreconcilable Differences? The Waning of the American Jewish Love Affair with Israel* (Hanover, NH: Brandeis University Press, 2001), 175. It was at this juncture that American Jews started to redirect their financial assistance to Israel from state to civil and political-society causes. This trend was reversed beginning in 2001 when perception of acute Jewish insecurity inside and outside Israel galvanized the United Jewish Communities' emergency campaign that quickly raised about $300 million "to help educate diaspora Jews about the [Middle East] crisis, keep them connected with Israel, and raise money to help Israel" (*Jerusalem Post*, June 27, 2002).

56. Aviel Roshwald, *Ethnic Nationalism and the Fall of Empires: Central Europe, Russia, and the Middle East, 1914–1923* (New York: Routledge, 2001), 110.

57. Tololyan, "Exile Governments," 183.

58. The diaspora was divided along class, religion, and political lines, and was influenced by the political and cultural pressures of the different surroundings in which Armenians lived. Unlike the Dashnaks, the diasporic bourgeoisie cooperated with Soviet Armenians in communal matters. See Razmik Panossian, "Between Ambivalence and Intrusion: Politics and Identity in Armenian-Diaspora Relations," *Diaspora* 7 (1998): 155–58.

59. Panossian, "Between Ambivalence and Intrusion," 159–60. The Soviets "portrayed the Armenian SSR as the homeland and exclusive source of national identity, where the nation was being conserved and advanced. . . . Soviet Armenia was presented as a concerned homeland providing cultural nourishment for the diaspora, so that the latter could preserve its weakening 'Armenianness' in foreign lands. . . . In this view, the earlier roles of donor and recipient were reversed. The homeland became the 'aid' provider, while the diaspora needed assistance for its national 'survival.' "

60. J. G. Libaridian, *The Challenge of Statehood: Armenian Political Thinking since Independence* (Watertown, MA: Blue Crane Books, 1999), 124.

61. Inspired by third world ideology and the international attention given to political terrorism in the Middle East and Europe, young Armenians in Lebanon established the Armenian Secret Army for the Liberation of Armenia (ASALA). In numerous acts of terrorism against Turkish facilities and diplomats (as well as against Western targets allegedly associated with the "fascist regime in Turkey"), ASALA's violence reenergized the Armenian cause in the international arena. The organization's visibility posed a challenge to the Dashnak older leadership, and the diasporic party responded by establishing its own terrorist arm known as the Justice Commando for the Armenian Genocide. See Anat Kurz and Ariel Merari, *ASALA: Irrational Terror or Political Tool* (Boulder: Westview, 1985).

62. Khachig Tololyan, "Cultural Narrative and the Motivation of the Terrorist," *Journal of Strategic Studies* 10, no. 4 (1987): 232.

63. This point was made by Armenian diasporic expert Khachig Tololyan in a letter to the authors, October 4, 1999.

64. Stephan H. Astourian, "From Ter-Petrosian to Kochman: Leadership Change in Armenia," Berkeley Program in Soviet and Post-Soviet Studies Working Group, 2000–2001, 18–19.

65. Hovann Simonian, "The Armenian Diaspora Gets Its Second Wind, as Relations with the Homeland Improve over the Genocide Issue," Transition Online-TOL, January 18, 2001.

66. Panossian, "Between Ambivalence and Intrusion," 171.

67. See the message from the Chairman of the Board of Directors of the Armenian Assembly of America in the 1998 Annual Report.

68. Libaridian, *Challenge of Statehood*; Astourian, "From Ter-Petrosian to Kochman."

69. A 1995 study of the World Bank shows that "in June 1994 the average wage in the state sector stood at about $2 a month—equivalent to one kilogram of meat—and $4 to $5 economy-wide; the average monthly pension was about $1." Cited in Astourian, "From Ter-Petrosian to Kochman," 8.

70. According to one estimate, diasporic financial transfers to Armenia from the West amount to $175 million annually, about 15 percent of the GDP for 1998. See Astourian, "From Ter-Petrosian to Kochman," 41–42. Even though American foreign aid budget is dropping, the Armenian lobby has managed to increase aid to Armenia and has turned its homeland into the second largest recipient (after Israel) of aid per capita. Armenia receives about $120 million annually, despite plentiful evidence of corruption and a patchy record on democracy and human rights. See *Washington Post*, January 24, 2001.

71. M. Lev Freinkman, "Role of the Diaspora in Transition Economies: Lessons from Armenia" (paper presented at the 11th annual meeting of the Association for the Study of the Cuban Economy, Coral Gables, Florida, August 20, 2001).

72. Ronald Suny, "Provisional Stabilities: The Politics of Identities in Post-Soviet Eurasia," *International Security* 24 (1999–2000): 158–59.

73. Gerard Libaridian, an Armenian-American who served as a senior foreign policy adviser to President Ter-Petrossian, argues that the politicization of the genocide by the diaspora "had served, wittingly or unwittingly, to create the mentality and psychology that Turkey, through its non-recognition of the Genocide, is likely to repeat it, that Turkey is the eternal enemy. If Turkey is the eternal enemy, then Russia is the eternally necessary friend. And this then creates pressures on your policy of independence." See *American Forum*, http://www.gomidas.org/forum/af2c (accessed February 15, 2007).

74. As Mehmet Ali Birand, a leading Turkish observer, has written: "What bothers the Armenians in the shops and markets is not whether Turkey will accept the Genocide allegations or not. They are more concerned with how to fill their stomachs and how to win their daily grind." *Turkish Daily News*, February 2, 2001.

75. Beilin, *His Brother's Keeper*, 72.

76. Freinkman, "Role of the Diaspora in Transition Economies."

77. Sue Gunawardena, "From British Sikhs to British Panjabis: The Reconstruction of Diaspora Sikh Identity and Homeland Politics" (manuscript, 1999), 31.

Index

Acton, Lord, 114, 166n44
Aliyev, Heydar, 186n49
America. *See also* United States
  anti-Semitism, 83
  Arabs and Muslims, 123
  Civil War, 19
  identity, 16, 26, 67, 84
  influence on diaspora activity, 66–67
  and Israel, 83–90
  Jews in, 54–66, 72–76, 79–100
  "Manifest Destiny," 45
American Israel Public Affairs Com-
    mittee (AIPAC), 87, 92, 108, 122,
    135, 180n109, 184n25
American Jewish Committee (AJC),
    83
Americans for Peace Now, 111
Amichai, Yehuda, 82
Anderson, Benedict, 111, 130, 182n7,
    185n33
Anti-Defamation League (ADL), 51,
    83
Anti-Semitism, 61, 67, 71, 83, 92, 104,
    134
  and anti-Americanism, 93
Arab-Israeli-Palestinian conflict,
    88–90, 111–20, 135
Arabs, 61, 70, 77, 78, 112, 134, 152
Arafat, Yasir, 49, 90, 91, 118, 120
Arian, Asher, 70, 173n6, 175n37,
    177n50, 178n66

Armenian Democratic Liberal Party
    (ADL-Ramgarais), 51
Armenian Revolutionary Federation
    (ARF), 51, 148, 184n21
Armenian State, 19, 128, 132–33,
    156–57, 161–62
  genocide, 14, 116, 120–22, 133,
    145–50
  "Greater Armenia," 52
Assimilation/assimilationist, 14–20, 22,
    67, 72, 78, 85, 88, 94, 104, 174n16
Astourian, Stephen H., 184n21
Asylum Seekers, 21
Atatürk, Mustafa Kemal, 14
Australia, 59
Authoritarianism, 45
Authoritarian regime, 12, 17–18,
    22–26, 44–52, 112, 128
Ayalon, Daniel, 96
Azerbaijan, 14, 116–22, 147–50,
    163n10, 163n21, 171n42, 186n49
  Section (907), 116

Ba'athism, 17, 25
Bakshi-Doron (Chief Rabbi), 80
Balkan, 12, 166n40
  nationalism, 27
Baltic States (post-Soviet policies), 12,
    166n40
Barak, Ehud, 60, 70, 78, 82, 88, 90–91,
    106, 111, 180n96